# THE
# PHARAOH

WITH 234 ILLUSTRATIONS, 172 IN COLOR

GARRY J. SHAW

# THE
# PHARAOH

## LIFE AT COURT AND ON CAMPAIGN

Thames & Hudson

*For my wife, Julie*

HALF-TITLE **A gilded and painted wooden figurine of Tutankhamun standing on the back of a feline, from his tomb in the Valley of the Kings. The king wears a pleated kilt, a wide collar that covers his shoulders and the tall White Crown of Upper Egypt; a rearing cobra, known as a uraeus, is at his brow, ready to spit fire at the king's enemies. He holds a staff in his left hand and a flail in his right. The striding black feline may represent the night sky, while the gilded figure of the king may identify him as the sun god.**

TITLE PAGES **Relief from the mortuary temple of Merenptah at Thebes showing mirror image figures of Amenhotep III. He is wearing the Blue Crown and steers a chariot and holds a bow. The pharaoh is protected by the vulture-goddess Nekhbet.**

RIGHT **Glass inlay depicting an early Ptolemaic king.**

First published in 2012 in hardcover in the United States of America by Thames & Hudson Inc., 500 Fifth Avenue, New York, New York 10110

thamesandhudsonusa.com

Library of Congress Catalog Card Number 2012933045

ISBN 978-0-500-05174-0

Printed and bound in China by Toppan Leefung Printing Limited

# CONTENTS

# PHARAONIC LIVES

Wearing his blue and yellow *Nemes*-headdress, the cobra at his brow, a long false beard beneath his chin, the crook and flail gripped in his hands above his knee-length kilt, Pharaoh is one of the most recognizable symbols of ancient Egypt. Since classical times he has been the subject of works of literature, religion and history, and today finds himself in films, documentaries and television series. In many of these incarnations, however, he is surprisingly characterless, reduced to a stereotyped image – commanding, powerful and stern upon his throne, the very picture of authority. Few have presented the pharaoh as an individual holding an office – a *human* with duties and expectations, family and friends, pets and pastimes. In this book, the lives of these men (and the occasional woman) who ascended the throne of Egypt will provide an insight into the experience of life as one of the most powerful individuals in the ancient world. How did someone become pharaoh? What did a pharaoh do each day? Was he an all-powerful despot, capable of commanding any act, or was he merely a figurehead? Did the kings really lead their armies into battle? How were they educated? What rituals did they perform? How was a pharaoh approached in audience? From Menes, the mythical founder of the Egyptian state, to the Roman emperors who ruled over a conquered land, each pharaoh represents a manifestation of the long-lasting institution that he embodied, giving us a glimpse into this fascinating and vanished world.

## From Menes to the Roman Emperors

To the Egyptians themselves, their kings were links in a chain that stretched back unbroken to a time when gods ruled the world. Archaeology, of course, presents a different picture, one in which different cultures across Egypt slowly merged over

One of four coffinettes from the tomb of Tutankhamun, used to contain the king's embalmed viscera. The king wears the *Nemes*-headdress, a rearing uraeus and a false beard, and holds a crook and flail in his hands – the symbols of a pharaoh.

a long span of time – known as the Predynastic Period – ultimately to be unified and led by a single individual. Chapter 1, **Pharaonic Kingship: Evolution and Ideology**, presents both the mythological and archaeological history of kingship, as well as the fundamental trappings and ideology that built up around the person of the king. How was a pharaoh identified? What were his crowns and regalia? Was the king a god, a demi-god or nothing but a man?

Once unified, Egypt was ruled by 31 dynasties of kings, encompassing a period of roughly three thousand years. The dramatic events witnessed and overseen by these pharaohs is the subject of Chapter 2 – **The Story of the Two Lands**. Each dynasty brought its own character to the office of kingship and had to deal with an ever-changing world. The great Old Kingdom kings built the first pyramids, but later watched as their authority waned in the face of increasingly powerful regional mayors. Following the fragmentation of the First Intermediate Period, Middle Kingdom pharaohs presided over a period of artistic experimentation and territorial expansion, before central authority was again lost and the Delta fell under the control of foreign settlers known as the Hyksos, forming the Second Intermediate Period. The New Kingdom was a time of great prosperity and empire, when such famous figures as Thutmose III and Ramesses II strode the corridors of power; Third Intermediate Period kings faced a fractured country and increasingly competed for territory, only to be overpowered once more by foreign rulers. From that time on, Egypt continuously fought to assert its independence from outside rule, enjoying both periods of high cultural renaissance and infighting, before Alexander the Great initiated a period of Greek-Macedonian rule that lasted until the Romans absorbed the country into their expanding empire.

Ideally, each new pharaoh was the son of his deceased predecessor, but this was not always the case. **Becoming Pharaoh** (Chapter 3) discusses the many paths to the throne, from those who might have usurped power, such as Amenemhat I of the Middle Kingdom, to the commoners who took the crown from dying, childless kings. Most royal princes, however, duly inherited the throne from their fathers. While enjoying lives of luxury and sport, these princes also received an education to prepare them for kingship. Some held positions in

The upper half of a copper statue of Amenemhat III; many unusual royal statues were produced during this king's reign.

government, acting as priests or military commanders, and were appointed as co-regents. At the death of his father, a crown prince awoke the next day as king, spending the following 70 days in mourning while funeral preparations were made. Once his predecessor had been buried, and on a day that signalled a fresh beginning, the new king was crowned amid much pomp and ceremony.

The experience of **Being Pharaoh** (Chapter 4) depended greatly on the period when the individual was ruling, but also on his personal character; some presented kingship as a burden (Senwosret III and Amenemhat III), while others revelled in its luxuries (Amenhotep III). Travelling from palace to palace, treated as a god, the king experienced a level of opulence far beyond the dreams of his subjects. This was a man who could not be touched for fear of divine retribution, who proclaimed decrees in lavish formal audiences, but who could also be met with in private for more candid discussions on policy. As supreme judge, his word was law, and although debate might be encouraged, his decisions were final. When not in political meetings, he took part in elaborate festivals, pleasing the gods in his role as intermediary between them and mankind so that Egypt might benefit. Yet not all existence revolved around administration and solemn ritual – entertainment and enjoyment were important parts of life too. At times, the king could relax and be amused by tales of past rulers and musical performances, or he could engage in sports, such as hunting or horsemanship.

Egypt is a naturally isolated country, with desert to the west and east, dangerous Nile cataracts to the south, and the Mediterranean Sea to the north, but warfare – either in retaliation against invasions or in order to secure trade routes and obtain luxury goods – was still a frequent event. As time progressed, expansionism and control became fundamental to the image of the kings, and they accordingly portrayed themselves as warrior pharaohs – men who led their armies into battle and exulted in their victories. But how true was this presentation? What precisely was the role of **Pharaohs on Campaign** (Chapter 5)? Did they actually fight alongside their troops? What role did they play in the military? How was the army organized? And what was life like on the march?

Even when not on campaign, pharaohs still spent much of their time travelling, touring the country and participating in festivals, all the while living at the expense of local mayors (called nomarchs). Certain **Royal Cities** (Chapter 6), however, were always regarded as home. Memphis, at the junction between the Two Lands – Upper and Lower Egypt – where the Nile Valley opens out into the Delta, was founded at the beginning of Egyptian history as the perfect location for kings to oversee the country, and retained its importance well into the Roman Period.

A pectoral displaying King Amenemhat III smiting enemies, protected by the vulture goddess Nekhbet above. This colourful pectoral was discovered in the burial of Princess Mereret, within the pyramid complex of her father, Senwosret III, and is now in the Egyptian Museum, Cairo.

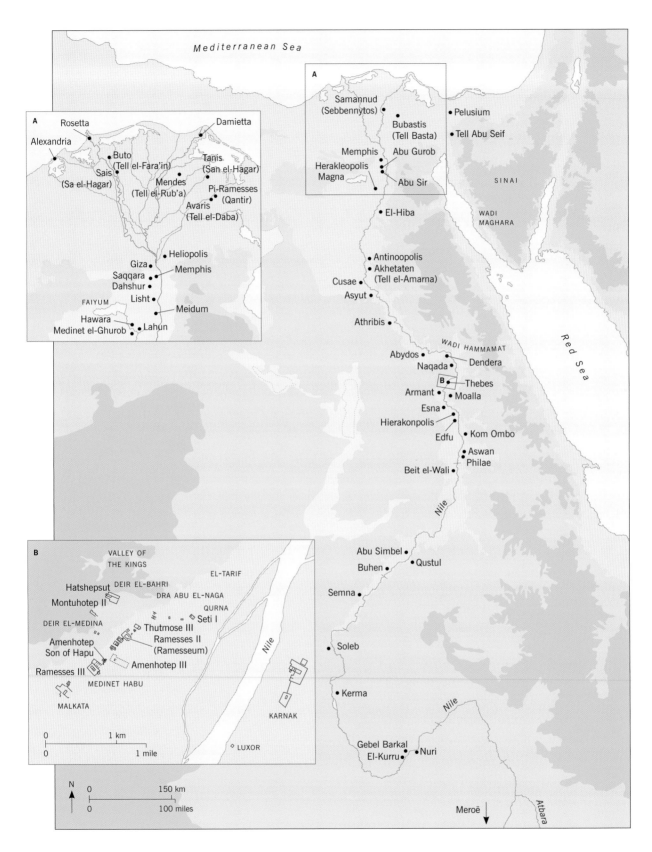

Mediterranean Sea

**A**

Samannud
(Sebbennytos)
Pelusium
Bubastis
(Tell Basta)
Tell Abu Seif
Memphis
Abu Gurob
Herakleopolis
Magna
Abu Sir
SINAI
WADI
MAGHARA
El-Hiba
Antinoopolis
Akhetaten
(Tell el-Amarna)
Cusae
Asyut
Athribis
Red Sea
WADI HAMMAMAT
Abydos
Dendera
Naqada
**B**
Thebes
Armant
Moalla
Esna
Hierakonpolis
Edfu
Kom Ombo
Aswan
Philae
Beit el-Wali
Nile
Abu Simbel
Buhen
Qustul
Semna
Soleb
Kerma
Gebel Barkal
El-Kurru
Nuri
Nile
Meroë
Atbara

**A**

Rosetta
Damietta
Alexandria
Buto
(Tell el-Fara'in)
Tanis
(San el-Hagar)
Sais
(Sa el-Hagar)
Mendes
(Tell el-Rub'a)
Pi-Ramesses
(Qantir)
Avaris
(Tell el-Daba)
Heliopolis
Giza
Memphis
Saqqara
Dahshur
FAIYUM
Lisht
Meidum
Hawara
Medinet el-Ghurob
Lahun

**B**

VALLEY OF
THE KINGS
EL-TARIF
Hatshepsut
DEIR EL-BAHRI
DRA ABU EL-NAGA
Montuhotep II
QURNA
Seti I
DEIR EL-MEDINA
Thutmose III
Amenhotep
Son of Hapu
Ramesses II
(Ramesseum)
Amenhotep III
Ramesses III
MEDINET HABU
Nile
MALKATA
KARNAK
LUXOR

0        1 km
0        1 mile

N

0        150 km
0        100 miles

Kings also founded new royal cities to act as their main place of residence, such as Itj-Tawy (Amenemhat I), Akhetaten (Akhenaten), today known as Tell el-Amarna, and Pi-Ramesses (Ramesses II), while Thebes, as cult centre of the state god Amun, rose to importance in the New Kingdom and continued to thrive afterwards. But in these great cities, with their slums, temples and markets, what public services did pharaoh provide for his people? And what were they like to live in?

In death, the pharaoh was surrounded by as much ritual and splendour as when he ascended the throne. From Early Dynastic Period burials hidden beneath whitewashed mounds and accompanied by the burials of sacrificed royal retainers, to the monumental pyramids, the dark, descending corridor-tombs of the Valley of the Kings and the later burials within temple precincts, royal funerary architecture evolved over the course of the pharaonic period. Chapter 7, **The Pharaoh in Death**, charts these changes in burial practices, recreates royal funerals of the Old and New Kingdoms, with their elaborate ceremonies and magnificent equipment, and describes royal afterlife beliefs.

**The Last Pharaohs** (Chapter 8) were Greek-Macedonian and then Roman in origin. The Ptolemaic Dynasty, which came to power after the death of Alexander the Great, ruled from Alexandria on the Mediterranean coastline. These were turbulent times, when Egypt again held a short-lived empire, and the kings enjoyed lavish lives in sumptuous palaces while trying to control the often rebellious native population and limit infighting within their own family. With the suicide of Cleopatra VII, Egypt became a Roman province, ruled by emperor pharaohs, few of whom actually visited Egypt. Nevertheless, their names were placed in cartouches and their images were carved on temple walls performing the traditional offering rituals for the gods. But of these Roman emperors, who truly was the last pharaoh?

ABOVE **The king (originally Hatshepsut, but usurped by Thutmose III) offering to Horus in the chapel of Anubis at the temple of Hatshepsut, Deir el-Bahri. The king was the intermediary between mankind and the gods.**

OPPOSITE **Map of Egypt, with the main sites mentioned in the text.**

## CHAPTER 1

# PHARAONIC KINGSHIP: EVOLUTION AND IDEOLOGY

The Egyptians traced their line of kings back into a mythological time, when the country was ruled in turn by gods, then demi-gods, spirits of the dead and finally by 'mortals', the first of whom was Menes. These mortal kings acted as intermediaries between mankind and the gods and embodied a divine office that was as integral to the cosmos as the annual Nile flood or the rising of the sun. Pharaonic kingship's actual beginnings are just as compelling as its mythology. For over 200 years archaeologists have been piecing together the history of Egypt's most distant past: a time before written records and grand monuments proclaimed the deeds of kings, when the country's culture was still developing. In this age, known as the Predynastic Period, the ideology and iconography of rule eventually crystallized in the person of one man – and a uniquely Egyptian vision of kingship was born.

## Myths

*The Book of the Heavenly Cow*, one of the Netherworld books associated with New Kingdom royal burials, provides a mythological origin for the first pharaoh and establishes his role in the cosmos. It presents the aged sun god Re ruling in person over his domain on earth; but, despite living in a world of plenty and perfection, mankind plotted against his authority, causing him to exterminate them as revenge. Before wiping out all mankind, however, the weary sun god felt pity for his creation and ceased the slaughter. He then ascended from the earth on the back of the goddess Nut, who had taken the form of a cow. After departing, Re reorganized the cosmos into three: the sky (formed from Nut); the earth; and the Netherworld (called the *Duat*). The earth was left an imperfect place, where the pharaoh, as Re's physical representative and deputy on earth, now governed in the sun god's place, charged with supporting the pillar of heaven and ensuring order and stability in the face of the ever-present threat of chaos.

Statue of the 4th Dynasty pharaoh Khafre, from his valley temple at Giza. The king sits upon a throne made in the shape of the hieroglyph for Isis, while the Horus falcon protects and enfolds his head with its wings. As each king in death becomes Osiris, the statue is thus actually a triad, showing Osiris, Isis and Horus.

Another myth significant to our understanding of Egyptian kingship is that of Osiris. The Egyptians believed that he once ruled on earth as a wise and kind god-king, but that his jealous brother Seth, desiring the kingship for himself, devised an elaborate plan to kill Osiris and take his throne. One evening, Seth held a party and invited numerous guests, including his brother. As part of the festivities, he produced a magnificent coffin and announced that whoever fitted it exactly could keep it for himself. Naturally, the coffin was designed in precise accordance with Osiris' measurements, so that when he lay inside it was a perfect match. With Osiris in the coffin, Seth slammed it shut, sealed it with molten lead and hurled it into the Nile. Adrift, sailing along the river, the coffin emerged into the Mediterranean and slowly found its way to Byblos in the Lebanon. Osiris' sister and queen, Isis, went in search of the coffin and found it entangled in a cedar tree, still containing the body of her husband. She returned the body to Egypt, only for Seth to hack it into 14 pieces, which he scattered across the land. Piece by piece, Isis again sought out the remains of her husband, but discovered that his phallus had been eaten by Nile fish. To reassemble Osiris fully she formed a substitute phallus from gold, and afterwards they conceived Horus.

Isis hid the child from Seth in order to protect him, but once fully grown Horus set out to avenge his father and reclaim the throne for himself. According to *The*

The goddess Isis (in the form of a falcon) is impregnated by Osiris after she has reassembled his body from pieces spread across Egypt by Seth. Horus, the child she conceives, stands to the left and Nephthys, sister of both Isis and Osiris, stands to the right. The Egyptians saw each king in death as Osiris, just as in life each king was Horus. A relief from the Temple of Seti I at Abydos.

*Contendings of Horus and Seth*, a New Kingdom tale, the dispute between the two rivals took the form of a series of legal hearings, with a tribunal of gods setting various tasks for both so that they could judge who was most worthy to rule. These tests frequently involved the young, intelligent Horus defeating the strong yet dim-witted Seth. In the end, Horus received the throne of Egypt and his father Osiris was given the kingship of the afterlife, while Seth was pushed to the desert as god of chaos. From that point on, every king in life was Horus and every king in death was Osiris, a myth eternally played out with each accession and burial. This story forms the backbone of Egyptian kingship, establishing the principle that the crown should pass from father to son, even in cases when the deceased king's brother might be better placed to take control of the country.

## The Predynastic Origins of Kingship: The Naqada Period

Archaeology provides evidence for a different picture of pharaonic kingship's evolution. Kingship over a unified Egypt first occurred by around 3100 BC, in the period known as Naqada III (3150–3000 BC). Before then, in Naqada I (4000–3500 BC) and Naqada II (3500–3150 BC), the country was divided up initially into small centres and then more generally into larger domains in Upper (southern), Middle and Lower (northern) Egypt. Over this long time, society became increasingly stratified, particularly in the south, leading to the emergence of an elite overseen by powerful chieftains, each ruling his own territory. The most important centres developed during Naqada I at Thinis, Naqada and Hierakonpolis, all in Upper Egypt, while a comparable elite only developed in the north by the end of Naqada II – significantly, the rulers there, based at Sais and Buto, identified themselves using Upper Egyptian royal iconography. By Naqada III, the major centres of Upper Egypt had coalesced and their material culture slowly spread northwards, replacing the indigenous material culture of Lower Egypt. Although there is no strong evidence for widespread warfare, prestige items dated to Naqada III are frequently decorated with scenes of conflict, prisoners and vanquished settlements, indicating that the Lower Egyptians did not simply accept the dominance of the south and offered some resistance. If so, they were unsuccessful, and by Naqada III the entire country had a uniform material culture – that of the north had completely vanished – and a single man ruled the country from the Mediterranean Sea down to Aswan.

During late Naqada II and Naqada III, burials with a royal aspect are found. Some of the graves in Cemetery T at Naqada are distinguished by their larger size and

The Battlefield Palette: a lion, perhaps symbolizing the king, defeats enemies, while birds prey on the fallen. The scene may commemorate violence between Egypt's north and south before final unification.

being lined with brick, and perhaps belonged to early chieftains. Similarly, at Hierakonpolis, Tomb 100 was lined with mud-brick and was decorated with painted scenes; among them is one of an individual smiting enemies with a mace – the traditional pose of Egyptian kings throughout the Dynastic Period and first evidenced during Naqada I on a painted pottery vessel from Abydos.

Kings of 'Dynasty 0' – a line of unrelated kings known to precede the traditional 1st Dynasty during Naqada III – were buried in cemeteries U and B at Abydos. Among the contents of tomb U-j was a small ivory crook, symbol of pharaonic rule, as well as ivory labels possibly with palace façade decoration, an emblem closely associated with the elite, which may show that large-scale construction was already being undertaken in the name of these proto-kings. Abydos Cemetery B, the later of the two burial grounds, is where the final kings of 'Dynasty 0' were buried, including Ka, Iry-Hor and Narmer.

So even at this early time the ideology and insignia of kingship were beginning to take shape – the first example of a Red Crown, which later symbolized Lower Egypt, is found in the Naqada I period at Naqada. Other marks of kingship are known from Naqada III: the first image of the White Crown, representative of Upper Egypt in the pharaonic period, decorates an incense burner from Qustul

Two ivory labels from tomb U-j at Abydos, showing a bird perched on a panelled building. These may represent an early form of *serekh* – a rectangular representation of the royal palace – however, if taken as a heron on a shrine they can perhaps be read as Djebaut, a location in the vicinity of Buto. Other labels found in the same tomb (below), of a Predynastic 'proto-king', display early hieroglyphic symbols.

The Scorpion Macehead, found at Hierakonpolis, displays the conventions of Egyptian art that would remain in use for the next 3000 years.

in Lower Nubia, while the first depiction of a king carrying a flail, an emblem of authority, is carved on an unprovenanced knife handle, now in the Metropolitan Museum of Art, New York. The next instance is found on a macehead from the time of King Narmer, found at Hierakonpolis.

By the end of Naqada III, Egyptian kings are depicted using conventions that would be familiar throughout the remainder of Egyptian history. The Scorpion Macehead, also discovered at Hierakonpolis, shows King Scorpion in the White Crown of Upper Egypt holding a hoe beside a canal. He wears a bull's tail and is attended by two fan-bearers, both shown on a much smaller scale. The king is thus the dominant figure and stands on a baseline, which provides order to the composition. His eye and torso are shown frontally, while the rest of his body is in profile, his arms and legs carefully separated to delineate them in full.

The Narmer Palette, again found at Hierakonpolis, displays King Narmer wearing the White Crown of Upper Egypt on one side, and the Red Crown of Lower Egypt on the other, implying that unification had occurred. On the first side, Narmer is shown smiting an enemy, holding him by the hair with one hand and raising his mace high with the other, ready to bring it down on his head (see p. 117). Before the king, the falcon god Horus perches on top of papyrus flowers, symbol of Lower Egypt, his talons gripping a rope attached to a prisoner's head. Behind the

This pot sherd, dated to Naqada I and now in the Ashmolean Museum, Oxford, bears the earliest known image of the Red Crown, which in the Dynastic Period symbolized Lower Egypt.

17

## WRITING A HISTORY OF THE PHARAOHS

When approaching literary and artistic evidence for pharaonic activity it must always be borne in mind that it was created to serve a particular purpose. The king was constantly surrounded by ritual, and there were rules not just for approaching him in life, but also in how he could be described and depicted in different contexts. As defender of *maat* (divine order) for the gods, he always acted for their benefit; as ultimate warrior, he was always a valiant leader, defending his troops.

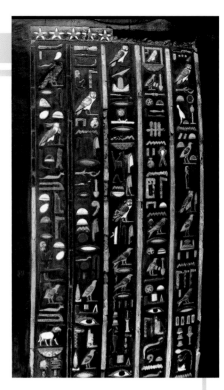

Vertical columns of hieroglyphic text inlaid with brightly coloured glass on the Ptolemaic coffin of Petosiris, now in the Egyptian Museum, Cairo. Strict rules governed the presentation of official texts in ancient Egypt.

*Maat* relied on uniformity – the repetition of age-old actions in the correct manner. Any occasion that could be described as an 'event' – something out of the ordinary – was placed under control to prevent it from being chaotic. Thus, when composing official texts for the king, scribes took documents – such as decrees and administrative papers – and overlaid the basic information with an embellished, idealized veneer, ensuring that each person behaved according to his proper place in the scheme of things. Nobles were bound by the same rules, describing their interactions with the king in a manner that best fitted the officially prescribed presentation. For example, courtiers directing construction projects say that they witnessed the king building monuments that they were actually responsible for, while soldiers were forbidden from saying that they killed enemies on the battlefield, for only the king could slay Egypt's enemies and protect the country. An understanding of these rules of presentation is key to approaching Egyptian history, and especially the history of pharaonic activity.

king, in his own register, is a small image of the royal sandal-bearer. In the register below are two defeated or fleeing enemies. On the reverse side is a procession: the king is again the largest figure, with a noble and four standard-bearers before him and his sandal-bearer behind. In front of them all, 10 enemies lie dead, their

Detail of the Narmer Palette showing the king in procession, with rows of decapitated enemies in front. Following artistic convention, the king is the largest figure in the scene. See also p. 117.

severed heads between their legs. In the register below are two mythical creatures with their heads intertwined, perhaps representing unification, while in the final register, a bull – probably the king – tramples an enemy and attacks a town.

With these two pieces, carved at the dawn of the pharaonic period, the conventions of Egyptian art, and especially those controlling the depiction of kings, were fixed and they remained unchanged for the next 3000 years. The king always wears a particular crown, performs good acts for the gods – smiting enemies or making offerings – and is the largest presence, demonstrating his premier position in human society. Scenes are divided into a series of registers, and all individuals are presented in their most perfect form. Striving for perfection and order was key to society, and the king was the guarantor of these concepts.

## The Ideology and Insignia of Kingship

The cosmos as perceived by the Egyptians was divided between the gods, the king, the spirits of the dead and humanity, with the pharaoh acting as intermediary between the divine and human spheres. Without a king to perform this function the gods would abandon Egypt, leaving the country to fall into ruin. Every king, as chief priest of all the gods, was expected to embellish or build temples and make endowments for their upkeep. He was depicted on their walls making offerings, emphasizing his role as donor to and appeaser of the gods, the only beings to which he was subservient. In return, the gods gave Egypt prosperity and peace.

The king's main duty was to ensure *maat*, a concept of divine order and justice that found its opposite in *isfet* – chaos. The king's very existence helped to guarantee that *maat* was established, but correct action was necessary to maintain it and keep it balanced, and it was through building temples, making offerings to the gods, protecting Egypt's borders and upholding the country's laws that he achieved this aim. To aid him, the king was believed to possess *hu* and *sia* – divine utterance and divine knowledge – as well as *heka*, divine magic. He was also assisted by an educated elite, who held key positions within Egypt's government. While each played his own role within the administration, all officials were ultimately responsible to the king, who passed commands down to them from the gods. As the head of this administration, the king appeared in audience to proclaim decrees and was responsible for the creation and maintaining of laws.

A gold-plated silver statuette of a pharaoh, possibly Seti I, offering *maat* – symbol of justice and order.

'Re has placed King N in the land of the living for eternity and all time; for judging men, for making the gods content, for creating Truth, for destroying evil. He gives offerings to the gods, and invocation offerings to their blessed spirits.'

The King as Sun Priest

A silver ring inscribed with the *nesu-bity* name (also called the throne name or prenomen) of Thutmose IV (Menkheperure) in a cartouche.

He was the ultimate judge in the land (though in reality this role typically fell to the vizier), and the only one allowed to impose a penalty of death or mutilation. As 'shepherd' of his people, the pharaoh guided and looked after Egypt's population, who lived on land that belonged entirely to him; any produce that derived from that land could be taken and redistributed by him as he saw fit.

As a mark of the king's unique position in society he was given special titles, clothing and insignia to differentiate him from the rest of the population. He had five names: the Horus name, which associated him with the falcon god Horus, son of Osiris; the Two Ladies name (*nebty*), connected to the tutelary goddesses of Upper and Lower Egypt, Nekhbet and Wadjet; the Golden Horus name, perhaps connected to the eternal nature of gold and therefore kingship; his birth name, preceded by the title Son of Re, connecting him with the sun god; and the *nesu-bity* name, literally meaning 'he of the sedge and bee'. This final name is typically translated as King of Upper and Lower Egypt, though in reality it may have designated the combination of the divine office of kingship (*nesu*) and the human, mortal ruler (*bity*). The last two names were enclosed in a cartouche – an oval-shaped motif that represented an elongated hieroglyph for 'eternity'. From the New Kingdom onwards the king is also called *per-aa* meaning 'Great House' or 'Palace'; this is the word that reaches us today as 'Pharaoh'. Reflecting the traditional division between north and south, and his dominance over both, the king could also be called 'the Lord of the Two Lands'.

In their own monumental inscriptions in tombs, courtiers most frequently refer to the king as 'His *Hem*', a word that Egyptologists have had difficulty translating. Most render it 'His Majesty', though this is purely for convenience's sake. In reality, *hem* designates the agent through which

Two wooden statuettes of Senwosret I: the one above, from the Egyptian Museum, Cairo, wears the Red Crown of Lower Egypt, while the one below, now in the Metropolitan Museum of Art, New York, wears the White Crown of Upper Egypt.

20

the divine kingship – something intangible and abstract – could be interacted with on earth. This has led to a wide variety of possible translations, including 'His Person', 'His Manifestation', 'His Agent' or 'His Incarnation'.

When the king appeared before his people he wore specific regalia. A variety of crowns are known from depictions, though none have been found archaeologically beyond a few diadems and headdresses, and so their actual material and size remain uncertain. Each crown connected the king with a particular aspect of divinity and power, and may have been regarded as a way of transferring authority from the gods to the king on earth. All were ultimately connected to the sun god Re, who gave them to the king as his deputy. By appearing as a divinity, the king associated himself with the gods.

The Red Crown (*Desheret* or *Weret*) was the symbol of Lower Egypt, and was linked to the morning light at dawn, when the sun is reborn. Its base, which curved to a peak at the rear, was seemingly formed of a bundle of reeds or was perhaps made from leather; a curling 'wire' coil emerged at the front. The White Crown (*Hedjet* or *Wereret*) represented Upper Egypt. Tapering from its base, this crown terminated in a bulbous peak, and, like the Red Crown, may have been fashioned from leather. The Double Crown (*Pa-Sekhemty*, 'the Two Powerful Ones') fused both the White and Red crowns, presenting the king as ruler of a united country. Associated with Osiris, and typically worn by the king when performing certain religious functions, the *Atef* Crown was similar in appearance to the White Crown, but had ostrich plumes attached to the sides (see p. 23). It may have been made from woven plant stems bound with golden bands. The Blue Crown (*Khepresh*), frequently shown worn by the king at war though not exclusively, was shaped like a helmet, and again perhaps made of leather; it was decorated with an elaborate arrangement of faience discs across its surface. The *Nemes*-headdress is first attested on a statue of King Djoser of the 3rd Dynasty, worn over a wig. This was a simple yellow- and blue-striped cloth, later worn on its own as a headdress that fell down loosely to the shoulders. For daily wear, this crown was connected to solar rejuvenation. The diadem (*Seshed*), with a uraeus – a rearing cobra – hanging beside each ear as well as one at the brow, was also probably worn by the king on a daily basis. An example of such a diadem still adorned Tutankhamun's head beneath his famous golden mask (see p. 77). A much simpler diadem, now in the Leiden Museum, is thought to have belonged to King Intef VI of the 17th Dynasty.

In his hands the king held the crook (*heka*) and flail (*nekhakha*), representative of his role as guardian and ultimate authority respectively; the former, a type of sceptre, probably derives from the crooks used by shepherds,

A uraeus, a rearing cobra (below), one of the symbols of kingship, and the royal diadem to which it is attached (bottom), thought to belong to King Intef VI; in Leiden Museum.

and the latter was perhaps an elaborate form of flywhisk. A false beard, tied to the king's chin by cords around the ears, associated him with the gods, and a uraeus was attached to a thin golden band that passed around his forehead, so that it reared at his brow. In religious texts, the uraeus acts as the king's divine guardian, spitting fire at his enemies just as a cobra spits venom. The king displayed his virility, and by extension the fertility of the land and its livestock, by wearing a bull's tail hung from the back of his kilt.

## The King's Divinity

The extent of the king's divinity has been a much debated topic. It was once thought that the Egyptians regarded their pharaoh as a pure god on earth – a superhuman being who spent much of his life performing arcane rituals. Although still popularly held today, this viewpoint is inaccurate. Early scholars based their opinions on analyses of religious texts alone, ignoring other relevant data. It was not until 1960, with a study by the French Egyptologist Georges Posener, that such views were challenged. Posener argued that if the king were a god, he was a god who could die, and one with limitations on his divine abilities. And, as the son of a god and a human mother, he could at best only be regarded as a demi-god. The Egyptians did indeed refer to their king as a *netjer*, a word typically translated as 'god', but he was a *netjer nefer*, a 'good god', rather than a *netjer aa*, a 'great god', the epithet associated with true divinities such as Osiris. There was thus a careful distinction between the two.

Although from the earliest periods the king was linked directly with the god Horus through his Horus name, from the 4th Dynasty he also began to be called the Son of Re. This is illustrative of the growing importance of the sun cult, but it also indicates that the king was slowly being removed from the full divine sphere – he was now the son of a god, dependent on his divine father. In literary tales, composed from the Middle Kingdom onwards, the king was not omniscient and was prone to human failings, such as anger and drunkenness. He had faults, just like any other human, and, unlike the gods, he enacted rituals each year to renew his powers and required a tomb to house his body after death. Yet the king was paramount in official ideology and any level of contact with him, no matter how slight, was highlighted in funerary biographies as an example of the individual's successful career. Despite his human weaknesses, to his courtiers the king was the 'breath of life, who makes all men live when he has shone on them'.

The upper half of a colossal statue of Akhenaten from Karnak. Despite the religious and artistic upheavals under Akhenaten, the symbols of kingship remained unchanged. Here the king wears the Double Crown above his *Nemes*-headdress, a uraeus is at his brow and a false beard hangs from his chin. He grasps the crook and flail in his hands.

How can we reconcile this image of a fallible mortal with that of a divine or semi-divine being? It is possible that the king was seen as fully human, yet played the role of a god during rituals. In which case he could be regarded as similar to a god, but not inherently divine. It can also be argued that it was the performance of ritual that conferred divinity upon him. In this interpretation he was a simple human when conducting daily business, but when dressed in the ritual accoutrements of kingship, performing acts for the gods, some of their powers were transferred to him and he partook of their divinity. What does seem certain is that during the coronation, when the king wore numerous crowns in succession and took the crook and flail, his nature changed: the mortal man was now imbued with a divine energy – the royal *ka*-spirit – and occupied an everlasting office (*nesu*). The human king might die and be replaced, but the kingship carried on forever, passing from one man to the next. In this manner, the divine kingship, with all its associated supernatural powers, was limited by its human, physical agent. Similarly, the gods were believed to inhabit statues in their temples at times of ritual, but the statues themselves could not perform supernatural acts. The statues, like the human body, constrained divine freedom, but did allow the gods, as intangible forces, to be interacted with by mankind.

Amenhotep III kneels before the god Amun-Re, who crowns the king with the elaborate *Atef* Crown on top of his *Nemes*-headdress, in a relief from Luxor Temple. At this moment, the king was imbued with the divine energy of kingship.

The king may also have been regarded as deputy to the sun god on earth. He was associated with the morning star, which the Egyptians saw as an emanation of the sun god because it appeared in the sky shortly before the sun rose; both were separate yet connected, one always appearing before the other. The German Egyptologist Rolf Gundlach has postulated that the kingship was divided into three parts: the person; the kingship of the ruling king; and Horus as the original sun god and ultimate sovereign, distant in the sky. According to this theory, Horus as sovereign is unable to act on earth and so transfers his powers to the king as his deputy. Clearly, the matter of the king's divinity is still a matter of debate and will probably remain so for many years to come.

## CHAPTER 2

# THE STORY OF THE TWO LANDS

In the 3rd century BC, not long after the death of Alexander the Great, a priest named Manetho was summoned to the royal court at Alexandria and commanded by Ptolemy I or II to compile a list of the pharaohs stretching back to the beginning of time. Diligently, Manetho divided his list of rulers into 30 dynasties (a 31st Dynasty was added by later writers), generally making his divisions when one family line ended and another began. In some cases, however, he regarded an event as so significant – such as the building of the first pyramid or the relocation of the main royal residence – that he created a further division. He also ignored co-regencies – times when two kings ruled simultaneously – as official ideology dictated that there could only ever be one pharaoh at a time. Despite such problems, Manetho's dynastic list still provides a useful framework for placing a ruler within a chronology, given that absolute dates remain to be established for much of Egyptian history.

Manetho's great work, which has only survived as excerpts quoted by later authors, can be supplemented by king lists from various periods of Egyptian history. The earliest known is carved on to the Palermo Stone (see p. 158), which dates to the 5th Dynasty and provides the names of kings, regnal years and the major events in their reigns up to that point. Subsequent lists provide more data, but come with their own biases, such as the removal of unworthy kings, and, like Manetho, they ignore co-regencies. Modern scholars have used these lists to refine and correct Manetho's work, and have also grouped his dynasties into longer periods. Spans of time when Egypt was politically unified are called 'kingdoms', and times when the country was divided, lacking a central unifying government, are called 'intermediate periods'. The first of these longer eras is the Early Dynastic Period.

Stele from the tomb of King Djet at Abydos displaying the king's Horus name. The falcon god Horus perches on a rectangular representation of the royal palace called a *serekh*. In the upper half is the royal name, carved within the palace's simplified ground plan, while the lower half is the niched facade of the palace's outer walls – a symbol of authority.

## The Early Dynastic Period (*c.* 3100–2584 BC)

By 3100 BC, Egypt – known as *Tawy,* 'the Two Lands', or *Kemet,* 'the black land', because of its fertile soil – was unified under a single king, a man traditionally known as Menes, but who is perhaps the historical King Narmer or Hor Aha. Whatever his identity may be, he was the first king of Egypt's 1st Dynasty, ruling from the mouth of the Delta down to Aswan in the south, with his main administrative capital at Memphis, where Upper and Lower Egypt meet. There is little information concerning the lives of these early rulers, but it is clear that, as noted in Chapter 1, over the course of this period the trappings, symbols and architectural setting of kingship became more prominent. Kings were increasingly set apart from their courtiers by the magnificence of their tombs at Abydos, the elaborate prestige items buried within, and the complicated rituals that formed around the kingship. One such ritual was the *Sed* Festival, in which the king was rejuvenated after 30 years of rule – an event depicted on an ebony label from the tomb of King Den, fourth king of the 1st Dynasty. Den's reign appears to have been a time of innovation: on an ivory label from Abydos he is the first to be shown wearing the royal uraeus, and the *nesu-bity* name (see p. 20 and p. 68) first appears.

Innovation occurred under subsequent kings too: Semerkhet, sixth king of the 1st Dynasty, was the first to use the *nebty* (Two Ladies) name, while the first depiction of the Double Crown is found in a rock-cut inscription in the western desert from the reign of Djet, third king of this dynasty, worn by the Horus falcon (it is first shown worn by a king in the following reign of Den). Government and foreign relations also evolved. It is probable that state taxation already existed under the 1st Dynasty, and military expeditions were sent into either Sinai or Palestine. Southern Palestine and Lower Nubia were occupied for much of the Early Dynastic Period, ensuring the smooth flow of luxury goods into Egypt. As time passed, however, Egyptian interest in Palestine declined and the sea trade route to Lebanon was preferred over the land passage.

Government continued to develop under the 2nd Dynasty, with the country now divided into a series of provinces called *sepat*

TOP **A tiny figure of King Den takes part in *Sed* Festival rituals in the top right corner of this ivory label from Abydos. Among the hieroglyphs is the first example of the *nesu-bity* (throne) name.**

ABOVE **Another ivory label of King Den shows the king wearing the first known royal uraeus, smiting an enemy; the text describes the 'first occasion of smiting the East'.**

LEFT **A statue of the 2nd Dynasty King Khasekhemwy, who wears the White Crown of Upper Egypt and is tightly wrapped in his *Sed* Festival robe. The statue, in the Ashmolean Museum, Oxford, is inscribed with the number of northern enemies killed during his reign, indicative of turmoil within Egypt.**

(plural *sepatu*) in Egyptian, but customarily referred to by Egyptologists using the Greek word, nomes. Little is known about the 2nd Dynasty kings themselves, however. The tombs of at least two of its rulers have been discovered at Saqqara, though the final two kings, Peribsen and Khasekhemwy, were buried at Abydos. This move of the royal cemetery was doubtless connected to political changes, and it is possible that a civil war erupted towards the end of the dynasty between north and south, as Khasekhemwy speaks of fighting northerners.

Despite possible political problems, over the course of this dynasty kingship continued to evolve: a small statuette of Ninetjer, its third king, shows him holding the crook (*heka*-sceptre), representing the first time this symbol of kingship was officially used, while fine royal statuary appears under Khasekhemwy, illustrating the increasing skill of craftsmen in the royal workshops.

## The Pyramid Age – The Old Kingdom (*c.* 2584–2117 BC)

The Old Kingdom, comprising dynasties 3 to 6, began with the accession of King Netjerikhet, better known today as Djoser. Although Djoser was related to Khasekhemwy, last king of the preceding dynasty, Manetho created a break at this point in his chronology because Djoser was the first king to build a pyramid, the famous Step Pyramid at Saqqara. This was such a momentous event that a new dynasty began – and with it also the pyramid age of the Old Kingdom. The administrative power required to command the resources necessary to construct a pyramid and its related structures led to the government becoming ever more complex, but this development was also aided in part by a lack of outside aggression and a high degree of self-sufficiency.

Not much is known of Djoser's immediate successors, as none managed to complete a pyramid or leave any significant imprint on history. And we have little more information about the 4th Dynasty kings, despite the fact that they left monumental funerary complexes, including the three pyramids at Giza, and a large amount of statuary from the time of Khafre onwards. Sneferu, first king of this dynasty, traded with Lebanon and launched campaigns into Nubia and Libya. He was also responsible for the first true pyramid – one with smooth sides rather than steps – at Dahshur, and was the first king to be called a 'good god'. During his reign and those of his successors most state resources were directed towards the construction of the royal pyramid complex, which had become a national project for the benefit of the god-king and was surrounded by the tombs of his highest courtiers. Throughout the 4th Dynasty, the royal family monopolized positions within the government – the office of vizier, for example, was held successively by royal princes. Any hope of promotion among the growing nobility depended entirely on the king's grace. Religious disputes may have arisen towards the end of this period: King Shepseskaf built his tomb at Saqqara in the form of a monumental mastaba, rather than a pyramid, perhaps indicative of an attempt to separate himself from the growing importance of the sun cult symbolized by the pyramid form. With Shepseskaf the 4th Dynasty line ended. Khentkawes, a queen mother who ruled as regent, was the next to hold power; it is unclear who her royal son was, but he was probably Userkaf, first king of the 5th Dynasty.

From the 5th Dynasty, royal family members ceased to play such an important role in the country's administration. King Djedkare Isesi altered the ranking system of the nobles and a second vizieral post was created for Upper Egypt, while provincial administrators were installed in the nomes and lived there permanently. This was intended to bolster central control, connecting the court and the periphery more directly, but in reality it was the beginning of the end for the Old Kingdom. Over the years, the provincial mayors built their tombs far from the royal pyramid, using artisans sent from the court, and began to retain local resources for themselves. Slowly, they created their own mini-courts in rural Egypt, and, by passing on their offices to their children, they effectively limited the king's choice in who held key positions across the land. The centralized state was in danger of breaking apart.

Further problems marked the start of the 6th Dynasty. According to Manetho, Teti, its first king, was assassinated by his guards, while his successor, Userkare, who probably usurped the throne, reigned for only a brief time. Userkare was followed by Pepi I, a son of Teti, who was confronted by both a harem conspiracy and the growing power of provincial mayors. He was succeeded in turn by Merenre and then Pepi II, the longest reigning of all pharaohs. Pepi's incredible 94-year reign was not enough to save the Old Kingdom from collapse, however. With its resources drained and faced by increasingly powerful provinces, the weakened central state limped into the First Intermediate Period and Egypt broke apart.

Throughout the Old Kingdom the pharaoh had been a distant personality. This was a time when kings did not feel it necessary to publish large inscriptions promoting their great deeds, when their human side was not dwelled upon, and when massive pyramids and austere statues promoted a sense of profound separation between the monarch and his subjects. The king is never depicted in private tombs, though interactions with him are mentioned; even if it was only a simple letter, any noble fortunate enough to receive a message from his king proudly recorded it on his tomb walls

Pepi I, depicted in a copper statue from Hierakonpolis and the larger of two statues of the king found at the site. Pepi survived a harem conspiracy against him.

for posterity. For non-royals, all success and initiative were related directly to the patronage and power of the pharaoh. After the events of the First Intermediate Period, this presentation of the king changed irrevocably; he would no longer be a distant god, instead he would be thoroughly involved in the very human business of war and government.

## The First Intermediate Period (*c.* 2117–2066 BC)

Following the ephemeral 7th and 8th Dynasties, power in the north of the country was held by rulers from Herakleopolis Magna, a city in northern Middle Egypt. These were the 9th and 10th Dynasties of Manetho. Little is known of these kings, not even their names in many cases or their reign lengths, though the dynasty was founded by a man named Akhtoy, described by Manetho as 'more cruel than all his predecessors'. While some kings of this period imitated Old Kingdom names in an attempt to link themselves with a glorious past, they left no large-scale monuments and failed to form a strong centralized state. Still, despite the fragmentation of the country, nomes under Herakleopolitan rule – effectively those north of Abydos – continued to display allegiance to the crown and spoke of events in terms of their connection to the king, just as in the Old Kingdom.

The situation was very different in the south. Here many nomarchs competed with one another for territory and resources, while owing at least nominal allegiance to the powerful family of Intef, based at Thebes. Each provincial ruler presented himself as a father looking after his family; they helped to clothe and feed their provinces, and boasted of their assistance to their citizens, promoting themselves relentlessly. Nomes formed their own armies, and local chiefs, such as Ankhtifi of Moalla, refer to leading troops in words similar to those used by kings in later periods. These men worked for their own aims and had no need to operate under the authority of a royal ruler.

Thebes grew in importance under Intef, son of Iku, head of the Theban nome and overseer of priests. He was the ancestor of the 11th Dynasty and was related to both Montuhotep I and his successor Intef I, men who styled themselves as kings south of Abydos. Intef I's own successor, Intef II, ruled for 50 years. He called himself King of Upper and Lower Egypt and Son of Re, though he did not take the full five-fold titulary traditionally held by kings of Egypt, nor did he depict himself wearing the traditional royal crowns. Nevertheless, he did initiate a programme of royal construction in temples under his control, setting a precedent for all future kings. He also received the allegiance of southern nobles, uniting their nomes under a single ruler. Despite his royal pretensions, Intef II's common origins are betrayed by his installation of a biographical stele within his tomb, a practice previously confined to non-royals.

The First Intermediate Period ended in a war between north and south. Intef II pushed his army into the Thinite nome, battling with the Asyut nomarchs loyal to the Herakleopolitans. In turn, the Herakleopolitans retaliated, achieving some success in the south before attempting to conquer Abydos. It was this that caused the Theban king, Montuhotep II, grandson of Intef II, to react, forcing his way northwards until he held sole control over the whole country. A second reunification had occurred and the Middle Kingdom began.

## The Middle Kingdom (c. 2066–1781 BC)

Montuhotep II was followed by two like-named successors, forming the second half of the 11th Dynasty. Their surviving monuments and known activities are restricted to Upper Egypt, showing either a lack of interest in or an absence of true control of the Delta region. Expeditions were sent to the Wadi Hammamat and Punt, and the administration of the south improved: the number of nomarchs was reduced, central government was strengthened and the office of vizier was again occupied. There was also a campaign into southern Palestine under Montuhotep II, indicative of strong central control. Montuhotep III's name is known from temple work in the south and from fortifications built to stop an influx of Asiatics – a continual problem during the Middle Kingdom. Little is known of Montuhotep IV, though it is possible that he was a usurper, since his name is absent from king lists and he was not related to the royal family.

Montuhotep IV's vizier, Amenemhat, is almost certainly the same person as King Amenemhat I, founder of the 12th Dynasty. He began his reign in Thebes, as shown by the abandoned construction of a royal tomb there, similar to that built by Montuhotep II at Deir el-Bahri. But sometime after his fifth year he founded a new capital, called Amenemhat-Itj-Tawy – 'Amenemhat-seizes-possession-of-the-Two-Lands'– in the vicinity of modern Lisht close to the entrance of the Faiyum Oasis (its exact location is unknown). This was a physical manifestation of his new beginning, a period that he called a 'renaissance'. By moving the capital north from Thebes he strengthened his control over the Delta, connected himself with the glory days of the Old Kingdom, and took up a better position from which to face the incoming Libyans and Asiatics – threats to Egypt's new-found stability, to which he also reacted by building a series of fortresses in the Eastern Delta called the 'Walls of the Ruler'. Such threats were not entirely limited to foreign incursions. Around 60 soldiers, dated to Amenemhat's reign and all slain during a siege, were found interred in a rock-cut tomb at Thebes, perhaps evidence of violence erupting within Egypt's borders.

Statue of King Montuhotep II, who re-unified Egypt at the end of the First Intermediate Period. He sits wrapped in his *Sed* Festival robes and wears the Red Crown of Lower Egypt.

The White Chapel of Senwosret I at Karnak exhibits extremely fine carving and exquisite detail, representing the high artistic achievements of the Middle Kingdom artisans.

Amenemhat himself may have been assassinated or mortally wounded by his own guards. Whatever the ultimate aim of this conspiracy, Amenemhat's son, Senwosret I, succeeded him to the throne.

During and after Senwosret I's reign, the Middle Kingdom developed into a period of high culture, when the language of Middle Egyptian was formalized and great works of literature were composed. Many sculptures of Senwosret I were carved and building work began in earnest at temple sites across the country. One inscription records that the king sent an expedition of 17,000 people to the Wadi Hammamat to procure stone for 150 statues and 60 sphinxes of himself, demonstrating the sheer scale of these undertakings. The administration was revamped too, and new titles appeared, including chamberlain and high steward. Lower Nubia, as far as Buhen, just north of the Nile's Second Cataract, became permanently occupied thanks to a series of fortresses, allowing the Egyptians to control the flow of trade north and exploit nearby gold-rich zones. After the end of the First Intermediate Period, warfare returned to being a royal prerogative, but its character had changed: the king was now portrayed as an aggressive warrior, threatening his enemies in lengthy tirades, rather than a silent symbol of order over chaos. Amenemhat II led campaigns into Nubia, as did Senwosret III, while

Senwosret II and Amenemhat III were more notable for their building works across Egypt. Amenemhat III in particular commissioned a wide variety of unique and unusual sculptures, including sphinxes that were later usurped by various kings.

Old Kingdom and First Intermediate Period thought were fused together to form a distinctly Middle Kingdom outlook. The administration, economy and military were all modified, and the bureaucracy was reorganized and expanded. Officials presented themselves as part of a patron-client model, while a sense of the ideal courtier emerged. And, although the king's position as intermediary between mankind and the gods remained unchanged, court literature and art now displayed his human side: these were kings with emotions and faults, able to recognize their mistakes and depicted in statuary as weighed down by the kingship and the appeals of their people. At the same time, the king's qualifications were emphasized – his divine origin, the good acts he performed for the population, his temple building and his aggression against chaos. Egyptians were urged to worship and obey him because of these good deeds and to express their loyalty to the crown. He in turn was anxious for his people, and, thanks to an expanding government and enhanced control over the provinces, had an even greater influence over their daily lives than ever before. The king was no longer a detached, untouchable man-god, but the holder of a multifaceted office at the head of a vast bureaucracy, affecting the lives of every man and woman in society.

Despite its apparent strength and stability, the 12th Dynasty ended with problems over succession. Amenemhat IV, son of Amenemhat III, had no heir, leaving Sobekneferu, probably a daughter of Amenemhat III, to rule as a female pharaoh. After her four-year reign, the 12th Dynasty came to an end and Egypt again began to fragment.

King Amenemhat III as a sphinx, one of a series of similar statues probably originally dedicated at Bubastis. Over time, these statues were usurped by various rulers and moved to new locations.

## The Second Intermediate Period (c. 1781–1549 BC)

The 13th Dynasty was a continuation of the 12th, though it is traditionally classed by scholars as part of the Second Intermediate Period. Over the course of this dynasty's rule centralized authority began to collapse and Egypt again became divided into small kingdoms, each ruled by its own 'king'. Avaris (modern Tell el-Daba), in the northeast Delta, was one such kingdom, ruled at first by a man named Nehesy and then by a number of ephemeral kings, some with Egyptian names, others with Asiatic ones – probably the descendants of prisoners of war settled during the Middle Kingdom, or traders. These kings are grouped together as the 14th Dynasty. The independence of this Delta kingdom barred the 13th Dynasty kings from trade with the Levant and beyond, while in Nubia an increasingly powerful kingdom based at Kerma, south of the Nile's third cataract, had already spread northwards, taking over Egypt's fortresses and buying the allegiance of the soldiers still remaining there. Increasingly weakened and surrounded by enemies, the 13th Dynasty eventually abandoned Itj-Tawy and moved the court to Thebes, while at the same time the 14th Dynasty was decimated by plague and famine.

A new line of rulers – the 15th Dynasty – filled the resulting power vacuum, entering Egypt as an invading force across the Sinai; these kings became known to history as the Hyksos – a Greek corruption of the Egyptian *hekka khasut*, 'rulers of foreign lands'. Having established themselves at Avaris, they expanded their power base, perhaps aided by an additional influx of Asiatic immigrants, so that they eventually controlled the entire Delta and as far south as Cusae in Middle Egypt. The 13th Dynasty then re-emerges as the 16th Dynasty at Thebes, but little is known of these rulers beyond brief accounts of war and strife, and their relationship to the succeeding 17th Dynasty is unclear.

Although relations with the increasingly Egyptianized Hyksos appear to have been generally amicable at first, the 17th Dynasty eventually began a series of campaigns against them with the intention of re-conquering the north. This was perhaps initiated by King Seqenenre Tao, whose mummy betrays a violent death (see p. 119). His successor, Kamose, then led raids northwards, leaving an account of his journey and successes, apparently as far as the Hyksos capital at Avaris. A lull in activity followed, when both Kamose and his Hyksos counterpart, Apophis, died, each leaving their thrones to much younger monarchs. Once old enough, the new pharaoh, Ahmose, took his army back to Avaris and pushed the Hyksos out of Egyptian territory, chasing them across the Sinai and besieging them at Sharuhen in southern Palestine for three years.

## The New Kingdom's Golden Age – The 18th Dynasty (*c.* 1549–1298 BC)

With the expulsion of the Hyksos, Ahmose could truly call himself King of Upper and Lower Egypt. From that moment on, unsurprisingly perhaps given the violent birth of the period, the 18th Dynasty witnessed an increased militarization of the state, and an expansionist policy became part of kingship, fuelled by the notion that Egypt could secure its borders by dominating surrounding lands. No longer content simply to sit within their traditional boundaries, Amenhotep I and his successor, Thutmose I, expanded deep into Nubia, reclaiming territory previously held during the Middle Kingdom, and then progressed further, completely crushing the kings of Kerma who had arisen during Egypt's absence from the region, and in so doing removed a major threat to Egypt's stability. In a display of power, Thutmose I next marched northeast towards the Euphrates, but did not clash with Egypt's great rival there – the Mitanni. With only a stele erected to mark his accomplishment, Thutmose left it to later kings – Thutmose III and Amenhotep II – to consolidate Egypt's control over the Levant. Unlike in Nubia, however, where an active programme of colonization occurred, in the Levant the pharaohs established a sphere of influence, with individual city states forced to pledge their allegiance to the crown. The Theban god Amun, who had grown in importance under the Middle Kingdom, now emerged as premier Egyptian deity. As national god, he was the main recipient of the vast amounts of wealth brought back from the pharaohs' foreign campaigns. Amun's temple at Karnak expanded with each passing reign; in return he granted Egypt further success and prosperity.

Although strength and power had always been an element of the pharaoh's image, 18th Dynasty kings emphasized their personal physical abilities in sport and on the battlefield more than any kings before them. Amenhotep II took this to its furthest extent, boasting of his strong arms, his ability to fire an arrow through a sheet of copper and his violent acts against his enemies. In this last aspect he excelled, being more brutal than any of his predecessors or successors. In one text he records that seven foreign princes were hung from the prow of his boat when he sailed back to Egypt, while in another he speaks of watching the villagers of two Levantine towns burning in a ditch. It was not only a king's strength that 18th Dynasty scribes extolled, his intelligence now also became a major focus. Ahmose is described at Karnak Temple as 'a disciple of the star Sirius, favourite of Seshat [...] Thoth is at his side: who has given him the knowledge of the rites. He conducts the scribes according to their exact rules'. The same text presents him as an expert in magic, a skill normally associated with sages. Thutmose III was 'more conversant with the regulations than the scribes', well informed in all matters, like Thoth, god of knowledge and writing, and is said to have issued a decree regarding public health after he 'had seen a "Protection-book" from the time of the forefathers'. Horemheb, last king of the 18th Dynasty, is also compared to Thoth in his coronation inscription. It is ironic then, that by highlighting these kings' intelligence and strength, the ancient scribes were simultaneously humanizing the kingship.

As well as securing their national borders, the 18th Dynasty kings also made sure of their family line. Acutely aware of the succession problems that had ended previous dynastic lines, their solution was to encourage intermarriage between members of the royal family. Royal princes now married their half-sisters – never their full sisters – and princesses were forbidden to marry commoners, a practice that continued until the reign of Ramesses II of the 19th Dynasty.

The so-called Colossi of Memnon, two great statues of Amenhotep III that marked the entrance to the king's immense mortuary temple on the west bank of the Nile at Thebes. Many great monuments were constructed under Amenhotep III, who ruled when Egypt was at the peak of its wealth and power.

By the reign of Thutmose IV, in the early 14th century BC, Egypt had established its territory to the south and northeast, and the country was free to enjoy the fruits of its success. Kings no longer had the opportunity to prove themselves at war (though they still described themselves as great warriors), leaving Amenhotep III to outdo his predecessors in sheer opulence and scale; under his rule, great buildings were constructed across the country and finely carved statues were commissioned, some colossal in scale.

Over the course of the 18th Dynasty the sun cult had grown in importance; Amenhotep III's palace at Malkata was even known as the 'Palace of the Dazzling Sun-Disc'. Amun was by now syncretized with Re as Amun-Re, and all other gods were inferior to the great distant disc in the sky. This religious focus crystallized to its most dramatic extent under Amenhotep III's son, initially known as Amenhotep IV but better known to history as Akhenaten, first king of the Amarna Period.

## Sun Kings – The Amarna Period

Comprising the final part of the 18th Dynasty, the Amarna Period was a time of great cultural upheaval. The first sign of the peculiarity to come was Amenhotep IV's decision to hold his *Sed* Festival on the second anniversary of his accession rather than the traditional 30-year mark. Then, at Karnak Temple, the king commanded four structures be built, all connected to the solar cult, especially the Aten ('sun disc'). As well as the prominence of the Aten on these early monuments, Queen Nefertiti also makes frequent appearances, often performing ceremonial acts beside Akhenaten, including smiting – a traditional prerogative of kings. The new structures built under Amenhotep IV were decorated in a new artistic style. All individuals, but especially the king, were depicted with exaggerated features: elongated faces, hanging bellies and wide hips supported on thin, spindly legs. There is as yet no absolute agreement on the meaning behind this artistic development, but it may represent a fusion between male and female characteristics.

The king's new constructions appeared at Heliopolis, Memphis and in Nubia, and possibly the Delta too. But in his fifth year Amenhotep took the decision to make a complete break with the past by building an entirely new city dedicated to the Aten on a site unconnected to other gods. This would be called Akhetaten – 'the-Horizon-of-the-Aten'. The king then sent out his followers to deface the name of Amun wherever it was found and changed his own name to Akhenaten ('Effective-for-the-Aten'). The old temples were closed and their funds diverted; the Aten would now be Egypt's one god, and the king would be the only individual with access to his divine teachings.

Despite the reforms, campaigns in Nubia and the Levant continued and the court remained in contact with the Levantine vassals, with a large-scale reception of foreign ambassadors occurring in Akhenaten's 12th year. Akhenaten died during his 17th year as king, to be succeeded by an ephemeral and mysterious individual known as Smenkhkare, who ruled for three years in association with Princess Meritaten, a daughter of Akhenaten. The kingship then fell upon Tutankhaten, a young son of Akhenaten. For the first three years of his reign art continued to be produced in the Amarna style. But the king then abandoned Akhetaten and moved to Memphis; from here, Tutankhaten – now Tutankhamun – reinstated the traditional temples with their cult of Amun.

Akhenaten revolutionized Egyptian religion and art. Under his rule, and for a short time afterwards, figures were portrayed with elongated faces, hanging bellies, wide hips and spindly arms and legs.

At Tutankhamun's death, aged just 18 or 19, perhaps the result of a combination of a strong strain of malaria and an infected leg, Egypt was left without a natural successor. His queen, Ankhesenamun, wrote a message to the Hittites – the new power in the northern Levant and eastern Anatolia – requesting that they send a prince to marry her, thereby uniting their two kingdoms and saving her from the disgrace of marrying a commoner. Prince Zannanza was despatched, but was murdered *en route*, enraging the Hittites and leaving an influential yet aged official named Ay – a man perhaps related to Queen Tiye, Tutankhamun's grandmother – to ascend the throne. He lasted just four years, but in that time attempted to mend relations with the Hittites and establish a successor. In the latter he failed, as General Horemheb, an influential military leader of the Amarna Period, was next on the throne. Under him, a series of large-scale building projects and administrative reforms were initiated.

## The Ramesside Period (*c.* 1298–1069 BC)

The Ramesside Period (Dynasties 19 to 20) began with the accession of a commoner. Having no son of his own, Horemheb selected a man named Pa-Ramessu from among the military ranks to be his successor – the latter already had both a son and grandson to succeed him. Horemheb ensured their succession by creating the title 'Royal Deputy'; he also made Pa-Ramessu his vizier, an act that Pa-Ramessu himself would emulate for his own son, Seti.

With the death of Horemheb, Pa-Ramessu became King Ramesses I. His new dynasty, the 19th, made no attempts to connect themselves with the preceding 18th Dynasty; quite clearly this was a new beginning. Nevertheless, the effects of that tumultuous time continued to be felt by post-Amarna kings. They did not form a distinctly individual version of the kingship, and even though the prestige of the office returned over the course of their tenure, it was no longer possible for the king to act entirely as he wished. Powerful officials now held a higher degree of influence over royal actions, guaranteeing that there would never again be another Akhenaten.

Ramesses I reigned for barely a year before his son Seti succeeded him. As prince, Seti had undertaken

The upper half of a colossal statue of Ramesses II from the Ramesseum, his mortuary temple at Thebes, now in the British Museum, London. Ramesses had one of the longest reigns of any pharaoh and is famous for his extensive building programme across Egypt (as well as for usurping the monuments of others) and his military campaigns in the Levant.

military duties for his father and held various priestly positions in the Delta. As king, he began a series of programmes of restoration of temples and tombs damaged during the Amarna Period, and began his own construction projects. Mines and quarries were reopened and campaigns were launched into Nubia and the Levant; territory was quickly won and lost, and it was left to his son, Ramesses II, to regain Egypt's past glory.

As king, Ramesses II's first campaign into Syria occurred during his fourth year, when he captured the important province of Amurru, only to lose it again almost immediately. Ramesses' reaction was to march back the following year in yet another attempt to re-conquer his lost territory. The ensuing battle of Kadesh in *c.* 1274 BC (see pp. 134–35) is one of the best recorded battles in Egyptian history, although it ended in stalemate. The territorial tug-of-war continued over the following years, but Egypt never again regained Kadesh. In Ramesses' 21st year Egypt signed a peace treaty with the Hittites, in which it was agreed that both Amurru and Kadesh would forever remain in Hittite hands. Although surely a blow to Ramesses' ego, the Levantine territory remaining in his possession was now secure, allowing trade to flow into Egypt. The situation was less stable on the western frontier, where Libyan incursions had become an increasingly frequent problem. In response, a line of fortresses was built along the edge of the Delta and into the desert to protect Egypt's territory. Ramesses initiated many other large-scale construction projects during his reign and embellished temples across the country, often usurping the work of earlier kings in the process.

Ramesses enjoyed a long reign, celebrating more than one *Sed* Festival. In total, 12 of his around 50 sons died before him, leaving Merenptah, already advanced in age, to ascend the throne. Famine was by this time sweeping the Near East, and the king sent grain supplies to the Hittites as a relief effort. This widespread food crisis may have been one of the causes of the movement of disparate Mediterranean groups, known to the Egyptians as the 'Sea Peoples', who decimated cities and towns across the Levant in their search for new land to inhabit. In Merenptah's fifth year these groups joined forces with Libyan tribes and attempted to invade the Delta, with the intention of settling there. Merenptah and his army, however, met them in battle before they could reach Memphis and defeated them in six hours – events dramatically described on the walls of Karnak Temple.

When Merenptah died, after only nine years on the throne, the 19th Dynasty faced a series of dynastic problems that led to its eventual decline. Seti II, Merenptah's son, became king, but competed with a rival called Amenmessu, who ruled south of the Faiyum Oasis for about four years after coming to power under unclear circumstances. Amenmessu's lineage is obscure; some scholars have argued

The Hittite version of the peace treaty agreed between the Egyptians and Hittites in the 21st year of Ramesses II's reign. It is inscribed in Babylonian cuneiform (the lingua franca of the day); Egyptian versions, written in hieroglyphs, were engraved on the walls of Karnak Temple and the Ramesseum.

that he was the son of Seti II and a queen called Takhat, while others see him as a vizier who seized power. Afterwards his name was erased wherever it was found, and the tomb he had begun in the Valley of the Kings was usurped. Seti II ruled for just six years, and the state of confusion continued.

Seti II's son, Seti-Merenptah, was his intended heir, but he never became king. Instead, a young boy with an atrophied leg called Siptah succeeded. Siptah's origins are uncertain, though he may have been a son of the usurper Amenmessu. Whatever the case, it fell to Seti II's principal wife, Tawosret, to act as regent. With the aid of a high official named Bay, she retained power and eventually assumed full royal titles shortly before Siptah's death. We are left in the dark about the end of her reign, but it surely cannot have been peaceful. The Egyptians refer to this time as one of anarchy and rebellion, and later tried to erase both her and Siptah from history. Fortunately, a king emerged at the head of a new dynasty to restore order.

This new king, the first of the 20th Dynasty, was Sethnakht. Little is known of him, except that he is said to have freed Egypt from the chaos that existed before his accession. He ruled for a short time before the throne passed to the last great king of the New Kingdom, his son Ramesses III. Ramesses attempted to emulate Ramesses II in every way that he could, even going as far as naming his children after those of his idol. Militarily, however, Ramesses III did not mount great campaigns into the Levant, though he did protect Egypt from two large-scale incursions by the Libyans and one by the Sea Peoples. Despite these great achievements, he may have been killed in a harem plot. The New Kingdom

Libyan captives tied in a variety of excruciating positions, from Medinet Habu, the mortuary temple of Ramesses III. Although Ramesses III never campaigned beyond his own borders, he successfully repelled two Libyan invasions of Egypt and one incursion by the Sea Peoples.

then entered decline: Libyan invasions continued; the Temple of Amun became an independent power thanks to its extensive land ownership and wealth, thus weakening royal authority; and tomb and temple robberies were a frequent problem. Ramesses III's eight like-named successors were ineffective, able to do nothing but watch as grain prices soared, mines and quarries closed, and the priests of Amun revelled in their power.

The New Kingdom's death knell came with the general Herihor, who in addition to his military rank took the titles of high priest of Amun and vizier, thereby uniting the land's most powerful offices. At Karnak Temple he also depicted himself as pharaoh, though his power was restricted to Thebes. This city now acted independently of the crown, ruled by Amun himself, his wishes interpreted by his high priests. Central power was lost and Egypt became divided, so that with the death of Ramesses XI, the great New Kingdom, born so violently 500 years earlier, quietly slipped into nothingness.

## Kinglets and Kushites – The Third Intermediate Period (c. 1064–664 BC)

'As for Pharaoh, Life!, Prosperity!, Health!, *how* shall he reach this land (Nubia or Thebes)? And of whom is Pharaoh, Life!, Prosperity!, Health!, superior still?' These despairing words, written in a letter from a general to his scribe in the last years of Ramesses XI's reign, show how far from the glory days of Ramesses II Egypt had fallen by the end of the New Kingdom. But the institution of pharaoh was a resilient one, and would again be resurgent.

Smendes, a man of unknown origin, founded the 21st Dynasty in the Delta in around 1064 BC. Under him, the city of Tanis, a hitherto small port, became the new major royal centre. At the same time, the Theban high priests ruled in the south, their territory extending as far north as El-Hiba, where they constructed fortresses. This state of actual division would last only for a short time, however. The northern throne passed from Smendes to Amenemnisu, and then to a man named Psusennes I, whose younger half-brother, Menkheperre, became high priest of Amun at Thebes. Through the intermarriage of the families of the Theban high priests and northern royals, a single family line in effect ruled the country, though official geographical divisions continued to operate. This reveals a major Third Intermediate Period alteration to pharaonic kingship: an acceptance among the ruling class of disunity. The Theban high priests, northern kings and various other Delta kinglets co-operated, with none making a push to assert themselves and re-establish a single kingdom.

When in *c.* 940 BC King Psusennes II, last king of the 21st Dynasty, died without heir, the throne passed to another powerful Delta dynasty. According to Manetho, this new dynasty – the 22nd – came from the city of Bubastis and were Libyan in origin. Over the course of the preceding 21st Dynasty, its members had grown in power and married into the royal family, while Shoshenq I, its first king, had been a general under Psusennes II. As pharaoh, he made efforts to reunify the country, campaigned in the Levant and placed members of his family in positions of high office. Shoshenq's political reforms had little long-term effect, however, and the provinces slowly became more independent. From the reign of Shoshenq III, sixth king of the dynasty, numerous individuals declared themselves king across the Delta. Consequently, the late 22nd Dynasty overlaps with the 23rd and the 24th Dynasties, demonstrating how fractured the kingship had become by this time.

In the midst of this chaos, a Nubian king called Kashta, whose territory extended as far north as Aswan, entered Egypt in a major display of power and domination. Seizing control of Upper Egypt only, he nevertheless proclaimed himself king of the entire country; from now on the Nubians began to see Egypt as an extension of their own territory. Shortly after Kashta's invasion, one of the various Delta rulers, Tefnakht, a man of Libyan descent, gradually expanded his sphere of influence across the Delta and into Upper Egypt. In response, Kashta's brother, Piye, marched an army into Egypt and headed northwards, aiming to curtail Tefnakht's power. Successful in his goals, Piye forced Tefnakht and the other Delta rulers to pay him homage before returning to Nubia in triumph. Little changed after Piye's incursion, however. Tefnakht continued to consider himself king and, in c. 727 BC, passed his 'crown' to his son Bakenrenef, a man reputed to be a famous lawmaker, according to Diodorus. The expanding power of Bakenrenef led Shabaqo, now king of Nubia, to march his army north and forcibly seize power. In the ensuing violence, Bakenrenef was captured and burnt to death, ending the 24th Dynasty. But again little changed, because Shabaqo, although now based at Memphis, simply left the Delta rulers to continue squabbling among themselves. Nevertheless, some semblance of central control had returned.

The Nubian 25th Dynasty brought their own traditions to pharaonic kingship. During their rule, it was acceptable for the crown to pass from brother to brother, rather than the traditional father–son succession. They also frequently depicted themselves with a double uraeus at their brow and wore cap crowns; the Blue Crown, so popular in earlier periods, is absent from royal art. On the other hand, many Egyptian traditions were retained. Titularies were based on those of Old Kingdom rulers and some of the Nubian kings were crowned at Memphis. Their statuary also shows a melding of Middle and Old Kingdom ideals, with strongly formed upper bodies reminiscent of the Old Kingdom, but with medial lines in the torso, similar to statuary of the Middle Kingdom. These kings were even buried under small pyramids, with associated chapels, in Nubia.

While the Nubians may have congratulated themselves over their easy victory, dark clouds were building on the horizon. Assyria had emerged as a major power in the east, and though Shabaqo initially enjoyed friendly relations with his Assyrian counterpart, Sennacherib, the situation quickly deteriorated. Ten years after Shabaqo's death, Taharqo was forced to defend Egypt's borders against the Assyrian ruler Esarhaddon. In the ensuing invasion, Assyrian sources claim that Taharqo was wounded five times at Memphis before the city fell. He then fled south, leaving his wife and family behind in Esarhaddon's hands. Now free to do as he pleased, the Assyrian ruler slaughtered entire villages, piling severed heads high, before taking Taharqo's wife, children, harem and possessions back to Assyria. On Esarhaddon's Victory Stele, Taharqo's son is even depicted with a rope tied around his neck.

The Assyrians set about obtaining oaths of allegiance from the Delta rulers, hoping to secure their opposition to any attempt by the Nubians to regain power. Necho of Sais was left to rule his territory as a vassal king of Assyria, while his son, who had spent time in Nineveh being educated at the royal court, was installed to rule Athribis. Taharqo then tried to retake the country, capturing Memphis and gaining the support of the Delta dynasts in the process. But his success was short-lived. Enraged, the Assyrians marched back into Egypt and again chased him south. This time he did not return, dying in Nubia in 664 BC. The Assyrians punished the disloyal Delta dynasts, although Necho managed to convince them that he had been unable to prevent the turn of events, and so was left in place as governor of Sais, and awarded Memphis too.

Taharqo's successor, Tanutamani, made the next attempt to bring Egypt back under Nubian control. He met with some success, managing to defeat the Assyrian-aligned Delta rulers and perhaps even killing Necho, if Herodotus is to be believed. Again, however, the Assyrians sent a large army to quell the rebellion, probably at the behest of Psamtik I, Necho's son, who had fled to the northeast. This time the Assyrians chased Tanutamani all the way back to Nubia, sacking and pillaging Thebes along the route. Tanutamani wisely remained there, and with Necho dead, the Assyrians placed Psamtik I on the Egyptian throne to rule in their name.

## The Late Period (664–332 BC)

When the Assyrians departed, Psamtik I was left behind as 'king' of Egypt. At first his authority was limited: in the north he was forced to contend with the various remaining unruly Delta kinglets, supported only by a single small Assyrian garrison based at Memphis, while in the south he faced powerful rulers, including Montuemhat, who controlled Thebes and remained loyal to the Nubians. But despite his upbringing at the Assyrian court, it was Psamtik who threw off the foreign occupier's yoke and unified Egypt, becoming first king of the 26th Dynasty, which initiated the Late Period. Psamtik achieved control of Egypt through diplomacy, backed by the threat of a powerful Greek military force provided by Gyges of Lydia, with whom he had forged an alliance. A key element of this peaceful takeover was the 'adoption' of Psamtik's daughter, Nitiqret, as successor to the position of God's Wife of Amun at Karnak Temple. From the reign of Osorkon III, the God's Wife had wielded an increasing level of political and religious influence, gained at the expense of the power of the high priest of Amun. It was her duty, as a celibate priestess, to establish her successor through adoption. However, this successor was always a daughter of the reigning king, ensuring a high degree of royal control over the temple, and, by extension, Thebes. Thus, when the Nubian God's Wife, Amenirdis II, adopted Nitiqret as her successor, Thebes' allegiance passed from the 25th Dynasty to the 26th without a single drop of blood being spilt. Once Egypt had been secured, Psamtik launched a campaign against Libya, where certain Delta princes were operating. After their defeat, he focused his attention on reforming the country.

The Assyrians now had little capacity to stop Psamtik, as they were caught up in political intrigues and wars closer to home. The power vacuum left by the ensuing collapse of their empire was quickly filled by the Babylonians, so that by the time of Psamtik's death, after roughly 55 years as king, both Egypt and the world around it had changed immeasurably. Neither the Assyrians nor the

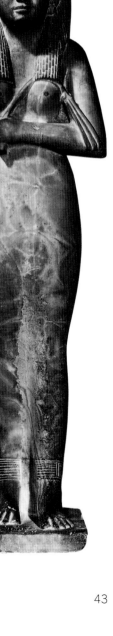

A calcite statue of the God's Wife of Amun, Amenirdis, daughter of the Nubian ruler Kashta. The office of God's Wife was particularly influential at Karnak during the Third Intermediate Period and early Late Period.

Nubians were players on the world stage, and Egypt had risen from being a fragmented province of a powerful empire to being the possessor of its own empire once again.

The kings of the Late Period were inspired by many previous epochs, but it was the Old Kingdom that attracted their attention most. They pursued an active policy of excavating Old Kingdom tombs and temples so that wall scenes and statues could be reproduced, while ancient texts were copied too. The kings also used traditional terminology to refer to themselves and based their titularies on those of Old Kingdom kings. While these kings were attempting to bolster their positions by emulating a golden age, their officials emphasized their independence of royal control, proclaiming responsibility for their own achievements. They drew on terminology from First Intermediate Period texts, and some even went as far as stating that pharaoh was dependent on them; something unthinkable in earlier times. Despite the 26th Dynasty's triumphs, the office of kingship was clearly in decline.

The caption:

The head of a Late Period king, most probably Ahmose II, who seized power from Apries; now in Berlin.

Psamtik's successor, Necho II, initiated a series of campaigns into the Levant. From 607 BC, this led to clashes with the Babylonians, who had been expanding their territory and planned to invade Egypt. Intention turned into action when Nebuchadnezzar's army marched across the Sinai, only to meet a heavily fortified Delta. Despite numerous confrontations, in countering the Babylonian aggression the Egyptians managed to protect their country and even regained some of their Levantine empire. Their luck did not last. Necho's second successor, Apries, was overthrown by one of his own generals – who became King Ahmose II. As king, Ahmose repelled another Babylonian invasion and then watched as a new nemesis emerged – Persia. After Ahmose's death, the Persians succeeded where the Babylonians had failed and invaded Egypt. According to Herodotus, Psamtik III, Ahmose II's son and successor, was captured and taken to the Persian capital, Susa, but only after his eldest son had been executed and his daughter enslaved. There, after attempting to launch an uprising, he was executed by being forced to drink bull's blood; with him died the 26th Dynasty. The 27th Dynasty (also known as the First Persian Period) would be another time of foreign occupation.

There is a great discrepancy in the way in which classical authors and Egyptian sources present the Persian occupation. Herodotus paints the Persians as despised and disrespectful of Egyptian traditions, while in Egyptian records they are portrayed as being at pains to follow customs. Whatever the case, it is clear that the Egyptians frequently rebelled against Persian rule, though this only resulted in greater repression by the Persians. One of the best documented rebellions was that of Inarus, under Artaxerxes I, between 463/2 BC and 449 BC. According to the Greek historian Thucydides, Inarus was the son of a king called Psamtik, perhaps Psamtik III. At one point Inarus secured control of the Delta, trapping the Persian army at Memphis with the help of the Athenians. Most of Memphis was then taken, until the Persian general Megabyzus arrived and the Egyptians lost ground. Large numbers of the Athenians were killed before reinforcements could arrive, while Inarus himself was either crucified or impaled.

Egypt was liberated in 404 BC by Amyrtaeus of Sais, sole king of the 28th Dynasty, the country having proved too distant from Persia to be effectively controlled. Little can be said of Amyrtaeus – there is one possible reference to him in the writings of Diodorus. According to an Aramaic papyrus, however, Amyrtaeus was defeated in battle by Nepherites of Mendes and then executed at Memphis. The 29th Dynasty, founded by Nepherites I, consisted of only four kings. This dynasty and its successor suffered from instability and the ever-present threat of another invasion by Persia. Nevertheless, kings of both dynasties continued their royal obligation of erecting monuments and chose names that mimicked those of the 26th Dynasty. Of the 29th Dynasty, only King Hakor reigned for any length of time; it seems that there was always a power-hungry would-be successor watching and waiting for his opportunity to usurp the crown.

Indeed, it is probable that Nectanebo I, first king of the 30th Dynasty, deposed Nepherites II of the 29th Dynasty in a military coup. Nectanebo's unusually peevish statements in the Demotic Chronicle – 'I have appeared in the golden crown; it will not be removed from my head … My coronation robes are on me; they will not be removed … the office of ruler is in my hand; it will not be removed from me; the sword is the office of ruler, which is the appearance as falcon' – may betray his fear that the 29th Dynasty might return and try to retake power in the same manner that he himself had usurped it.

The 30th Dynasty was a period of prosperity and renewal. Its three kings acted as true pharaohs, undertaking building projects across the country and involving themselves in religious cults. But conflict at home and abroad remained a recurrent problem. To protect Egypt from Persian invasion, Nectanebo I fortified the eastern Delta, but he was still forced to

A basalt slab displaying King Nectanebo I making an offering. Probably from a temple at Sais or Heliopolis, it is now in the British Museum. The 30th Dynasty kings reigned during a time of renewed prosperity, but were plagued by the ever-present threat of Persian invasion.

repel a large-scale assault. To ensure his line of succession, he installed his son Teos (Djedhor) as co-regent. Teos did indeed inherit the crown, but he did not wear it for long. A military rebellion led by his nephew Nectanebo II forced him into exile, and he spent his remaining days in Persia, under Artaxerxes II.

Nectanebo II's reign saw one last glorious flowering of traditional Egyptian civilization. The arts prospered and the temples and their cults benefited from his patronage, but he could only resist Persia's forces for so long. The Persian army, said to be led by Artaxerxes III in person, was assisted by a defector who was familiar with Egypt's defences. The Persians penetrated the Delta at multiple points and the great fortifications fell quickly, followed by a series of towns. Nectanebo escaped to Memphis and prepared for a siege. As the Persians marched they took Pelusium and Bubastis, along with many other cities. Sensing imminent defeat, Nectanebo fled to Nubia never to return. The Persians entered Memphis and the second Persian occupation, sometimes called the 31st Dynasty, began.

## THE DEMOTIC CHRONICLE

**The failures of the final Late Period kings – from Amyrtaeus to Nectanebo II – were explained by the Egyptians of the early Ptolemaic Period as the result of divine punishment for not behaving in accordance with the will of god. The pharaohs, who from the start of Egyptian history were always in harmony with the divine, were now thought to be just as fallible as anyone else, their fates inexorably linked to their actions in life.**

The Demotic Chronicle, a text from this time, provides a list of good and bad rulers and their consequent fates. Good kings were expected to 'walk the path of god', and could achieve this by first performing the proper coronation rites, protecting Egypt's borders, ensuring the country flourished and by providing offerings for the gods. Kings who abandoned the law were removed. Amyrtaeus is said to have ordered violations of the law and as a result was forced to relinquish the throne. Similarly, of Nepherites I it was said '(Only) a few days are what were given to him, himself, because of numerous sins which were done in his time'.

Divine retribution could affect descendants too, as was said to be the case with Nepherites II: 'Because the law was abandoned under his father, a crime was made to reach his son after him'. It is unimaginable that a Khufu or an Amenhotep III would have been judged in this manner; such kings were the embodiment of divine order.

The evolution of Egyptian kingship over 3000 years is thus the evolution of the king's relationship with the divine and mankind's relationship to the king, their relative positions shifting in accordance with the realities of political life. Changes in the style of the evidence, and its preservation, allow us to observe these shifts. One must feel almost sorry for these Late Period kings because of the judgments meted out to them by their succeeding generation. Facing threats not only from a powerful foreign empire but also from within their own courts, and living in an age when the great deeds and artistic achievements of Egypt's most ancient pharaohs were idolized, they could not escape comparison with their, by then, mythic predecessors – the Ramesseses and Senwosrets, who gazed sternly down at them from ancient temple walls, speaking of great victories over impossible odds and absolute power over their courtiers. Given the realities of their time, could a Nectanebo or Nepherites ever truly 'walk the path of god'?

The Persians left a satrap in charge of their affairs and ruled as they had done during the 27th Dynasty – from afar. According to Diodorus, their regime was cruel and ruthless in its plundering of the wealth of the temples. It is fortunate for the Egyptians, then, that this dynasty was torn apart by internal intrigues at court. In Diodorus' account, Artaxerxes III, the great king who had taken Egypt, was poisoned by his vizier Bagoas, though other evidence suggests that he died of natural causes. Artaxerxes' son, Artaxerxes IV (Arses), then came to power, but he too was poisoned by Bagoas, leaving his successor, Darius III, to turn the tables and poison Bagoas first. During these events, in around 338 BC, an individual called Khababash appears to have rebelled against Persian rule in Egypt, which left him in control of part of Egypt and with the title of king. If indeed he followed Nectanebo II (and this can be disputed), he was the last native ruler of Egypt until the 20th century AD. But the Persians remained the true rulers of Egypt until the last months of 332 BC, when Alexander the Great entered Egypt and was welcomed as a liberator. This act initiated a new phase in Egyptian history, when the office of pharaoh was first occupied by Greek-Macedonians and then by Romans. Given its own unique character, the story of the Graeco-Roman Period – pharaonic kingship's final gasp – will be told in Chapter 8, 'The Last Pharaohs'.

The stele of Djedherbes, the son of a Persian father and an Egyptian mother, displays a mixture of artistic styles representative of both his parents' homelands, and probably dates to the 27th Dynasty. Found at Saqqara, it is now in the Egyptian Museum, Cairo.

## CHAPTER 3

# BECOMING PHARAOH

**Ideally the kingship passed from father to eldest son, imitating the passage of the crown from Osiris to Horus. In reality it was rarely this straightforward. Usurpation, obscure family lines, assassination and childless kings could all cause confusion for the hereditary line.**

## The Royal Bloodline

Children are the lifeblood of any royal dynasty; knowing this, each pharaoh ensured that he fathered numerous offspring. King Ramesses II, for example, had over 100 children – in fact he had so many sons that they were granted their own huge collective tomb in the Valley of the Kings, today known as KV 5. Unlike non-royals who could only have one spouse at a time, kings were free to marry as many women as they wished; of these, however, only one could hold the title of Great Royal Wife. Her first-born son was the most prestigious of all the royal children and would be next in line to the throne. Yet the high child mortality rate meant that it was never assured that a son would reach adulthood. Disease was common later in life, too, so that even a healthy adult crown prince might not live to become king. The title of 'eldest royal son' could thus pass at any time along the line of succession, ultimately often designating the eldest surviving royal son rather than the first-born male. It was therefore prudent to prepare all princes for the possibility of one day ascending the throne.

## The Birth of a Prince

Kings were believed to be quite literally the sons of gods. The female pharaoh Hatshepsut relates that the god Amun-Re was her father and that he had taken the form of King Thutmose I to have sexual intercourse with her mother, Queen Ahmose. Amenhotep III relates a comparable story at Luxor Temple, citing himself as the god's divine offspring. Although only known from the New Kingdom, the divine birth legend probably has its origins in the Old Kingdom and so formed a

A colossal granite statue of Ramesses II as a young boy, protected by the Canaanite god Hauron in the form of a falcon, now in the Egyptian Museum, Cairo. According to Egyptian custom, the child Ramesses is depicted naked, with his finger to his mouth and a side-lock of hair falling from the right side of his head.

major element of royal ideology. Egyptian kings also state that they were predestined to rule. 'God has given to him (the king) wisdom already in the womb', relates the 5th Dynasty physician Niankhsekhmet, while Senwosret I proclaimed at Heliopolis, 'He (the god Horakhety) has set me to be shepherd of this land … I am a king by virtue of my being, a sovereign to whom the office is not given; as a fledgling I conquered; I lorded in the egg; I controlled as a youth … The land was given to me, its length and breadth; I have been nursed as a born conqueror.'

In *The Romance of Setna and the Mummies*, known from the Graeco-Roman Period, when Pharaoh is informed about his daughter's pregnancy 'his heart became exceedingly happy' and he sent gifts to her from the royal treasury. However, such joy would always be accompanied with anxiety, especially when it was a Great Royal Wife who was pregnant. To ensure the safety of both the mother and child a special birthing room was prepared, decorated with images of the protective deity Bes – a leonine, bearded dwarf believed to guard new mothers and children. Magical charms placed around the room provided further protection, and spells were read aloud by priests to counteract the presence of any malevolent forces. Precautions of a more practical nature were also taken, as the Egyptians used their extensive medical knowledge to help bring the new prince into the world unharmed. When giving birth it was normal for the mother to squat balancing on two bricks, with her hands on her knees; she might also drink beer to help ease the labour pains.

Papyrus Westcar, a series of literary tales set in the Old Kingdom, describes the birth of three royal princes in fictional terms. The goddesses Isis, Nephthys, Meskhenet and Hekat enter the mother's birthing chamber disguised as dancing girls, along with the god Khnum, who pretends to be their porter. Isis stands before the mother, with Nephthys behind, while Hekat is said to hasten the birth. When the time came, each child 'slid into her (Isis') arms, a child of one cubit, strong boned, his limbs overlaid with gold, his headdress of true lapis lazuli'. Isis announces the name of each in turn, and the umbilical cord is not cut until the placenta has appeared and the child has been cleansed and bathed. After Meskhenet's proclamation that each child would be a king of Egypt, Ruddedet, the mother, 'cleansed herself in a cleansing of 14 days'. This was a time of isolation. Images of

The conception of Hatshepsut, from her divine birth scenes at Deir el-Bahri. The god Amun sits on the left, while Hatshepsut's mother, Queen Ahmose, is on the right. The pair are held aloft by two goddesses who sit upon a lion-bed – a symbol of resurrection.

women in this phase show them naked except for a collar and girdle, with their hair tied up, attended by female servants. In *The Story of the Two Brothers*, from the New Kingdom, after a queen has given birth, a wet nurse and nannies are assigned to the child, a practice typical among all elite women.

## Wet Nurses

Wet nurses are known to have been part of the royal court from as early as the Old Kingdom, although at that time they were not associated specifically with royal children. It is only in the 18th Dynasty that the title of royal wet nurse was introduced, disappearing again at the end of it. *The Papyrus of Ani*, a wisdom text dated to the New Kingdom, suggests that there was a suckling period of three years, which kept the child safe from contaminated water and thereby improved a prince's chances of survival. If a wet nurse's own children grew close to the future king they might be honoured with the rare title: 'foster brother/sister of the Lord of the Two Lands'. One such child was Mutnofret, whose mother had been nurse to Amenhotep II. Many of these children went on to prosper if the prince became king, with a large number finding positions in the Temple of Amun at Karnak.

A wet nurse's unique relationship with her young charge could also lead to other special privileges. Hatshepsut's nurse, Sitre, and perhaps also Senetnay, nurse of Amenhotep II, were two of only a few commoners buried in the Valley of the Kings, a clear sign of their importance to their respective monarchs. Sitre was also honoured with the gift of a life-sized statue from the royal workshops (now very fragmentary), perhaps given as a posthumous honour. The statue depicted the nurse seated with a miniature image of Hatshepsut as an adult, dressed in full regalia, on her lap. This was the first of a new form of statuary, which broke with tradition by allowing a commoner to be shown in physical contact with the king. In all other similar examples, however, it is a royal tutor who is shown with a prince or princess, rather than a royal nurse.

Despite the clear importance of royal wet nurses, there is little evidence to reconstruct how they came to attain their positions, since information about their lives typically derives from the tombs and votive objects produced for their husbands and sons. At the start of the 18th Dynasty they may have been chosen from among the royal family, but most later nurses appear to have been the wives of nobility.

A limestone flake with a drawing showing a woman suckling a child, probably from Deir el-Medina. She is depicted in the conventional manner for a woman during her 14 days of cleansing: her hair is bunched up above her head and she is naked except for a few items of jewelry.

## Royal Tutors

Once old enough, probably from the age of about four, princes and princesses began their formal education, guided and looked after by one or more specially appointed royal tutors. Although from textual records we know that tutors were a fixture of royal palaces from the Old Kingdom (Kaemtjenet of the 5th Dynasty, for example, states that he educated a royal prince), tutors specifically associated with individual royal children are only found in the 18th Dynasty. Almost 50 tutors are evidenced from this time, with the position itself developing over the course of the period. A tutor was part of his charge's life until he or she reached adulthood. Ahmose Pennekhbet began his work as tutor to Princess Neferure, daughter of Hatshepsut, 'when she was a child upon the breast', while Min of Thinis is depicted in his tomb teaching Amenhotep II as a young man. As time passed, each tutor progressed from being guardian to educator.

At the start of the 18th Dynasty royal tutors were drawn from the ranks of experienced officials, men of the royal court who had spent their lives involved in various aspects of the administration and had proved their worth to the king. The vizier Imhotep, who served under Amenhotep I, relates that he was chosen, 'because of the greatness of his (the King's) praises', while Senenmut, an influential high steward under Hatshepsut, states that he became tutor to Princess Neferure, 'because of my excellence on behalf of the king'. Other royal tutors, such as Paheri of El-Kab, his father, Itruri, and Min of Thinis, were important nomarchs (provincial mayors), while some even had a military background, such as Ahmose Pennekhbet, who had served in the wars of the early 18th Dynasty, although he had progressed from the military to the treasury by the time of his appointment.

Later in the 18th Dynasty, however, roughly from the reign of Amenhotep II, the office of tutor became increasingly formalized. It was no longer a position awarded to long-serving officials in addition to their primary duties (or when in semi-retirement), but became a professional career in itself, with the office divided between basic royal tutors and the higher-ranking overseer of tutors. Although the overall governmental rank held by these later individuals was not high, their proximity to the king and thus personal influence gave them a much greater degree of power than might be expected. As with royal nurses, the sons of tutors benefited from their parents' special connection: Sennefer and Amenemopet, the sons of Ahmose-Humay, tutor to Amenhotep II, became mayor of Thebes and vizier respectively, no doubt as a result of their youth spent with the prince. The latter was even buried in the Valley of the Kings (KV 48), close to the tomb of Amenhotep II.

Royal tutors, also like royal wet nurses, could be honoured with the gift of statues from the royal workshops, as well as the right to depict themselves in their tombs in scenes of personal contact with the king. Of all the 18th Dynasty royal

The royal tutor Senenmut holding Princess Neferure, daughter of Hatshepsut. This is one of many statues showing this tutor and his charge together.

tutors, the high steward Senenmut had the most 'tutor and child' statues bestowed upon him. Intriguingly, there are also 'tutor statues' for individuals not known to be royal tutors from any other source, which suggests that while such men may have performed this role, the lack of an official title reveals that it was not a formal position. It is possible that they were a teacher for only a short time, and perhaps for a specific subject unique to their personal experience.

It is not clear why the office of royal tutor became so prominent during the 18th Dynasty, though it is likely that it is related to the frequent absence of the king from Egypt. This was a period of empire building, when the pharaoh spent long periods of time accompanying his army into Nubia and Syria-Palestine. So unlike in other periods, when the tutors would be working under close royal supervision in the palace, in the 18th Dynasty the king was not always there to ensure that his children received a proper education. It comes as no surprise, then, that young princes were put in the care of respected, knowledgeable and, above all, highly trusted members of the administration. These were men who were given the specific privilege of being *royal* tutors, charged with shaping the minds of Egypt's future rulers and acting as their personal guardians.

## The Children of the Royal Nursery

Royal children grew up and were educated in the *kap*, a word often translated as 'royal nursery'. This was a secure and extremely private area at the rear of the palace reserved for personal royal affairs – only those with special access could enter, and anything that occurred within was treated with great secrecy. The New Kingdom official Amenhotep Son of Hapu referred to himself as 'one who hears the words of the secret *kap* … an official to whom something is confided'. The Late Middle Kingdom Papyrus Boulaq 18 gives the titles of those with freedom of access to this part of the palace, including the 'people of the house of nurses', 'children of the royal nursery', 'magicians of the royal nursery' and 'children of the nursery of the private quarters of the king'.

Children of the high elite, who were educated with the prince in the royal nursery, proudly displayed this connection for the rest of their lives, regularly including the title 'child of the royal nursery' in the lists of offices held in the course of their careers. Though this specific title is only known from the 18th Dynasty, the privilege of a youth spent with the royal children had been extended to elite children from at least the 5th Dynasty, when the official Ptahshepses is recorded as having been brought up among the royal children of the palace within the harem. In such a situation bonds could be formed between the royal princes (especially the crown prince) and future high-ranking courtiers, bonds which served to strengthen the future government. The children of the royal nursery could even use their prestige to act as a judiciary body: a marriage contract was signed by the children of the royal nursery, while a man petitioned a council made up of children of the royal nursery to ensure that his slave would have continual access to the royal palace.

To be so close to the king and educated with the royal princes was not necessarily a fast-track to key governmental positions. Some graduates of the royal nursery went on to hold quite low-ranking occupations, such as butler, fan-bearer and royal scribe, though interestingly they came from relatively low-status families: the shipbuilder Iununa was the son of the chief of carpenters of the king, Hemesh, while the draughtsman Nebseni carried on in the same profession as his father. Although low in administrative rank, however, the role of butler or fan-bearer required an individual who could be trusted, as it involved close proximity to the king.

A wall painting from the tomb of the high priest of Amun, Menkheperreseneb, at Thebes, showing foreign envoys with young children. The sons of vassal kings were often brought up at the Egyptian court in the New Kingdom.

But most children of the royal nursery did go on to occupy high- and middle-ranking positions: one for example, became high steward – responsible for the king's affairs – while another became viceroy of Kush (see p. 107) – the official who controlled Egypt's empire in Nubia. Some achieved important religious positions, including one Amenhotep, who became the high priest of Hathor-in-the-Midst-of-Thebes, and Kamose, the chief of the royal pure-priests in the Domain of Amun.

Many foreign princes, the sons of Egypt's vassal kings in Syria-Palestine, were also educated in the royal nursery from the time of Thutmose III onwards; as the author of one of the Amarna Letters (diplomatic correspondence inscribed on clay tablets found at Tell el-Amarna; see p. 131) relates: 'I have sent my son to the king, my lord, my god, my sun!' This gave the pharaohs influence over the often rebellious vassal kings of their empire and also ensured that the next generation of Levantine rulers had a strong and loyal connection to Egypt.

## An Education Fit for a King

What were the king's children actually taught in the private quarters of the royal nursery? Although no preserved text details the content of a royal child's curriculum, we can assume that it was similar to the standard education given to scribes in the less prestigious schools attached to temples and administrative buildings.

Pharaohs were certainly literate. In the story known as *The Prophecy of Neferti* the king takes a papyrus roll and a scribal palette so that he can write down

Neferti's words, while the 5th Dynasty vizier Senedjemib Inti states that the king wrote to him, 'with his own fingers'. Amenhotep II is also said to have composed a letter to his viceroy of Kush, Usersatet, 'with his own two hands'. Young princes must have begun to study writing as soon as they entered the palace's nursery, since literacy was the most important part of a scribal education. They first learnt the hieratic system of writing – a cursive form of hieroglyphic script used for all administrative documents and day-to-day business – before progressing to hieroglyphs, the more formal script used in temples and tombs. Normally, only students who entered the priesthood were expected to learn hieroglyphs, but it was an important necessity for the crown prince, who was training to become the highest priest in the land. In fact, given the arcane nature of much that the king was expected to know, it is likely that a prince underwent additional 'higher' training within the temples, learning restricted knowledge from the priests; some princes certainly held offices in the temple administration.

It was normal for scribal students to read and memorize the classic literature of ancient Egypt as a fundamental part of their education. Stories such as *The Tale of the Shipwrecked Sailor* and *The Eloquent Peasant* both entertained and taught basic writing skills, while wisdom texts (known as *sebayet*, 'Teachings') such as *The Maxims of Ptahhotep* would impart the highest morals to their young minds and equip them with the etiquette necessary for court life. *The Teachings for King Merikare* was written as if by a king for his son and stresses the responsibilities of kingship – something a crown prince would certainly have needed to be aware of. The prince is urged to respect his nobles and his people, not to be overconfident, not to punish unjustly, and to encourage loyalty through a good disposition. He is told the importance of knowledge and to learn from the words of his predecessors, and, perhaps above all, to be 'proficient in speech, so that you may be strong, for the strength of a king is his tongue. Words are mightier than any struggle.'

For at least a thousand years, teachers also used the *Kemyt* – a form of 'textbook', which is full of idioms and formulae and includes introductions to model literary letters and even a tale of travel – as part of their basic curriculum. Students would learn these texts by heart through copying and recitation. A popular text to learn was *The Satire of the Trades*, a composition that compared the highly prestigious life of a scribe and its relative ease to the pains and problems of other professions; no doubt this was intended to motivate and focus students on their work. But if a student's concentration did waver, his teacher was free to motivate him with violence, as one text relates: 'a boy's ear is on his back, he listens when he is beaten'. There is no evidence as to whether such punishments were inflicted upon royal princes; it is possible that their special status gave them immunity from the thrashings that their more unfortunate schoolmates had to endure.

Students wrote on wooden boards covered in gesso, which could be wiped clean and re-used, or on ostraca (sing. ostracon) – broken pieces of pottery – which were available in abundance. Papyrus was expensive to produce and so was only used for formal documents. Whether on a writing board or ostracon, the teacher would take the student's copy of the text and write his corrections over any mistakes that he found. In addition to writing and literature, the crown prince also studied mathematics, while royal tutors are recorded as having taught physical education to their students too: the tutor Min, mayor of Thinis under Thutmose III, is shown in his tomb instructing the young Amenhotep II how to fire arrows, a lesson that the prince is said to be enjoying (see also p. 112), while the First Intermediate Period biography of Khety describes swimming as part of the education of princes and nobility. *The Blinding of Truth by Falsehood*, a New Kingdom literary tale, relates that schoolboys also practised the art of war.

A major stage in any prince's life was his circumcision, as this was an initiation ceremony into manhood. The only images of a royal prince's circumcision are among the divine birth scenes carved on temple walls during the New Kingdom. One version, in the Temple of Mut at Karnak, depicts a young prince being held by his thighs by a kneeling woman, while a man squats in front performing the operation. It is uncertain at what age circumcision actually occurred, though it probably coincided with puberty.

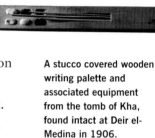

A stucco covered wooden writing palette and associated equipment from the tomb of Kha, found intact at Deir el-Medina in 1906.

A relief depicting the circumcision of young boys, from the 6th Dynasty tomb of Ankhmahor at Saqqara. Circumcision was an important rite of passage as it marked the change from child to adult.

## A Princely Life

For much of Egyptian history the activities of royal princes are enveloped in a cloak of silence; rarely, however, certain personalities and events do emerge, providing a fleeting insight into their lives. It is recorded that crown prince Amenmose, in the fourth year of Thutmose I's reign, went off, 'enjoying himself' shooting arrows, while the young Amenhotep II is presented in his Sphinx Stele as an expert in rearing horses. Before becoming king, Thutmose IV enjoyed riding his chariot in the desert near Memphis, shooting arrows at copper targets, and hunting game and lions with his friends. Thutmose was also responsible for ordering repairs on the Sphinx at Giza when only a prince. Prince Thutmose, a son of Amenhotep III, was apparently a pet lover – he had a sarcophagus made for his favourite cat (see p. 110). Khaemwaset, fourth son of Ramesses II, is often cited as being the first Egyptologist because he spent much of his time restoring the monuments of the Old and Middle Kingdoms, already ancient in his day, often leaving inscriptions to record the work he had undertaken. Ramesses IV states that in his youth he was occupied with trying to understand the policies of god; he immersed himself in ancient writings in search of old rituals, as he was concerned with the proper ritual way of approaching the divine.

Despite the lack of extensive detailed evidence, we thus get a picture of royal princes leading a life of learning, relaxation and sport, no doubt taking part in the same activities as their non-royal friends – listening to recitals of Egyptian tales set

A procession of the sons of Ramesses II. Ramesses had around 50 sons, many of whom served in the army. Merenptah, Ramesses' eventual successor, is 13th in the full row in this relief.

to music, attending banquets, hunting in the desert and marshes, and playing board games, such as *senet* – whether as adolescents, teenagers or adults (see also p. 115).

It wasn't all play, however. In the early Old Kingdom, especially in the 4th Dynasty, princes could be appointed to positions of high responsibility, acting as expedition leaders, overseers of construction projects and viziers. It was only with the political reforms of the 5th and 6th Dynasties that members of the royal family ceased to hold the top positions in the land, leaving these offices to non-royal members of the elite. From this time on, princes are no longer mentioned in administrative texts, although they are shown in pyramid temple reliefs, where they are identified only by name and sometimes with low-ranking priestly titles. The tombs of some late Old Kingdom princes are known, but they are no more elaborate than those of contemporary officials. Princes are even more obscure in Middle Kingdom evidence, being almost completely absent from administrative records and with hardly any of their burials known.

During the New Kingdom, however, princes who reached adulthood during the reigns of their fathers were normally awarded reasonably high positions. Prince Amenmose, son of Thutmose I, was overseer of the army; Amenemhat, the first-born son of Thutmose III, was an overseer of cattle in the Temple of Amun at Karnak, while Thutmose III himself had been a priest of Amun before becoming king; Amenhotep, son of Amenhotep II, was a *sem* (funerary) priest; and Thutmose, son of Amenhotep III, was responsible for the sacred Apis bulls at Memphis and acted as high priest of Ptah in that city. Despite these princes being more visible in the archaeological record, most of their burials are still unknown, although some were interred in their fathers' tombs in the Valley of the Kings.

More extensive evidence for offices held by princes is found in the Ramesside Period, when the aforementioned Khaemwaset was working as high priest of Ptah at Memphis and high priest of Re at Heliopolis. Some remains (now lost) discovered at the Serapeum – the catacombs of the sacred Apis bulls at Saqqara – were identified as belonging to Khaemwaset on the basis of inscriptional evidence, though they may in fact have been the remains of a bull, arranged to simulate a human burial. Temple reliefs and inscriptions, also of Ramesside date, show that princes could sometimes accompany their fathers on campaign and often held military titles. Certainly, the young Ramesses II accompanied his father, Seti I, during his wars in the Levant, learning valuable military skills that he later used to his advantage during his own wars. Seti himself had led military campaigns when serving his elderly father, Ramesses I. Similarly, Ramesses IV was commander of the army when a prince, but also refers to spending time in the law court (*kenbet*), where he silently observed the proceedings in order to gain insight into judicial affairs.

Prince Khaemwaset, fourth son of Ramesses II, served as high priest of Ptah at Memphis and high priest of Re at Heliopolis. He is often cited as the first Egyptologist because of his particular interest in restoring monuments of the Old and Middle Kingdoms.

## CO-REGENCIES

Co-regency – when two kings ruled simultaneously – was technically against the traditions of Egyptian kingship, which dictated that only one pharaoh could rule at any one time. Nevertheless, the first co-regency appears to have occurred in the Middle Kingdom, between either Amenemhat I and his son Senwosret I, or Senwosret I and Amenemhat II.

Following the tumult of the First Intermediate Period, ensuring a clear line of succession must have become a priority. But in addition to any overall dynastic advantages of a co-regency, it also gave the crown prince an opportunity to experience his future role first-hand, gaining valuable on-the-job training.

Deciding whether or not a co-regency occurred for certain kings has been a major problem for scholars attempting to recreate Egypt's chronology; some even argue that co-regencies did not occur at all until the Ptolemaic Period.

A block from the Red Chapel of Hatshepsut at Karnak, displaying Thutmose III and Hatshepsut side by side as kings (see p. 93).

Thus, except for the early Old Kingdom and parts of the New Kingdom, there is very little evidence for princes playing an active role in the day-to-day running of the country, and it was not until the 21st and 22nd Dynasties, during Egypt's Third Intermediate Period, that princes again played a more active role in public office. For most of Egyptian history, royal princes are simply names connected to a specific king, but about whom nothing is known.

Irrespective of whether he held a particular governmental office or spent his time at leisure, at some point in a crown prince's life, the king – his father – would die, propelling him to the highest position in the land. At this moment his life and very nature would change irreversibly. He would now simultaneously be high priest of all gods, intermediary between heaven and earth, a symbol of order and control, the highest authority and decision-maker in the land, and the ultimate warrior. He would no longer simply be a man, but a pharaoh.

## Usurpation and Assassination

Although it was strictly against royal ideology for someone to usurp the throne – kingship being inherited by the eldest son in an unbroken line – for the power-hungry the supreme authority embodied by the crown was often too tempting to resist. Kings faced assassination attempts, dynastic unrest and military coups from the start of Egyptian history – probably more often than the evidence currently allows us to see. The reality of life as king must have been stressful, knowing that potential conspiracies lurked around every corner and behind every door.

The 6th Dynasty in particular appears to have been a troubled time. Manetho recounts that King Teti, first ruler of this period, was murdered by his bodyguard. An ephemeral king called Userkare then appears to have successfully usurped power, only to be replaced by Pepi I – the rightful heir – who removed Userkare's name from any monuments that recorded his existence. Pepi himself faced a harem conspiracy that attempted to remove him from the throne but was ultimately thwarted. The only information concerning this event derives from the tomb of the contemporary official Weni, who states: 'when there was a legal case in secret in the royal harem against the royal wife, the "great of affection", His Majesty had me proceed to hear it on my own. No vizier or official was present apart from myself … I alone together with just one other judge and mouth of Nekhen put it down in writing … never before had anyone like me heard the secrets of the royal harem ….'

'Maintain your vigilance against those who should be subordinate to you, but who turn out not to be so, men in whose loyalty one can place no trust; do not let yourself be alone with them. Put no trust in a brother, acknowledge no one as a friend, do not raise up for yourself intimate companions, for nothing is to be gained from them.'

*The Teachings of Amenemhat for his son Senwosret*

It is almost certain that Montuhotep IV's vizier, a man called Amenemhat, became Amenemhat I of the 12th Dynasty, perhaps by violent means, only to be killed himself later in his own reign. This assassination is mentioned in a didactic text known as *The Teachings of Amenemhat for his Son Senwosret*, in which the king, speaking from beyond the grave or in his dying moments, states that it was his harem and personal bodyguard that made the attempt on his life. Consequently, Amenemhat's advice to his son is to be cautious of those around him, though in this case, the rightful successor, Senwosret I, did ascend the throne, showing that the plot was ultimately unsuccessful, even if the king himself was killed.

The second half of the New Kingdom was also eventful. Only two years into the reign of Seti II, a man named Amenmessu seized control of Egypt south of the Faiyum, though Seti II soon regained full control. Upon Amenmessu's disappearance from history, those who served him also vanished. Usurpation could also be more insidious. Seti II was succeeded by the young King Siptah, but due to his youth, Queen Tawosret held effective power in association with an influential royal adviser named Bay. This man overstepped his bounds, referring to himself as 'one who placed the king on the throne of his father' – a veritable kingmaker. Bay is also shown as equal in size to Tawosret on one monument, representing their equal authority, and even began a tomb for himself in the Valley of the Kings (KV 13). For his efforts, Bay was executed in Siptah's fifth year as king, an event recorded on an ostracon from Thebes which refers to him as 'the great enemy'.

In the reign of Ramesses III, the women of the harem planned an attempt on his life; it is unclear whether he was killed, but surviving records of the ensuing trials on various papyri detail those involved and the punishments meted out. The conspirators' aim was to place a lesser prince called Pentaweret, a son of Queen Tiye, on the throne in place of the rightful successor – Ramesses IV. Those involved were high ranking, including members of the treasury and army, royal cupbearers, magicians and scribes from the House of Life, and a chamberlain; this role of this last individual was apparently to recruit people to the conspiracy. The plotters from within the royal harem were thus joined by others from outside, who were expected to raise arms against the king both physically and supernaturally. Using a stolen book of magic from the royal library, one of the conspirators created wax figurines to harm the royal bodyguard magically, while wax gods were also created to attack the king himself. Other magicians conjured forces to counteract the positive magic normally used to keep the king safe. Once apprehended, the conspirators were treated harshly: many were sentenced to death or forced to commit suicide, others were mutilated, their noses and ears cut off, while those that had knowledge of the plot but did nothing to prevent it were also punished, along with their wives.

Accounts by classical authors provide a rich and detailed source of information on the troubled reigns of kings in the Late Period. Pharaoh Ahmose II of the 26th Dynasty took the throne by force from Apries, following the latter's defeat at the

Siptah receives life from the god Re-Horakhety in tomb KV 47 in the Valley of the Kings. This king ordered the death of the chancellor Bay, an influential adviser who ruled in all but name alongside Queen Tawosret during Siptah's youth.

## FOREIGNERS AS KINGS

Egyptian ideology made a strong distinction between Egyptians and foreigners. Egypt was the land of *maat* – order, control and justice – embodied by the pharaoh. Beyond its borders was chaos, always threatening to overpower order. Foreigners were a manifestation of this chaos, and so, during the various periods when Egypt was under foreign occupation, dealing with the contradiction of having an enemy on the throne must have posed serious problems.

In the case of the Hyksos – the rulers of the Delta during the Second Intermediate Period – this situation led to rebellion. But in the Third Intermediate Period pharaohs of foreign origin were more accepted. The Libyan rulers had been settled in Egypt for some time; though Egyptianized they retained much of their foreign identity, including their distinctive names, such as Osorkon and Shoshenq. The 25th Dynasty Nubian pharaohs were equally Egyptianized and portrayed themselves according to accepted conventions, though with some differences. The Persians too were depicted in much the same way as earlier kings. It seems that to the Egyptians living in the 1st millennium BC, as long as an individual was crowned according to traditional custom and behaved in the expected manner, then, irrespective of his origin, he was pharaoh.

The golden funerary mask of King Shoshenq II from Tanis. Shoshenq was a king of Libyan descent and proudly displayed his foreign heritage through his distinctly non-Egyptian name.

battle of Momemphis. Apries then fled the country, spending three years in exile, possibly in Babylon, before returning to Egypt backed by the Babylonian army. His plan to retake the crown was not to succeed, and he was again defeated by Ahmose II, and, according to Herodotus, was captured. Apparently, Ahmose II treated his prisoner well, refusing to kill the deposed king and permitting him to live in the royal palace at Sais. However, as Herodotus relates, 'The Egyptians objected to the injustice of maintaining a man who was his – and their – worst enemy, and persuaded Amasis (Ahmose II) to surrender the prisoner. They strangled him.' Ahmose II then buried Apries with full honours at Sais, despite all that had occurred between them. Another tale of Late Period usurpation is recorded by Plutarch, who relates that King Nectanebo II of the 30th Dynasty came to power after initiating a military coup, turning King Teos' Athenian and Spartan commanders against him. Deserted by his army, Teos fled and spent the rest of his life in Persia.

Herodotus, who visited Egypt during the Persian Period, records the story of an assassination attempt on a fictional King Sesostris – a combination of Ramesses II and the various Senwosrets (Sesostris is the Greek version of Senwosret) of the Middle Kingdom. According to this story, Sesostris, on returning home from abroad, was invited to a banquet by his brother, who had been acting as viceroy. Sesostris attended the banquet with his sons and wife, but his brother piled wood around the building and set it alight. To escape, Sesostris' wife suggested that he lay two of their six sons on the fire in order to make a bridge for the others. While these two sons were burned to death, he and his other children were saved; he later took revenge on his brother.

A late literary tale, *The Instruction of Ankhsheshonqy*, also relates a plot to assassinate a king. This was a large conspiracy involving 'the guards, the generals, and the great men of the palace', but the king was informed about the impending attempt on his life by one of his courtiers during the night. After hearing the news, he was unable to sleep. First thing the next day, the plot's instigator was burned on an earthen altar built at the door of the palace, along with his servants and anyone involved in the conspiracy. Ankhsheshonqy himself, who knew of the plans but was not involved, was imprisoned.

## The Royal Accession

At the death of the king, when 'the falcon had flown to heaven', the palace gates were closed and the courtiers bowed their heads in sorrow. The crown prince came to the throne the next morning, but his official coronation would not take place until full, proper arrangements could be made. The accession day could be a time of amnesty. The fictional *The Instruction of Ankhsheshonqy* presents the pharaoh celebrating his accession day by releasing all but one of the inmates from the prison at Daphnae.

> 'Menkheperre [Thutmose III], justified, went up to heaven and united with the sun disc; the body of the god joined him who had made him. When the next morning dawned the sun disc shone forth, the sky became bright, the King of Upper and Lower Egypt ... Amenhotep II was installed on the throne of his father.'
>
> Inscription of Amenemhab

The period between accession and coronation was a dangerous time, when 'the king who will rule' progressed around the country as part of a journey called 'The Creation of Order in all Provinces'. Based on a possible interpretation of a text that one scholar has dubbed the *Mystery Play of the Succession* but which is more widely known as the *Ramesseum Dramatic Papyrus*, the king sailed along the Nile and visited numerous cities, making offerings to the local god as he went.

According to the 'Mystery Play', an enactment of the coronation took place at each location, which tied the king to these major centres in a ritual manner in preparation for his full coronation. These 'performances' were all part of the king's re-establishment of order following the death of his predecessor.

The king and court also entered a period of mourning that lasted until the burial of the deceased king. During this phase the king was expected to let his beard grow. Consequently, some New Kingdom representations depict him with facial stubble, while one scene appears to show him crying, with red lines visible beneath his eyes. According to Herodotus, it was an Egyptian custom to let the hair and beard grow during the period between the death and burial of a loved one; it was also normal for people to abstain from eating and drinking excessively.

This ostracon bears a sketch of an unshaven king wearing the Blue Crown; as it was an Egyptian custom to remain unshaven from the day of a relative's death until the funeral, he is probably in mourning.

## The Coronation Ceremony

Once the necessary rituals had been conducted and the deceased king had been buried (see Chapter 7), the day eventually came for the coronation itself. When, where and how this occurred changed over the years, and no complete account has survived to guide a reconstruction. Nevertheless, it would be timed to coincide with an important date, such as new year's day, representative of a fresh beginning, while Memphis, as traditional royal residence, was the location for many, including Taharqo's coronation in the 25th Dynasty. Horemheb, however, was crowned at Thebes (at Luxor Temple) in the 18th Dynasty, as was Shabitqo again in the 25th Dynasty, and different pharaohs no doubt chose other major centres depending on the period in which they reigned.

In the Early Dynastic Period, the coronation ceremony focused on a ritual reunification of the Two Lands, though exactly what this entailed is unclear. One major element was certainly a ritual circuit of the great White Walls of

Drawing of a relief from Medinet Habu showing Ramesses III accompanied by the goddesses Wadjet and Nekhbet and the souls of Pe (Buto) and Nekhen (Hierakonpolis) during his coronation. These souls represent the king's Predynastic predecessors.

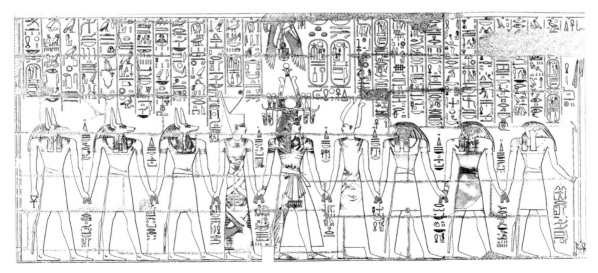

Ramesses III is crowned by Horus and Seth, deities important in the coronation ceremony.

Memphis, symbolizing the king's authority over the entire country. In later periods the first part of the ceremony involved the ritual purification of the king by priests representing the four cardinal points; by pouring water on the king they transferred their power to him. At this time, the king was also anointed with various oils and was symbolically suckled by a goddess, signifying rebirth – his transformation from man to god. Horus and Seth then brought an empty carrying chair, which was used to transport the king to the shrines of Upper and Lower Egypt, known as the *Per-Wer* and *Per-Neser*. Along the way he was acclaimed by priests acting as the souls of Pe and Nekhen, mythical ancestors of the king from the cities of Buto and Hierakonpolis respectively.

Within the two shrines, the king was crowned by the gods, receiving a different crown from each. Amenhotep II is particularly specific in his account of the crowns he received: 'He assumed the Two-Great-of-Magics; the Double Crown has united about his head, the *Atef* Crown about his brow, his countenance being adorned with the Upper Egyptian Crown and the Lower Egyptian Crown. He has assumed the Headband and the Blue Crown, and the *ibes*-headdress; the two great plumes are upon his head, and the *Nemes*-headdress has enveloped his shoulders; the assemblage of the diadems of Atum, which have been assigned to his image in accordance with the command of the creator of the gods, Amun, the primeval god who has crowned him.'

Coronation depictions from Hatshepsut's Red Chapel at Karnak Temple show the king kneeling before Amun; these scenes are virtually identical, except that in each Hatshepsut wears a different crown. However, all the various crowns are said to be a 'crown of Re', connecting them with the sun god. In his coronation inscription Horemheb speaks only of *Weret-Hekau* ('the Great of Magic') being established at his brow as his uraeus, and of the Blue Crown (*Khepresh*) being placed upon his head by Amun himself. At this moment, the divine royal *ka*-spirit combined with his mortal body, altering his very being.

Hatshepsut kneels before the enthroned Amun-Re, who places the Blue Crown on her head. Standing in front of the kneeling king is the goddess Amunet. Relief from the Red Chapel of Hatshepsut at Karnak.

Ramesses II receives the royal flail and the promise of many jubilees from Amun-Re as part of his coronation, depicted in the Great Hypostyle Hall in the Temple of Karnak.

The king was next presented with a scimitar and other regalia, such as the crook and flail – symbols of his power – followed by the presentation of a casket said to contain a document that confirmed his right to rule. At some point in the ceremony, probably after the actual coronation, the king performed a ritual circumambulation of the city walls, just as Egypt's earliest kings had run a circuit around the walls of Memphis. He also received the 'inheritance of Horus' through a ritual involving anointing, hymns to Horus and eating bread made in the shape of the hieroglyph for 'office'; he then made offerings to his royal ancestors. A ceremony called 'uniting the Two Lands' may have occurred next, followed by the proclamation of the king as legitimate successor by a priest dressed as Thoth. The gods then ratified this decree, and the king was led before them for blessings. Thoth proclaimed the royal titulary, before inscribing the years of the king's rule on the sacred persea tree (*ished*), accompanied and aided by the goddess Seshat. The king now fired arrows to the four cardinal points and freed four birds. The final stage of the ceremony was a large and sumptuous banquet. Afterwards, letters were sent out to officials across the country detailing the king's full titulary to be used in royal oaths.

BELOW **During his coronation ceremony Thutmose III fires arrows to the cardinal points, assisted by the god Seth.**

## THE ROYAL TITULARY

During his coronation the king was assigned four names – the Horus, Two Ladies, Golden Horus and *nesu-bity* (throne) names – in addition to the one that he was given at birth. These names could be completely original or be borrowed from a royal predecessor, but all were meant to emphasize policies that the king intended to achieve during his reign.

Amenhotep III's Two Ladies name was 'one who established laws and made the Two Lands peaceful', reflecting internal policies, while his Golden Horus name was 'the great-of-strength, one who has struck down Asiatics'. He also copied elements of Thutmose III's titulary, thus connecting himself with his illustrious ancestor: Amenhotep's Horus name was 'the victorious bull who has appeared in truth', whereas Thutmose III's was 'the victorious bull who has appeared in Thebes'.

Royal names were normally anticipatory, but they might also reflect achievements from before the coronation: Seti II's Golden Horus name was 'the one great of dread in all lands', while his Two Ladies name was 'the strong-of-sword, one who repelled the Nine Bows', perhaps referring to battlefield victories when he was crown prince. Kings could also change their names as their reigns progressed, often following major political events: Montuhotep II, who reunited Egypt by defeating the Herakleopolitans, was originally the Horus 'the one who sustained the heart of the Two Lands', but changed his Horus and Two Ladies names in his 14th year to 'the divine one of the White Crown'. Then, before his 39th year, his Horus and Two Ladies names became 'the one who has united the Two Lands'.

It is unclear who devised the royal titulary. An inscription at Karnak Temple from the reign of Thutmose III states that the god Amun-Re chose the king's names; perhaps the temple priests composed a variety of names and placed them before the oracle of the god to select from. A text from the reign of Hatshepsut relates that the lector priests set her royal titulary. At other times the king himself may have chosen the names, or if he were too young it is possible that the queen regent and influential officials together decided on them. Certainly, Udjahorresnet, a Late Period priest at Sais, official and chief physician to Cambyses, relates that he composed the royal titulary for that Persian pharaoh.

ABOVE **The royal cartouches of Horemheb, from his tomb in the Valley of the Kings (KV 57).**

LEFT **A gold ring inscribed with the *nesu-bity* (throne) name of Thutmose III – Menkheperre.**

Although accounts of the coronation are quite brief and focus their attention on the actions of the king and gods, a large staff of officials must have participated in the ceremony. One such individual was the chamberlain (*imy-khent*) Semty the Younger, who served under Amenemhat II in the Middle Kingdom. He records that

In this relief in the Great Hypostyle Hall at Karnak pharaoh Ramesses II, wearing his Blue Crown, kneels before the god Amun-Re, while behind him Thoth inscribes the leaves of the sacred persea tree with the years of his reign.

he was privy to the secrets of the king's adornment, and specifically mentions his role in relation to the royal crowns. He was 'Priest of the South Crown and North Crown, Khnum-servant of the king's adornment, who fashions the Great-of-Magic, lifts up the White Crown in *Per-Wer*, chief Nekhebite and servant of the Red Crown in *Per-Nu* (also called *Per-Neser*), hand-in-hand with the Wise One, one whose coming is awaited as Adorner with the Crown, in making-appear-in-glory Horus, lord of the Palace'. Similarly, a New Kingdom official called Amenhotep states that he was 'the chamberlain and greatest of anointers, who adorned the king in the *Per-Wer* and made festive the Lord of the Two Lands in the *Per-Neser*'.

Once the coronation ceremony was completed, *maat* was re-established and life continued as it had always done. Order had returned following a period of chaos, as a text from the time of Ramesses IV relates: 'Oh happy day! Heaven and earth are in joy, (since) you are the great lord of Egypt! Those who had fled are come back to their cities; those who were [hidden] have emerged; those who were hungry, they are sated and content; those who were thirsty are drunken; those who were naked, they are clad in fine linen.'

## CHAPTER 4

# BEING PHARAOH

Having united with the divine *ka*-spirit of kingship, the newly crowned king was now raised to the highest position in society. As king, his life revolved around ensuring that *maat* was enforced, that Egypt's borders were safe and that the gods received their due offerings. His life was dominated by ritual, whether at home in the palace or travelling around the country. He issued judgments and decrees, and, if he so wished, could accompany his army on campaign.

## Awakening in the Palace

The pharaoh woke up each morning in his bedchamber at the rear of his palace, mirroring the location of the god's sacred shrine in the innermost part of every temple. His bed, which sloped towards the foot end, was low and wooden, its legs terminating in exquisitely carved lion's paws. Covered in thick blankets, the bed was raised up in an alcove at the rear of the room, below a small window high in the ceiling to let in cool air. Pharaoh's head lay upon a headrest – shaped like an upturned crescent moon on a base – on which a linen pillow was placed. Such headrests could be quite elaborate; one from Tutankhamun's tomb took the form of two ducks' heads reaching to the base with their beaks.

Opening his eyes and staring at the ceiling, the king saw a line of five painted vultures of black, white and red, their wings spread wide against a yellow background, their heads facing the chamber's entrance; each represented the goddess Nekhbet. Beneath their wings were his own epithets and names. The vultures were framed by a band of small, red-centred rosettes, followed by an outer chequerboard pattern of yellow, red and green. The chamber's walls were painted with images of the god Bes alternating with another chequerboard pattern. Below, against a yellow background, were large alternating images of the hieroglyphic signs *ankh* (life) and *tyt* (connected to the goddess Isis), standing upon baskets representing 'all'; these were separated by vertical bands of red, white and green.

Pharaoh Menkaure, wearing the White Crown of Upper Egypt, a false beard and a *shendyt* kilt, stands with the goddess Hathor to his right and the personification of a nome to his left. This is one of a series of triads found during excavation of the king's valley temple at Giza.

The excavated bedchamber of Amenhotep III at Malkata in Thebes, on which this reconstruction is based, bears similar decoration to that known from other palaces of the same period – pleasing geometric shapes, protective imagery and scenes of nature were all popular subjects for palace chamber walls, ceilings and floors. But what furniture filled the king's bedroom? Nothing was found archaeologically at Malkata, but a reconstruction can be made based on the funerary objects of Queen Hetepheres of the 4th Dynasty and the furniture found in New Kingdom elite and royal burials. Gilded wooden chairs, tall wooden stands supporting vessels, oil lamps resting on pedestals, and chests containing linen and clothes would all have been present. A gilded wooden canopy surrounded Hetepheres' bed, hung with curtains for privacy; despite living over a millennium later, Amenhotep III may have enjoyed similar luxury.

Just beyond the royal bedchamber's wooden door, the king's personal bodyguard stood throughout the night.

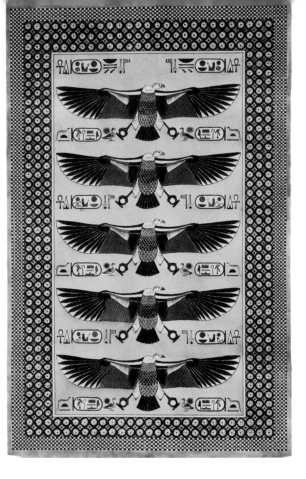

ABOVE **A reconstruction of the elaborately painted ceiling of Amenhotep III's bedchamber at Malkata. The vultures represent Nekhbet, the goddess of Upper Egypt, who grips *shen*-rings of eternity in her claws.**

ABOVE **Paintings of *ankh*-signs and *tyt*-knots alternate along the wall of the king's bedchamber at Malkata.**

RIGHT **A painted ivory headrest from the tomb of Tutankhamun, decorated with the face of the god Bes at its sides and with legs in the form of ducks' heads gripping the base with their beaks. Bes was an apotropaic deity, who protected mothers in childbirth, children and people while they slept.**

This individual changed daily, a practice referred to in the Ptolemaic Period *The Instruction of Ankhsheshonqy*: '(it was) his (Wahibre-Mekhy's) evening for spending the night in the portico of the resting place in which pharaoh was'. Tomb scenes from Tell el-Amarna depict guards standing at each doorway in the royal palace. While he slept, the pharaoh was well protected.

**Furniture from the tomb of Queen Hetepheres, wife of King Sneferu and mother of Khufu, from Giza. Among the objects were a bed with a headrest, chairs and a bed canopy.**

## Morning Ablutions

At Malkata, outside the king's bedchamber lay a robing room and bathroom, all of which were situated behind a small reception room with its own throne dais. This appears to have been a standard plan, as a similar layout is known at the rear of Merenptah's palace at Memphis (see p. 80) and in the small ritual palaces attached to New Kingdom royal mortuary temples. It would seem that after emerging from his bedchamber the king passed through his robing room, briefly through his reception room, and into the bathroom, where a stone screen wall provided privacy while a servant poured water over him. The best-preserved royal bathroom was found within Merenptah's palace. Its stone-lined walls were decorated with royal cartouches, a cornice ran along its top and protective symbols were below. A latrine with a stone screen wall was found in an adjacent room. From the bathroom, the king moved to his robing room, which at Malkata had a ceiling decorated with front-facing bulls' heads within interlocking spiral patterns and rosettes.

As in many court societies, the daily actions of the king, no matter how mundane, took on a ritualized charge. Each act involved special etiquette and required officials to organize and oversee it. The chief of secrets of the House of the Morning – the palace sector associated with the king's bathing, dressing and shaving – was charged with ensuring that the king's washing and rising proceeded correctly each day. In the Old Kingdom, many officials were attached to the House of the Morning, including those associated with the grooming of the king – men who supervised his manicure, shaving, hair, anointing and purifications. In the Pyramid Texts (see p. 168), the shaving of the king was conducted by a god called Dwa-wer, emphasizing the ritual role of this action.

Appearance was important to high-class Egyptians, and kings were no different. The pharaoh's body was expected to be clean shaven at all times, unless he was in mourning, so that typically he wore a wig made from human hair provided by his director of wigmakers. Tutankhamun's shaving equipment was stored in a white box in his tomb; it bears an inscription that reads, 'The equipment of His Majesty Life! Prosperity! Health! When he was a child. Contents: Copper handled-razors, knife-razors, and ewers; linen.' Despite the clear importance of shaving the body, many of the New Kingdom royal mummies still display their original hair, indicating these kings had not shaved near the time of their death.

In the morning, while being prepared for his day, the king's skin was moisturized with pure oils and fats, and lime or natron was used in place of soap. The king also used scented ointments, whether on daily business or when performing particular rituals. Senemiah, an official who served under Hatshepsut, states that he specifically chose the oils the pharaoh used during her rituals, oils that helped her to appear as a god.

Kings applied eye makeup (called kohl), which was made from green malachite until midway through the Old Kingdom and galena thereafter. The mineral was ground up and mixed with water to form a paste, which was stored in small pots and then, from the Middle Kingdom onwards, applied with a thin stick.

Cosmetic items from Tutankhamun's tomb appear to have been used during his life, including his kohl pots and kohl sticks. He was also buried with ointment containers; one particularly elegant example was carved from ivory in the shape of a trussed duck with a swivelling lid. Two elaborate cases for mirrors were also found in his tomb, though their contents were missing.

## The Royal Wardrobe

Just as statues of the gods were clothed each morning by particular priests, so various officials were in charge of clothing the pharaoh. A Middle Kingdom official named Montuhotep, for example, states that he was the 'great lord of the royal wardrobe who approaches the limbs of the king'. Others refer to being associated with the royal linen and the handling of different crowns and headdresses, holding positions such as director of all royal loincloths, the keeper of the crown, and the one who adorns Horus.

In official art the king is depicted wearing a variety of crowns, elaborate pectorals, a kilt held by a belt, sandals and a bull's tail. There can be no doubt that he dressed in this manner for some ceremonial occasions as these depictions must have some basis in reality, but did he dress this way in daily life? It is a difficult question to answer, both because of the idealism in official portraiture and because the clothing worn by the pharaohs has rarely survived. Still, the tomb of Tutankhamun as well as scattered further examples do provide some clues.

Made to encircle the whole torso, Tutankhamun's corslet, formed of a collar of semiprecious stones and a pectoral above bands of 'feathers' picked out in faience and agate, is a particularly elaborate item of clothing from his tomb, and was perhaps worn during particular ceremonies; other items, however, were more

OPPOSITE ABOVE
A reconstruction of the painted ceiling of the royal robing room at Malkata.

OPPOSITE BELOW An *ankh*-shaped mirror case from the tomb of Tutankhamun. Two mirror cases were found in the king's tomb, both empty, and one ivory mirror handle – its silver or gold mirror disc was probably stolen by ancient tomb robbers.

BELOW The elaborate corslet of Tutankhamun: glass beads form the 'feathers' in the lower half of the corslet, while above them on the front a pendant displays Tutankhamun in the presence of the gods Amun, Atum and the goddess Iussas. The main feature of the rear pendant is a solar scarab flanked by rearing uraei.

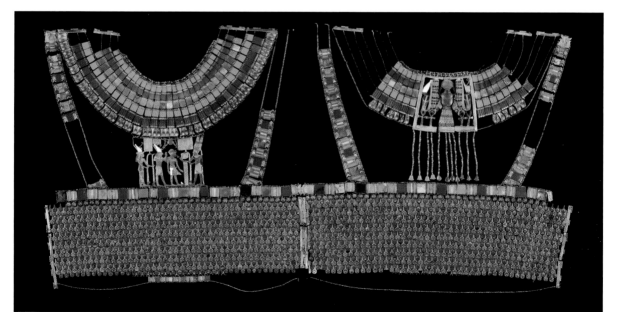

suited to daily wear. Bag tunics were typical of the
New Kingdom, and one knee-length tunic made
from a single folded piece of plain linen decorated with
applied bands featured a tapestry woven collar in the shape of an
*ankh*-sign and had a royal cartouche among its decorations. Various
embroidered bands at the bottom of the tunic display female-
headed winged sphinxes, gryphons, palmettes and hunting scenes
with ibexes and dogs, while others consist of geometric patterns,
including zigzags, squares and chevrons. This tunic, perhaps in
Syrian style, probably served a ceremonial purpose but is unlike
anything known in official art. Another tunic from the tomb made
of yellow linen features green and brown stripes and bands of flying
ducks across the chest, with similar bands of walking ducks or geese
at the sides and bottom. Further fragmentary items of clothing were
decorated with sequins, rosettes and cartouches. Plainer examples of
bag tunics were also found, though most had some form of embellishment,
as well as more than 50 loincloths with associated over-kilts. These show that
the king could dress just like any other noble, as similar examples are known
from private tombs and even the workmen's village at Tell el-Amarna.
Nevertheless, even if the style of his clothes was similar to that of his
subjects, the king wore the finest grade of linen – 'royal linen' – far higher
in quality than the lesser 'fine thin cloth', 'thin cloth' and 'smooth cloth'
below it.

Old Kingdom pharaohs wore their kilts in a unique style – the so-
called 'royal fold' – to emphasize their special position. Statuary from this
time presents the king with his kilt wrapped around from left over right in
a clockwise fashion, and tucked in at the front. In contrast, the elite only ever
present themselves with their kilts wrapped in an anticlockwise fashion.
By the Middle Kingdom, however, the elite could use the 'royal fold' too.

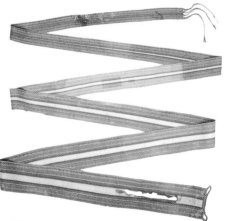

ABOVE **A modern reproduction of the
'Syrian' style knee-length tunic of
Tutankhamun. The collar is in the
shape of an *ankh*-sign, while geometric
patterns and animals were embroidered
at the bottom.**

LEFT **An elaborate sash that probably
belonged to Ramesses III, now in the
World Museum, Liverpool. It is long
enough to have been wrapped around
the body multiple times.**

Cloaks and robes were also among the clothing found in Tutankhamun's tomb, including one decorated with gold and faience daisies, and one with a leopard-skin pattern. The king was also buried with sashes, tasselled belts and rolls of cloth and bandages, which may have acted as sashes; some display the royal cartouche, including one tapestry woven sash formed of nine plaits. Another sash, probably originally from Thebes and which some scholars argue belonged to Ramesses III, is woven in red, blue, yellow and natural flax, and displays a pair of bands, zigzags, dots and rows of *ankh*s, as well as the king's name and a reference to the second year of his reign (now decayed). It is long enough to have been wrapped multiple times around the waist, just like those depicted worn by the king in battle scenes. Such elaborate sashes are typically associated with royalty, with much plainer types seen on statues of the high elite.

Most of the items of headgear in Tutankhamun's tomb were badly deteriorated when discovered, and no crowns were among them beyond a single diadem, still in place on the king's mummy. In art, this form of diadem, called the *Seshed*, consists of a simple headband with a cobra wrapped around it, rearing at the front. Two golden ribbons fall down at the back, as if the headband had been tied, and two further ribbons hang beside the ears, sometimes also decorated with rearing cobras. On Tutankhamun's example, the rearing cobra's body writhes over the crown of the head, giving support, rather than wrapping around the headband, and a vulture has been added at the brow. Beneath the diadem on the king's head was a fragmentary *khat*-headdress (a form of kerchief tied at the back, like the *Nemes*-headdress), with associated vulture and cobra, held in place by a golden headband; beneath this again was a skull cap. Tutankhamun's skull cap was made of fine white linen, with two uraei picked out in faience and gold beads; such skull caps may have been used to protect wigs or shaven heads.

OPPOSITE RIGHT **A modern reconstruction of a typical linen robe from the tomb of Tutankhamun. In reality, as opposed to official art, the king's daily dress was probably little different from that of his courtiers.**

RIGHT *Seshed* **diadem (above) found on the body of Tutankhamun, perhaps representative of the king's daily wear, and (below) a scene from the tomb of Prince Khaemwaset, a son of Ramesses III, from his tomb in the Valley of the Queens, showing Ramesses III wearing the same form of royal diadem and a fine linen shirt covered in sequins, similar to fragmentary examples in Tutankhamun's tomb.**

Accessories in the tomb included 27 tapestry woven gloves with *rishi*-feathered patterns, the finest of which could be attached to the wrist with tape, and 93 examples of footwear. Some of the latter were quite simple – made of rush or papyrus and undecorated – while others were crafted of wood with veneer. Examples of leather sandals had patterns in bead-work and gold; they could also be decorated with images of Nubian and Asiatic prisoners.

Overall then, it would seem that the depictions of the king in art are a faithful representation of what he may have worn on certain occasions. However, the more unusual clothing in Tutankhamun's tomb suggests that in reality the king could wear a much wider variety of styles, some quite plain and practical, others more decorative.

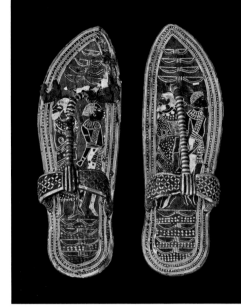

Wooden sandals from the tomb of Tutankhamun: bound foreign enemies are depicted on the inner soles, so that each time the king took a step he trampled on his foes.

## Breakfast and Morning Duties

Scented with ointments and having dressed in appropriate attire for his morning activities, the king might next feel the need to eat. He is said to have taken his meals in an area of the palace called the 'Mansion of Life' (discussed further below). Particular officials were connected with the royal breakfast, though perhaps only in an honorary manner. Many were of high rank, such as one individual called Nefersheshemre of the 6th Dynasty, who held the offices of vizier, overseer of royal document scribes, overseer of all the works of the king, first under the king, staff of the *rekhyt*, pillar of *kenmut*, and overseer of every royal 'breakfast'. Another official of the same dynasty, Geref, was 'the priest of the pyramid of Teti, overseer of the two cool rooms of the Great House, overseer of every royal "breakfast" which the sky gives and the earth creates'. Whether purely honorary or not, these individuals felt the need to emphasize their association with the king through the food he ate. It is unclear what the Egyptians ate for breakfast (though it no doubt included bread), and even the number of meals eaten over the course of an average day remains a mystery. From evidence supplied by ritual texts, however, it is probable that the pharaoh ate a light meal in the morning, followed by two larger meals for lunch and dinner.

After eating, the king received news on the current state of Egypt. According to the Greek historian Diodorus Siculus, 'In the morning, as soon as he (the king) was awake, he first of all had to receive the letters which had been sent from all sides, the purpose being that he might be able to despatch all administrative business and perform every act properly, being thus accurately informed about everything that was being done throughout his kingdom.' Diodorus continues, 'For there was a set time not only for his holding audiences or rendering judgments, but even for his taking a walk, bathing and sleeping with his wife, and, in a word, for every act of his life.'

Although he was writing in the 1st century BC, Diodorus may not have been far from the truth. A text inscribed in the tombs of a number of New Kingdom viziers records that each morning the vizier met with the king to update him on the state of the country. This was the final stage of a ceremony in which the vizier and chancellor first met at the flagstaffs outside the main gate of the palace and informed each other of pressing business under their jurisdiction. The vizier next opened the gates and doorways of the palace so that people and goods could enter and leave. Only then would he proceed to his meeting with the king. Despite what is written in viziers' tombs, it seems that the vizier was not the only person invited to this morning meeting, as *The Prophecy of Neferti* describes the inner court coming before the king for a similar morning audience, to pay homage 'according to their daily custom'. So the king appears to have met with his closest advisers each morning to discuss the affairs of Egypt and receive updates on any pressing matters. But what do we know about these meetings, and how did one approach the pharaoh?

## Entering Before Pharaoh: Audience Chambers and Throne Rooms

Kingship thrives on ceremony; authority must be acknowledged in order to exist. In ancient Egypt the court met frequently. Small-scale meetings took place in the private royal throne room, perhaps between the king and a single courtier since many individuals record that they were summoned at any hour to advise the king. Much grander audiences, known as 'Sittings of the King', were held in the palace's great columned hall, which served as the point where the inner private sectors of the palace met the more accessible and businesslike outer areas. At these larger events, officials were rewarded, appointments were made and decisions were announced. Even more imposing ceremonies might be held in the palace courtyard, when the king would emerge at his Window of Appearance and hand out rewards to the assembled multitude gathered below.

Whatever the size of the occasion, those coming before the king had to prepare themselves properly and follow a strict ritual code. We must imagine the courtiers of the New Kingdom riding to the palace in their chariots – status symbols as much as a means of transport – before disembarking at its imposing gateway, which was flanked by flagpoles set within a great niched wall. There they were checked by guards before they could progress within the palace grounds. Naturally, only people of a certain rank were allowed to enter: the Old Kingdom official Kaihap Tjeti relates with surprise, 'When I was appointed as sole companion, I was allowed to enter the royal house – (this) was not done as a favour for any other person'. Clearly this honour was not bestowed upon all 'sole companions'. Purity was an essential part of the ceremony. The ship's commander in *The Tale of the Shipwrecked Sailor* is told to wash himself before entering into the royal presence, while the 25th Dynasty Victory Stele of King Piye relates that it was forbidden for those who were uncircumcised or had eaten fish to enter the palace.

We get a picture of the procedure of a royal audience from the 18th Dynasty stele of the herald Intef, as it was his job to control those who could come and go before the king. First, Intef relates, the courtiers were brought into a waiting area to prepare themselves. At the correct time they would stand up and be counted, before being arranged according to rank. They were then hushed – fittingly for the location they were in, the Place of Silence. Suitably quiet and formally arranged, next came the moment of 'ushering in', an act conducted by the seal-bearer of the king in the Quban Stele of Ramesses II. Remembering to bow as they passed the chamber's doorkeepers, the officials found themselves in the audience area, standing in their two rows before the royal throne, still arranged according to rank. Their silence continued, for they could only speak when given permission.

Within the palace of Merenptah at Memphis, which is regarded as constructed specifically for ceremonial occasions, courtiers passed along a single straight axis through a paved peristyle court and a 12-columned vestibule before reaching the main entrance to the throne room. It was probably in such a vestibule that they were organized by men like Intef before their 'ushering in'. From this point there were three routes to the throne room: the procession could either continue along the main axis through grand double doors held in bronze sockets, or enter through one of two side entrances flanking the main axis. Given the need to place the courtiers in two rows, it is possible that each line used a different side entrance to process up to the throne, leaving the main central double doors for the king's sole use.

What did this throne room look like? Merenptah's throne room contained six columns topped with open papyrus capitals. Halfway up each column were panels showing the king performing various acts, such as offering before Ptah or slaying enemies. Inscriptions inlaid in blue faience ran around the bases and vertically up the columns, providing the titles and names of the king. Shafts of light flowed in through windows high up near the ceiling. Although little of the wall decoration was preserved, plants representing Upper and Lower Egypt and hieroglyphic inscriptions appear to have featured prominently. Ramesses II had one of his throne rooms decorated with large panels depicting foreigners in relief.

Merenptah's throne room was modest in size, and would only have been able to contain a relatively small number of courtiers at any one time. At Malkata, however, Amenhotep III's Palace of the King had two large, open audience halls,

A plan of the palace of Merenptah at Memphis. Courtiers probably prepared themselves in the vestibule before progressing into the throne room for an audience with the king. The king's private apartments were located behind the throne room.

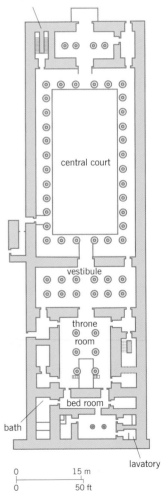

window of appearance

central court

vestibule

throne room

bed room

bath

lavatory

0      15 m
0      50 ft

each complete with its own throne dais, in addition to a smaller, more private throne room and a great hall attached to the royal apartment. One of these audience halls was decorated with an image of a court lady, while behind the throne dais was a painted scene of wild animals in the desert. The chamber's ceiling was decorated with rows of vultures, just like the king's bedchamber.

The floor in Merenptah's Memphis palace was decorated only with geometric border designs, but other palace remains provide more detail of what a typical floor may have looked like in the New Kingdom. At Malkata, for example, the floor of the great hall just in front of the throne room was decorated with a large scene of a pool with a wide border. A more complete version was found during excavations at the Great Palace of Akhenaten at Tell el-Amarna. The pool scene here was decorated with wavy lines, ducks, lilies and fish; its inner border had images of plants and animals and its outer border bouquets of flowers and piled offerings. A long pathway cut through these scenes, displaying alternating images of bound prisoners and the Nine Bows – symbolizing all foreign enemies; this may have been for the king's personal use, allowing him to trample on his enemies as he walked.

The royal throne dais was the focal point of any throne room or audience chamber. The remains of multiple daises from the time of Ramesses II were found

Amenhotep III enthroned beside Queen Tiye, in a relief from the tomb of Kheruef at Thebes. The royal couple are seated within an elaborate kiosk, surmounted by rows of protective rearing cobras. Amenhotep sits upon a block throne, used on sacred occasions.

during excavations at Pi-Ramesses, modern Qantir. One had a solid core overlaid with a veneer of elaborate faience tiles. Two sets of steps rose to the platform, one at either side, with each entrance flanked by large faience rearing lions gripping a foreign enemy and biting his head. The small steps were decorated with alternating

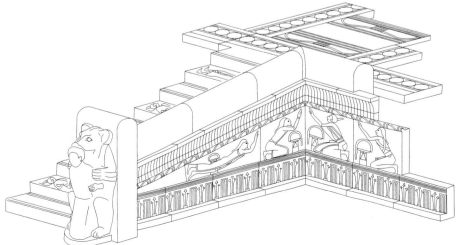

A reconstruction of the throne dais of Ramesses II at Pi-Ramesses. A rearing lion bites the head of a prisoner at the foot of the steps and vassals prostrate themselves at the sides.

images of bound prisoners and the Nine Bows. On the sides of the dais were images of vassals prostrating themselves. Both Merenptah's throne dais at Memphis and Amenhotep III's at Malkata appear to have been similarly decorated.

The throne that sat upon such platforms normally took one of two forms, but both types were made from precious materials such as ebony and gold. On 'sacred' occasions the block throne was used. This was a basic square box, its sides perhaps decorated with a feather pattern, symbols of unification or *serekhs* – representing the royal palace and power – with a low back, which could take the form of a protective falcon. For secular occasions an elaborately carved and gilded chair was used. This was flanked by images of lions, their legs supporting the seat and their tails rising at the back. The king's feet rested on a footrest, also decorated with images of Egypt's enemies. A baldachin or canopy protected the throne, its supports carved in the form of papyrus columns and its roof topped by rows of rearing cobras, each wearing its own sun disc.

## The Moment of Audience

And so the courtiers, arranged in their two rows according to rank, found themselves nervously filing into either a small throne room for a private ceremony or into a large audience hall for a royal proclamation. The dim light, passing through the high window slats, was supplemented by the bright flicker of oil lamps on tall stands. The king entered last, dressed in regalia suitable to the occasion and with a crown reflecting his particular role that day. He stepped on representations of his enemies as he ascended the throne dais, rising like the sun to the highest point in the room, before seating himself upon his throne. The courtiers dropped to the floor and prostrated themselves, kissing the ground before their king, their arms raised in a gesture of adoration. Then, once again standing, they listened to the royal announcement – perhaps the initiation of a building project or the declaration of a campaign. Courtiers describe the awesome effect the king's speech had on them at such events – in *The Tale of Sinuhe* the pharaoh's voice overwhelms Sinuhe's senses and the royal children say that he can give breath to the breathless.

In their autobiographies courtiers present the experience of meeting the king as pleasurable. They extol the king's wisdom and heap praise upon him, while saying that he provided rewards and appointments. Overall the event is described as calm and placid, and only rarely is he said to 'rage' at his courtiers. However, literary tales and other sources provide a different viewpoint. Here courtiers display fear and helplessness before an unpredictable, aggressive king. This unpredictability was a particular anxiety for those bearing taxes or tribute. If there was a deficit the official in charge could be beaten, but an even worse fate might befall the unfortunate courtier charged with bringing tribute if the king failed to be impressed, as one model letter relates: 'Remember the day of presenting the tribute when one has to pass before the king beneath the Window (of Appearance), the officials standing in two rows in front of His Majesty Life! Prosperity! Health!, foreign princes, having travelled from every foreign country, their goods standing there ready to be seen [...], but you are frightened and stunned, your hand grows weak, and you do not know whether death or life lies before you.' Another letter from the Ramesside Period relates: 'As to the one who reaches the Broad Hall of the King's House, Life! Prosperity! Health!, it is very much like a wave of the sea: (only) one survives, while a thousand die'.

If it was a smaller meeting involving the inner court, organized so that a particular decision could be taken – perhaps relating to matters of policy, the decision to go to war, or a high level appointment – there was a strict protocol for making statements: the highest ranking spoke first, followed by the lower ranking, but the former were explicitly not allowed to stop the latter speaking. Decisions were taken after discussion, with the pharaoh listening to his courtiers' advice. 'It happened', relates *The Instruction of Ankhsheshonqy*, 'that Pharaoh did not do anything except for something on which he had consulted Harsiese son of Ramose, the chief physician'. Hesi, an official under King Teti of the 6th Dynasty, relates in an inscription in his tomb at Saqqara: 'because of my efficiency, His Majesty used to ask my advice among the officials, even though I was only a judge and inspector of scribes'. But the final decision on any matter was the king's alone.

Courtiers were forbidden to touch the king. Some, however, were given special privileges when in the king's presence, such as the vizier Ptahshepses who (perhaps referring to King Shepseskare) recorded that, 'When His Majesty favoured him

The king in his carrying-chair is held aloft by servants during a procession to the temple, led by the newly appointed vizier Useramun.

because of the things (which he had done), His Majesty allowed him to kiss his foot – he did not allow him to kiss the ground'. The Old Kingdom vizier Washptah was also invited to kiss the king's foot. That touching the king's body or regalia without his express permission could have disastrous consequences is neatly illustrated by a text from the 5th Dynasty tomb of the *sem* priest Rawer, telling of an occasion when he had an encounter with King Neferirkare during a ceremony on a boat. He was: 'at the feet of His Majesty in his noble office of *sem* priest and keeper of ritual equipment. The *ames* sceptre which His Majesty was holding blocked the way of the *sem* priest Rawer. His Majesty said to him, "Be well!" – thus spoke His Majesty. His Majesty said: "it is the desire of My Majesty that he be very well, and that no blow be struck against him."' It seems that either Rawer had disrupted the ceremony by tripping over the king's sceptre or he had touched the king's body, but the king officially and magnanimously pardoned him to save him from a beating.

Once the audience or meeting was over, the officials were escorted out of the royal presence; Intef relates that this was his duty. If a royal appointment had been made, the promoted individual might then progress to the temple to give thanks or perhaps to ratify the king's decision before the god. On such occasions the king might accompany the courtier, carried in his palanquin under military escort and to the sound of musicians, as depicted in the tomb of the 18th Dynasty vizier Useramun.

## The King as Lawmaker and Judge

Among the many subjects that might be discussed by the king and court during a royal audience were legal matters. Although officials make reference to enforcing laws and viziers judged legal cases according to the 'law which is in his hand', only the king was sanctioned to make laws. According to Diodorus, the king's role as ultimate lawmaker and judge dated back to the time of Menes, first king of a united Egypt. Regularly in texts throughout the pharaonic period, the king refers to himself creating laws: Thutmose III says that it was he 'who laid down the correct laws'; Amenhotep III is one 'who establishes laws … more than the hook of the balance … he expels falsehood from every land'; while in his restoration stele, Tutankhamun is called one 'who is knowledgeable like Re, [ingenious] like Ptah, perceptive like Thoth, a decreer of laws, who is efficient of commands … and excellent of statements'. Officially the king was responsible for every decision, every law and every command. He was divinely inspired in these acts, the gods commanding him and he commanding the people.

Indeed, the pharaoh's word was the law, but the extent of his own personal involvement in legislation no doubt varied depending on individual personality and interest. Some royal decrees (*wedj-nesu*) are quite explicit in presenting the king as lawmaker. Horemheb, at the end of the 18th Dynasty, for example, is shown as dictating the content of a major decree to his scribe, who dutifully notes down a long list of commands aimed at fixing a series of administrative abuses. After being sealed in the king's presence, the content of the edict was inscribed on stelae erected at Karnak Temple and Abydos, and no doubt in countless other places too. This was common practice as a way of displaying and advertising royal announcements; the original document was stored in a local archive, while the more durable version stood publicly viewable for all to see – if not understand. Still, the description of Horemheb's personal dictation is surely fictional – a form of personalized introduction to the bland list of official directives that followed – as it is rather unlikely that the king simply invented, on the spot, a long and detailed list of commands without any prior discussion with his courtiers. Little, therefore, can be gleaned on the pharaoh's true role in legislation from this source.

> 'The kings were not allowed to render any legal decision or transact any business at random or to punish anyone through malice or in anger or for any other unjust reason, but only with the established laws relative to each offence.'
>
> Diodorus Siculus

The earliest physical example of a royal decree dates to the first year of the reign of King Shepseskaf (the content is 4th Dynasty, though the stele itself may be a later copy of the original). It reproduces exactly in stone the format of decrees known on papyrus, the earliest of which dates to the 5th Dynasty and was found at Abu Sir. As well as displaying a standardized layout, these decrees followed a conventional composition. First, the Horus name of the king was given in a vertical column, followed by the name and titles of the recipient in a horizontal line at the top. The content of the decree followed in vertical columns next to the king's name, forming the main body of the text and ending with the statement that the decree was 'sealed in the presence of the king himself' and the date. The conventional layout and the fact that many of the Abu Sir papyri are known to have been glued together in long rolls suggests that they were mass-produced and rubber stamped. Decrees of the New Kingdom contain little more personality, being mainly brief edicts connected to temple construction and endowment. They provide scant insight into the king's personal role in their formulation and execution, merely presenting him in his idealized role as champion of the gods. There are very few examples of a king commanding those around him for purely self-interested reasons, though the most notable are inscribed on the 'commemorative scarabs' of Amenhotep III, in which the king orders that a lake be dug for Queen Tiye, and that cattle be herded into an enclosure with a ditch so that he could hunt them. However, these relate to the king's authority over those surrounding him, not to overall lawmaking. From preserved royal commands it is thus hard to discern the extent of the king's true role as lawmaker – he may have played an active role or he may not.

As well as ultimate lawmaker, the king was also ultimate judge in the land. Papyrus Rylands IX describes 26th Dynasty priests accused of murder being brought before the king for judgment, while the Tomb Robbery Papyri of the 20th Dynasty present the king as receiving reports on the trials of the accused. Although the vizier headed these investigations, the convicted were left in prison 'until Pharaoh our lord should decide their punishment'. Such punishments could be brutal, with penalties of death and mutilation being set by the king alone. Horemheb's Edict is very specific about the punishments for particular offences: for example, if a servant of the Chamber of Offerings took a boat to be used by the kitchens of Pharaoh from a member of the army or anyone else in Egypt, his nose was cut off and the man despatched to *Ta-rew* – the site of Tell Abu Seif near modern el-Kantara – where people were sent for forced military service or labour; abuses by the army and overseer of cattle regarding cattle-hides were punishable by 100 blows and five open wounds and the confiscation of the stolen hides; a judge of the council found to have punished an innocent man was sentenced to death. Similarly brutal punishments were set down in a decree of Seti I at Nauri in Nubia. Impalement was a popular method of execution, as was burning. *The Instruction of Ankhsheshonqy* relates, 'Pharaoh caused an earthen altar to be built at the door of the palace. He caused that Harsiese son of Ramose be placed on the brazier with absolutely every person who belonged to him and with every person who had agreed to the misfortune of Pharaoh.' It seems that in cases of high treason, the king could not only order the death of an individual, but of his whole family too.

Normally, if a matter were to be judged by the king it was brought to the vizier in writing first and he might then deal with the matter himself. One papyrus, however, suggests that the king could ignore this procedure if he so wished: 'he was put before Pharaoh, he was not brought to us in writing'. Diodorus notes that making petitioners send their pleas in letter form was a way of trying to hold fair hearings of disputes, as it prevented the judges from being swayed by eloquence and allowed less articulate petitioners to be judged equally. Legal matters were usually dealt with in small local courts (*kenbetu*), while more serious matters were directed to the vizier as head of the Great *Kenbet*. Although in theory the king could be reached by the persistent petitioner, this must have been a rare event.

A large commemorative scarab from the reign of Amenhotep III. Such scarabs may have been presented as gifts to officials and foreign elites in Egyptian-held territories, and as offerings to the gods in temples.

## Managing Egypt

By the New Kingdom, the king stood at the apex of a vast bureaucracy – effectively divided between administration, military and priesthood – for which he had the responsibility of choosing the highest officials. *The Teachings for King Merikare* relate: 'Do not distinguish between the son of a man of rank and a commoner. Take a man on account of his actions.' This reflects the ideal that a person should achieve his position through merit rather than birth or influence, though this was contradicted by funerary wishes for a son to succeed his father in his position. In reality, it is unlikely that the king was always free to choose those who served him. In periods when the kingship was re-establishing itself or weakened, powerful noble families could place their own people in high office in exchange for continuing loyalty. There are times, however, when it is clear that a king had full control over his elite. Under Amenhotep II, the positions of vizier, mayor of Thebes, high steward in Perunefer and viceroy of Kush were all held by the king's childhood friends, men of noble background certainly, but whose families had never before attained the highest offices in the land. They surely rose to prominence because of Amenhotep II's personal influence, no doubt at the expense of more established family lines; before this, for example, the vizierate had remained in the same family for three generations.

ABOVE **Ramesses II leans down from his window of appearance to appoint Nebwenenef to the position of high priest of Amun at Karnak.**

It was also often the case that a person's actual authority might far exceed his official position, while some titles might effectively be meaningless. Responsibilities were also spread across different areas, with men simultaneously holding administrative and military or priestly titles. At times of a strong monarchy, simply having the king's ear and being a trusted friend might make someone the most influential person in the land. One such individual was Amenhotep Son of Hapu, a man of relatively humble origins who rose to become one of Amenhotep III's most trusted advisers after spending most of his career in obscurity in the town of Athribis. His official titles identify him as scribe, overseer of construction works and overseer of recruits (a position that allowed him to harness manpower for royal construction projects), but he also played an important ritual role for the king and was involved in his *Sed* Festival celebrations. Amenhotep's compositions, inscribed on his statues, are complicated and unusual, a sign of the high intelligence that must have impressed the king and led to his sudden rise. He was so admired that he received the unique honour of his own private mortuary temple at Thebes, and was subsequently deified and worshipped by the Egyptians of the Late Period.

Although the structure of government evolved and changed over the course of three thousand years, certain offices remained important throughout. Just below the king was the vizier, sometimes two – one for the north and one for the south. This office existed from the Early Dynastic Period and was held by royal sons until the end of the 4th Dynasty. The office holder was identifiable by his special dress – a long robe that came down to the ankles and was raised as high as the arm pits – and a symbol of *maat* that he wore around his neck, tucked into his robe. It is fortunate that a text known as *The Duties of the Vizier* has survived on the tomb walls of some New Kingdom viziers, as this outlines the many roles these individuals played. The vizier was head of the civil administration, deputy to the king and manager of the palace; consequently 'It is he who hears every decree of the king'. He was also responsible for taxation and the punishment of officials, as well as the king's security when travelling. New Kingdom viziers also managed Deir el-Medina, the village where the artisans who cut and decorated the royal tombs in the Valley of the Kings lived with their families.

Below the vizier were various important individuals, among them the overseers of the treasury, who organized state assets. The treasury also kept an archive of official documents, including those relating to land ownership. The military had its own chief general, while palace affairs were overseen by the chief royal steward or chancellor (depending on the period). In the New Kingdom there was also a government department in charge of livestock and a granary department. The newly annexed Nubian territory was given a viceroy, called the king's son of Kush, and there was an overseer of foreign lands for the Egyptian empire in the Levant. Supporting all offices was a vast army of scribes; these were the clerical officers who recorded land ownership, trials, commodity movements and military activities, among many other things.

Just as the king was presented in an idealized manner, members of the bureaucracy, too, measured themselves against particular models. They would often extol their moral behaviour in tomb inscriptions, hoping to entice passersby to stop and leave offerings or, at the very least, to recite the prayer of offering. One lengthy text, known as *The Great Hymn*, clearly expresses the attributes of a perfect courtier, relating that he should rise early, not speak arrogantly or argue with his superiors, do what the king loves, and refrain from speaking of the palace's internal affairs with the public. *The Teachings of Ptahhotep* also describes the proper conduct of an official before a superior, and so provides an indication of how a courtier should act before

OPPOSITE BELOW **A statue of the influential official Amenhotep Son of Hapu as a young scribe. A papyrus roll is unfurled across his crossed legs, emphasizing his learning, and his belly has rolls of fat, showing his success.**

BELOW **A statue of the vizier Imeru-Neferkare, who served the 13th Dynasty pharaoh Sobekhotep IV.**

the king, 'If you are in the audience chamber, stand and sit in accordance with your position which was given to you on the first day … the audience chamber tends towards strict etiquette.' The text further goes on to state: 'Your silence is more profitable than babbling, so speak only when you know that you are qualified (to do so). It is only the proficient who should speak in council, for speech is more difficult than any craft, and only the competent can endow it with authority.'

These rather formal accounts of behaviour can be contrasted with other, more relaxed presentations. As we have seen, kings grew up with the sons of officials at court, in many cases forging strong bonds with men who would serve them throughout their lives. Amenhotep II wrote to his viceroy of Kush, Usersatet, to offer friendly advice at the time of his friend's absence from a royal dinner. Courtiers regularly speak of their rise to power in terms of the king's special attention to them and he is even presented as showing personal kindness to certain individuals. One such (anonymous) individual, buried at Giza, records, 'Now with regard to the period when he was ill, His Majesty brought for him a carrying-chair from the residence so that he might supervise from it the work for which he was responsible. His Majesty also had set up for him an escort.' The king also sent for help when the courtier Washptah collapsed during an official site inspection, demanding that a carrying-chair, held aloft by ten men, be brought and that chests full of magic books be fetched to help cure him.

## GENERAL ORGANIZATION OF GOVERNMENT IN THE NEW KINGDOM

King

| Dynasty | Internal Government | | | | Foreign Territories | |
|---|---|---|---|---|---|---|
| Great Royal Wife | **Royal Domain** | **Army** | **Temples** | **Civil Administration** | Overseer of (northern) foreign lands | Viceroy of Kush |
| Crown prince | Chancellor | Commander-in-chief | Overseer of priests of all the gods of Upper and Lower Egypt | North and South Viziers | Vassal kings | Deputies of Wawat and Kush |
| Relatives | Chief steward | Chief deputies of northern and southern corps | High priest of Amun | Overseers of the treasury | Battalion commanders | Battalion commander of Kush |
| | Chamberlain | General officers | God's Wife of Amun | Overseer of the granaries | | |
| | Bureaucracy | | High priests of other gods | Overseer of cattle | | |
| | | | Priesthoods and bureaucracy | Bureaucracy, judiciary and police | | |
| | | | | Village chiefs, town mayors and councils | | |

A life spent in loyal service to the king continued to be of benefit in the afterlife. 'The one whom the king loves will be a well-provided spirit', states *The Loyalist Instruction*, but 'there is no tomb for anyone who rebels against His Majesty, and his corpse shall be cast to the waters'. Furthermore, a happy king might donate a sarcophagus or false door to his devoted servant's tomb; these would be produced in the royal workshops and so be of the highest quality – a welcome gift, given that courtiers had to finance their own, often quite elaborate final resting places.

## Royal Women and the Harem

The king could marry as many women as he wished, but there could only be one Great Royal Wife, whose power derived from her connection to the king. She lived with the king in the private apartments of the palace, travelled with him and played an important ritual role. Queens are shown praising the gods in scenes on the walls of temples and could hold priestly titles, acting as the female equivalent of a high priest during temple rituals. They could even be likened to certain goddesses, such as Hathor, Isis or Mut, while the title of God's Wife of Amun, an office with its own administration, connected them closely with the divine from the New Kingdom onwards (see also p. 43). In the Old and Middle Kingdoms, queens were set apart in a funerary context as well as in life, being buried in miniature pyramids alongside the larger ones of their husbands. In the New Kingdom there was a separate burial site for queens and royal children, now known as the Valley of the Queens, close to the Valley of the Kings. Furthermore, just as the king was distinguished by his appearance, so were his wives. From the Old Kingdom, queens are frequently depicted wearing a vulture headdress, the two wings hanging down at each side of the head, with a rearing cobra at the brow. From the 13th Dynasty double plumes might be added too, while Queen Tiye of the 18th Dynasty also added the horns and sun disc of the goddess Hathor.

As another mark of his special status, not only could the king have multiple wives, something forbidden to commoners, but he was also free to marry his half-sisters or even his daughters, as was the case with Amenhotep III and Ramesses II. This was following divine practice – brother and sister Osiris and Isis had married to produce Horus, so the king could marry within his own family. On a practical level, it kept power within the family line. Marriages were also made for other pragmatic reasons, such as diplomacy. In the New Kingdom it became common for kings to marry the daughters of important foreign kings in order to cement relations between powers and ensure treaties were adhered to. Thutmose IV, Amenhotep III and Akhenaten are all known to have married Mitanni princesses, while Amenhotep III married a Babylonian princess. Ramesses II, once the peace treaty had been signed between Egypt and Hatti, married two of the daughters of

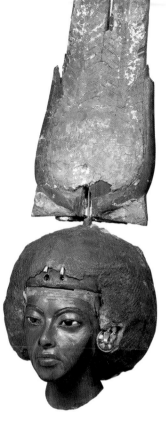

Head of a statue of Queen Tiye, the Great Royal Wife of Amenhotep III, now in Berlin. She wears a combination of the horns of the goddess Hathor, a double-plumed headdress and a sun disc. The head was found at Medinet el-Ghurob, where a harem palace stood.

King Hattusili III. In addition to their slaves, livestock and luxury goods, foreign princesses entered Egypt with a vast entourage; Gilukhepa, the Mitanni princess who married Amenhotep III, arrived with 317 ladies-in-waiting, according to the inscription on large scarabs made to commemorate the event.

The daughters of Levantine vassal kings were also sent to Egypt to join the king's harem, as one letter records: 'send your daughter to the king, your lord, and as presents send 20 healthy slaves, silver chariots, and healthy horses'. These women frequently vanish from the historical record after entering the harem; the Babylonian king, Kadashman Enlil, wrote to Amenhotep III to enquire about the whereabouts of his sister, as no one had seen or heard from her for some time. Kings could also marry commoners. Amenhotep III married a woman named Tiye, who was the daughter of Yuya, chief of chariotry and high priest of Min, and Tuya, chief of the harem of Min and Amun. Despite her common origins, Tiye's name is often mentioned alongside Amenhotep III's in official inscriptions and she is also depicted beside him in private tomb scenes and on colossal statuary. Thutmose III and Amenhotep II also married non-royals.

In contrast, from the beginning of the New Kingdom through to the reign of Ramesses II, royal women were forbidden to marry commoners, ensuring that the royal bloodline – and more importantly royal power – did not become diluted. It was especially prohibited for a royal daughter to marry a foreign king, 'from time immemorial no daughter of a king of Egy[pt] is given to anyone' wrote Amenhotep III to the Babylonian king Kadashman Enlil. It was thus a major break from tradition for Ankhesenamun, widow of Tutankhamun, to offer to marry a Hittite prince after her husband's death. Courtiers were allowed to marry royal daughters in certain periods, however; so for example Ptahshepses, in the Old Kingdom, married King Userkaf's eldest daughter, Khamaat, 'for His Majesty wished that she be with him more than with any other man'.

In an ancient Egyptian context, the word 'harem' is not used in the Ottoman sense of an inaccessible 'prison' for royal concubines; rather it was a self-contained palace, often built in the countryside. The best evidenced example is the harem of Medinet el-Ghurob (ancient Mi-wer) in the Faiyum Oasis, which is known to have housed large numbers of women, both royal and non-royal. These women, unlike those in the Ottoman harem, were allowed to come and go as they pleased, although the relative isolation of Medinet el-Ghurob ensured that they had little contact with the outside world. The harem palace must have been quite large to accommodate the number of women living there – not only the queens, but also senior court ladies, nurses and royal attendants. As noted above, 317 ladies accompanied the Mitanni princess Gilukhepa to Egypt during the reign of Amenhotep III, and all would have needed rooms in a royal harem palace.

Wooden statuette of the mistress of the harem Tiye, now in the Metropolitan Museum of Art, New York. Harem women had an army of servants to help them with their daily business.

## QUEENS AS KINGS

Some queens played a prominent political role: Queen Ahhotep of the early 18th Dynasty, for example, oversaw political affairs while King Ahmose was in his infancy, ruling as Queen Regent. Furthermore, although it was firmly against the ideology of kingship, some queens took royal titles and ruled as king.

This tended to occur at times of dynastic trouble, such as at the end of the 12th and 19th Dynasties (Sobekneferu and Tawosret respectively; the existence of a Queen/King Nitoqris reigning at the end of the 6th Dynasty is questionable as she is absent from Egyptian sources and only mentioned by Herodotus and Manetho), or at the end of the Ptolemaic Period (Cleopatra VII). But Hatshepsut, perhaps the most famous queen to become king, ruled during a period of relative stability in the middle of the 18th Dynasty.

Hatshepsut had been the Great Royal Wife of King Thutmose II, but as she had no son, on the king's death the throne passed to a prince born of a minor royal wife called Iset. Thutmose III was crowned, but he was still a young boy and so Hatshepsut – as most senior royal

ABOVE **The head of a colossal statue of Hatshepsut from Deir el-Bahri. Hatshepsut is one of only a few women ever to become pharaoh.**

RIGHT **Cylinder seal of the female pharaoh Sobekneferu, bearing four of her five royal names; now in the British Museum, London.**

family member – ruled as Queen Regent. Over the course of many years she slowly assumed royal prerogatives one by one until eventually she presented herself as a true king, chosen as successor by her father, Thutmose I, before his death. Technically, both Hatshepsut and Thutmose III ruled as co-regents, their cartouches sometimes appearing side by side on monuments, but Hatshepsut was the real power.

During her rule, Thutmose III was not locked away, however; rather, he appears to have led the army on at least one campaign into the Levant, indicating that if he so wished he could have used his military influence to overthrow Hatshepsut. As this did not happen, it must be assumed that the two ruled in co-operation; and, although her name was expunged from many of her monuments following her death, this was not until much later in Thutmose's sole reign and into the reign of Amenhotep II.

Many harem women must have been involved in weaving, as shown by numerous objects related to spinning and weaving found at Medinet el-Ghurob. The fine linen produced was not only used by the harem women themselves, but was also sent to the royal court. The women also held their own farmland, kept livestock and were supported by a team of officials who lived in small towns near the palace. Harems were thus self-sustaining centres of production as much as homes for royal ladies. But they were also luxurious. Records detailing jewelry, made of stones such as malachite and lapis lazuli, show that the women did not lack the finer elements of life, and there were also vast quantities of flowers. Harem palaces were used by the king and his entourage as a base during his travels around the country, like a countryside retreat.

## Rituals and Festivals

Writing in the 1st century BC but describing the lives of the most ancient kings of Egypt, Diodorus Siculus was surprised to find that the pharaoh did not have complete autocratic power, but instead was bound by a daily routine of cultic behaviour. While it is unlikely that Diodorus' account can be trusted in most of its details, it is certain that the Egyptian kings did live their lives ruled by ritual and religious practice. The king was, after all, both chief priest of all the gods and intermediary between them and mankind, and an initiate into the secret rites of the temples. In this role, it was his duty to perform the daily rituals before each god: to open the sanctuary, purify the chamber by burning incense, and clothe and feed the divine statue, before finally sweeping away his own footsteps as he respectfully left the sanctuary.

Drawing of a relief at Medinet Habu of Ramesses III cutting a sheaf of wheat, one of the rituals the king had to perform during the Min festival.

In reality, these rituals were performed by the priests of Egypt's many temples, men who acted as royal deputies. So, despite the fact that the king is depicted performing ritual acts on the walls of every temple in Egypt, it is difficult to ascertain how often he personally performed these rituals. Did he, when spending a month at Memphis for example, visit the Temple of Ptah each day to make offerings, or did he leave this work to the temple priests? *The Teachings for King Merikare* certainly stresses that the king should 'don his white sandals' and perform the monthly service within the 'holy place', while the Nubian king Piye, on his Victory Stele from Gebel Barkal, provides a particularly detailed account of his visit to the Pyramidion House of Re within the Temple of Ptah, referring to his robing, cleansing and viewing of the god's barques. But this was not a daily event, just one of his many stops along the way from Nubia to the Delta. Indeed, Egypt's kings were always on the move, attending various festivals and feasts across the country, such as the festival of Min in which the king

A relief from Medinet Habu showing Ramesses III making offerings to the god Min.

ceremonially cut a sheaf of wheat and released four birds to the cardinal points. It is probable that the king stopped at temples en route to such festivals, visiting the gods in their 'homes'. Many royal stelae begin by citing the king as in a particular location 'doing the praises' of a certain deity, as if he had just arrived there. Thutmose IV, when travelling in the south of Egypt, relates how: 'every god of Upper Egypt held a bouquet to his nose', indicating a progression from temple to temple, and he makes reference to performing the 'festival of Washing the Image, having stopped in the town of Behdet'.

Although the king might send deputies to certain festivals, just as the priests deputized for him on a daily basis in the temples, there were particular events that he always attended personally. In the New Kingdom the most important annual event was the Opet Festival at Luxor Temple in Thebes. The temple was dedicated to the cult of the royal *ka*-spirit, the force created at the moment that the king was conceived and which united with his mortal body at the time of his coronation (see p. 64). The ceremony began with a procession from the Temple of Amun at Karnak to Luxor Temple. The statue of Amun was carried in his barque from his

The sphinx-lined avenue that connects Karnak and Luxor Temples – the pylon entrance to Luxor temple can be seen in the distance. The pharaoh and the barques of the gods progressed along this avenue during the annual Opet Festival.

sanctuary, along with the statues of his wife, Mut, and their son, Khonsu, as well as the barque of the royal *ka*-spirit. Together they progressed along an avenue, lined with sphinxes, that connected the two temples, stopping at various shrines on the way. Within the temple, the king performed several ritual acts, including a circuit for Amun-Min and the presentation of offerings for Amun-Re, before receiving the Blue Crown from Amun-Re. Only the king, Amun and the barque of the royal *ka*-spirit were then allowed to pass into the sanctuary at the rear of the temple, where the king consecrated meat before the god's barque shrine. With each of his ritual acts, the king became more closely associated with the royal *ka*-spirit until their identities completely merged; at this point he was ready to enter the presence of Amun. He poured libations and burned incense for the god and in the process

OPPOSITE ABOVE **A panel depicting the 3rd Dynasty king Djoser performing *Sed* Festival rites, from his South Tomb at Saqqara. Similar scenes are found beneath the Step Pyramid itself.**

OPPOSITE BELOW **Detail of a label showing the 1st Dynasty King Den performing a ritual circuit during the *Sed* Festival.**

was divinized and made young again. He was then ritually re-crowned with the White and Red Crowns. This ceremony proclaimed and renewed the king's legitimacy by displaying his unification with the royal *ka*-spirit and Amun-Re's acceptance of him as ruler. When the ceremony ended, the king emerged from the dark inner sanctuary of the temple into the sunlight to be met by throngs of people, celebrating his renewal. He then either sailed back to Karnak Temple with the statues of the gods, or progressed back along the sphinx-lined avenue.

Another major royal celebration was the *Sed* Festival. This ceremony, enacted to demonstrate the king's continuing fitness to rule, dates back to at least the 1st Dynasty, as seen in an ebony label of King Den, which shows the king running a ritual circuit between two sets of three markers (see also p. 26). As part of the ceremony, the king wore a tightly wrapped ceremonial robe decorated with coloured squares; such a robe can be seen worn by King Khasekhemwy on statues now in the Egyptian Museum, Cairo, and in the Ashmolean Museum, Oxford, though the colourful decoration has disappeared. Full-scale stone replicas of the shrines associated with the *Sed* Festival form part of King Djoser's funerary complex, built in the 3rd Dynasty, while a statue of Djoser, found at the northern side of his pyramid, shows him wearing his *Sed* Festival robe. *Sed* Festival scenes also appeared

on the walls of later pyramid complexes, though no further attempts were made to recreate the physical setting as Djoser had done. Much later, in Demotic and Greek texts, the *Sed* Festival was known as the 'Feast of 30 Regnal Years' because the celebration traditionally occurred after 30 years of a king's rule, and then at regular intervals (typically every three years) afterwards. Ramesses II had 13 or 14 such jubilees while Amenhotep III had three. However, some kings did not wait for the full 30 years before holding their first festival; Montuhotep II appears to have held one after two years as king, as perhaps did Akhenaten, while, at the other extreme, Pepi I waited until his 36th year. Some kings refer to fictitious celebrations on their monuments, recording them in the hope that they might reach their 30-year point. The celebration itself was held in different locations, dependent on the whim of

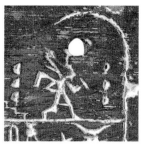

the king. Amenhotep III built an entire palace district at Malkata purely for his *Sed* Festivals, while Ramesses II held his at Pi-Ramesses. In most cases, however, the festival was probably held at Memphis.

There are four major sources for a reconstruction of the *Sed* Festival rituals: scenes from the Sun Temple of Niuserre at Abu Gurob; Amenhotep III's temple at Soleb in Nubia (as well as the tombs of his courtiers); Akhenaten's inscriptions from East Karnak; and depictions from Bubastis from the reign of Osorkon II. Despite these sources, the order of events and the meaning of the rituals are still not fully understood; some rites may even have been conducted multiple times. As far as can be ascertained, the first stage of the festival, which could last for months either side of the anniversary of the king's accession, consisted of assembling the statues of Egypt's major gods from across the country at the ceremonial location. After a torchlight procession at dawn, during which the two thrones and divine shrines were purified, the gods were installed in their shrines according to whether they came from the north or south. The shrines themselves also differed architecturally, depending on which half of the country they represented. This north/south division was a theme throughout the jubilee; even the palanquin on which the king was carried changed depending on whether he was approaching the gods of Upper or Lower Egypt. He was re-crowned first with the Red Crown and then with the White Crown, seated upon a double dais – the thrones back to back or side by side.

Once the king had made offerings to the gods – one by one in each of their shrines – and received their blessings for his continued rule, his courtiers pledged their allegiance to him and he performed a ritual circuit between markers representing the extent of his kingdom. This was the most important part of the ceremony as it proved his fitness to be king of Egypt. The ceremony also included many other rituals, such as a procession of lion-legged furniture; the driving of cattle around the city walls four times; a procession of the god Min; ritual combat between men representing the people of the ancient centres of Pe and Dep; and the release of birds and firing of arrows to the four cardinal points. Amenhotep III tried to ensure that his *Sed* Festival followed tradition, but he also included some innovations. He commanded that a huge artificial lake, Birket Habu, be dug at Malkata beside his palace, on which the evening and morning barques of the gods (as well as the king's own barque) sailed to the palace, and then later to their shrines, where cattle were sacrificed. At dawn on the day of the jubilee, the king and his courtiers raised a *djed*-pillar – a symbol of stability – before a statue of Osiris.

In addition to such major festivals, one of the king's main ritual roles was to build temples for the gods. The foundation ritual ideally included the king as master of ceremonies; however, as with other rituals, in most cases a priest acted in his stead. A complete foundation ceremony lasted between seven and 14 days, and although elements of the procedure are known, their order is debated. It is likely that the initial ceremony was held at night under a new moon, so that the stars could be seen for the alignment of the temple. The king and his followers, including a priestess playing the role of the goddess Seshat, sank poles into the ground at points marking the four corners of the temple. Next came the 'Stretching of the Cord', the most important part of the ceremony and the name by which the entire foundation ritual was known to the ancient Egyptians – *pedj shes*. This involved the king tying a cord around the four poles so that the temple's dimensions were clearly delineated. Using this outline, a foundation trench was then cut deep enough to reach groundwater and the king moulded mud-bricks, which he placed in the trench along with model tools, offerings, the sacrificial heads of a goose and bull, and corner stones. Sand, regarded as ritually pure, was also shovelled into the trench.

Once the temple was completed, the king or priest performed a month-long series of rituals. First, the building was purified with natron and whitewash; then the 'opening of the mouth' ceremony was performed in each room, allowing the temple to be officially used for cult practice. Finally, the statue of the temple god was placed in its sanctuary. A banquet was then held for the priests and artisans.

## Interacting with the Gods

As part of their role as mediator, kings presented themselves as receiving commands directly from the gods and passing them to the people; the gods were thus integral in the decision-making process – as Hatshepsut states, 'I did not plan a work without his (Amun's) doing'. But how did the king communicate with the gods? One way was by oracle, which quite possibly played a role in religious life

Horemheb kneels before the god Atum in a gesture of offering, in a statue in Luxor Museum. Although superior to all mankind, the king was subservient to the gods, pleasing them with offerings and passing on their commands to his people.

The Dream Stele of Thutmose IV, below the Great Sphinx at Giza, describes the god Re-Horakhety-Atum as appearing to the king in a dream when he was still a prince.

from the Old Kingdom. In pre-New Kingdom times, however, the gods tended to make their divine wishes known through dreams. Senwosret I, for example, is told in a dream to build a temple at Elephantine. Later kings could also interact with the divine when asleep. On his Dream or Sphinx Stele, erected between the paws of the Great Sphinx at Giza, Thutmose IV relates how as a prince he fell asleep beside the ancient monument, which by his time had already become buried under sand. In Thutmose's dream, the god Re-Horakhety-Atum spoke to him, promising him the kingship if he were to uncover the Sphinx's body and restore it. Similarly, Merenptah was visited by Ptah in a dream and handed a sickle-sword – a symbol of the god sanctioning war against the Libyans. Kings also speak of being divinely inspired by the gods and could feel their presence in *biayet* ('signs from god' or 'miracles'), such as a comet witnessed by Thutmose III when on campaign.

Oracles certainly become increasingly prominent in the historical record during and after the New Kingdom. This might be evidence that the practice only began in this period, but it perhaps reflects changes in the presentation of kingship, revealing that it was now permissible explicitly to describe the king before the god as oracle. In the 18th Dynasty, Hatshepsut was commanded by Amun to send an expedition to the land of Punt, while Amun himself is said to have guided the young Thutmose III to the 'station of the king' – effectively signalling his future kingship – at Karnak. Both Hatshepsut and Ramesses IV also refer to the god announcing their future kingship. Oracles could thus (retrospectively) be presented as legitimizing a king's reign. The king also approached the god when making temple appointments, as was the case with the priest Nebwenenef under Ramesses II. And it was a common practice to secure divine sanction before sending out the army – Thutmose IV, for instance, consulted an oracle before initiating a small-scale campaign in Nubia.

## The Provisions of the Lord: Finances and Food

The king technically owned all land in Egypt and imposed taxes on those living on his property to support the government's needs. To ensure that each person was taxed correctly, the vizier kept records of field boundaries and land and livestock ownership. Each year, after the Nile flood, he sent out officials called 'scribes of the mat' to measure each field and estimate its yield; this estimate was later compared to the actual yield following the harvest. As money did not exist, taxation was taken in the form of goods, such as grain, or as labour on state projects. Goods were stockpiled and redistributed by the government to support society's 'non-producers' – bureaucrats and military men – and to feed labourers. A special general tax levied on towns and districts purely for the benefit of the king is recorded in the tomb of the vizier Rekhmire (18th Dynasty); such extra income-raising efforts appear to have been quite rare, however. Additional supplies were also requisitioned by local mayors when the royal court passed through their territory (see p. 158). But it seems this system was open to abuse, leading Horemheb to issue a royal decree to lessen the demands placed on local mayors at such times.

In addition to general taxation, the palace also raised revenue from directly owned land and resources. Papyrus Boulaq 18, dated to the late Middle Kingdom, names three sources for 'the Provisions of the Lord': the Sector of the Head of the

A scene from the sarcophagus of Queen Ashayet, in the Egyptian Museum, Cairo, showing porters carrying grain into a granary, overseen by a seated official.

South; the Bureau of the People's Giving; and the Treasury. Special withdrawals from these supplies were called *inu*, a word that has variously been translated as 'tribute' or 'official gifts'. *Inu* was typically brought as gifts to the pharaoh by foreign dignitaries. Since it was for his personal use and existed outside the normal redistributive system, it can be regarded as his 'privy purse'. Kings used *inu* to feed members of the court, to donate to temples and to pay necropolis workmen, among other things. Reports on *inu* were made to the vizier and it was stored in the treasury, in a place called the *ges-per*, where it was divided according to place of origin rather than object type.

Palace records from the time of Seti I detail specific amounts of wheat used for the king's bread supply. The wheat was taken from the 'granary of Pharaoh' to the bakery, which was personally overseen by the mayor of Memphis. These records were particularly detailed, so that all the grain – which could easily go 'missing' – was accounted for. From these lists it can be seen that between 100 and 190 sacks of wheat were delivered each day to the royal bakery, and every few days between 2000 and 5000 small loaves of bread were sent to the palace. A damaged scene in the tomb of Ramesses III in the Valley of the Kings depicts a royal bakery. A large quantity of dough is kneaded underfoot by servants in a great trough before being taken to the court baker, who formed it into unusual shapes – one loaf is in the shape of a calf, others are spiral. The smaller loaves appear to have been baked, while some might have been fried. A royal kitchen is depicted in Ramesses III's tomb, with details showing drying meat and a young man stirring the contents

This scene, from the tomb of Ramesses III, depicts the hustle and bustle of a royal bakery and the various shapes of the loaves produced, including one in the form of a calf.

of a giant kettle. Nearby, a butcher catches blood from a slaughtered animal in a bowl and another cuts up a carcass. The storage rooms at Malkata palace were decorated with stands bearing food and fattened cows, while the royal butler Suemnut, who lived under Amenhotep II, is shown in his tomb inspecting the drink supply of the royal residence, including a particular form of cream ale in the royal kitchens.

Food and drink consumed by the king were called *ankh nesut* (royal victuals) and were made separately from those intended for palace guests and staff, or even the royal family. In one business document *ankh nesut* seem to have been a by-product of festivals at the pyramid complex of Senwosret II, which were delivered to his residence from the temple. Similarly, in Papyrus Boulaq 18, a constant item of delivery to the palace is *ankh nesut* from the Temple of Amun. This suggests that the king's personal food was prepared to the same level of ritual purity as food for the gods, reflected in the epithet 'pure of hands' applied to royal butlers.

The amount of supplies listed appears to be enough for three meals each day for the king alone – 100 items of bread and 10 *des*-jugs of beer. Such numbers may seem extravagant, but the scale of each item was likely very small, and, although this food was made specifically for the king's consumption, in their biographies officials brag about receiving food from the king's table, especially from his *abu-ra,* a word often translated as 'breakfast' though perhaps more generally meaning his first main meal of the day. Ineni, an overseer of works in the early 18th Dynasty, says, 'As I am in the favour of His Majesty daily, I am supplied from the king's table with bread of the king's "breakfast" and beer, and likewise fat meat, vegetables and various fruits, honey, cakes and wine, as well as oil'. Senemiah, under Hatshepsut, states, 'one brought me servings at the time of day and night with things of the king's own "breakfast"'. Clearly, receiving food from the king's own table was a notable royal favour.

A painted scene from the Theban tomb of the royal butler, Suemnut, who is described as 'pure of hands'. Food is piled high before him as his sustenance for eternity.

## ROYAL HEALTH IN THE NEW KINGDOM

'Give thanks for your blessings, and pray [to the gods] for your health', advises *The Teachings for King Merikare* – the king might embody the everlasting divine kingship, but he was still susceptible to the same physical ailments that affected any other mortal in society. Unlike the vast majority of the population, however, the king was attended by his own private doctors.

In the Old Kingdom there is a hierarchy of physicians connected with the palace in general, but in later periods they are specifically called physicians of the king and had their own overseers. Some were specialists, such as the oculist of the palace, the physician of the belly in the palace, and chief of palace dentists; there was also the chief physician of the Mansion of Life. Physicians treated patients by using a combination of magical spells, amulets and practical remedies. They believed that internal problems could be caused by the gods, malignant deities, demons or the evil eye, and that illness could be the result of harmful substances called *wehedu*

entering the body and infiltrating the *metu* – a word that describes all stringy tubes within the body, be they veins, arteries or tendons. These *metu*, it was thought, were connected to the heart, and all bodily fluids, including air, passed through them.

Treatments existed for physical injuries, including broken bones, while the Ebers Papyrus lists 700 prescriptions for internal diseases associated with specific organs. Whether facing a stomach complaint, a snake bite, or the need for a method of contraception, the Egyptian doctors could suggest a solution.

Analyses of the New Kingdom royal mummies have helped to shed light on the daily health problems faced by the pharaohs. King Ahmose, who was delicately built, had arthritis in his knees and back, and, against normal custom, had not been circumcised, leading some scholars to argue that he may have been too weak to endure the process. His wife Ahmose-Nefertari suffered from scoliosis, a condition that causes curvature of the spine. The body once identified as Thutmose I, but now

### SELECT NEW KINGDOM PHARAOHS AND THE DISEASES/CONDITIONS THEY SUFFERED FROM

| Pharaoh | Conditions | Pharaoh | Conditions |
|---|---|---|---|
| Ahmose | Arthritis of knees and back | Seti I | Arteriosclerosis |
| Thutmose II | Frail | Ramesses II | Arthritis of the hips |
| | Covered in scabs | | Arteriosclerosis of the arteries in his feet |
| Thutmose III | Scabs | | Abscesses in his jaw |
| | Calcification of his intervertebral discs | | Lost teeth |
| Hatshepsut | Overweight | | Ankylosing spondylitis or diffuse idiopathic skeletal hyperostosis |
| | Cancer | Merenptah | Overweight |
| | Diabetes | | Fractures in his femurs |
| Amenhotep II | Compression fracture in vertebrae(?) | | Arthritis |
| | Scabs | | Bad teeth |
| | Ankylosing spondylitis | | Arteriosclerosis |
| Thutmose IV | Pelvic tilt | Siptah | Clubbed left foot (caused by polio or cerebral palsy?) |
| | Contracted a fatal illness? | | |
| Amenhotep III | Overweight | Ramesses III | Overweight |
| | Abscesses of teeth | Ramesses IV | Well-worn teeth |
| Tutankhamun | Malaria | Ramesses V | Smallpox |
| | Lame foot | | Inguinal hernia |
| Ramesses I | Fractured left thigh bone | | Bubonic plague(?) |
| | Malformed ear (severe ear infection?) | | |

thought to be non-royal, possibly suffered from a pelvic fracture and was found to have an arrow in his chest. Thutmose II was frail and covered in scabs, possibly as a result of an illness, while his son, Thutmose III had similar scabs. Thutmose III's body also revealed calcification of his intervertebral discs; in some cases this can restrict movement and cause pain, but is not always the case. The body of a royal lady, now thought to be Hatshepsut, was apparently obese in life; she suffered from cancer, an incisional hernia, a slipped disc and diabetes. Amenhotep II may have had a compression fracture in his vertebrae, though this has not been confirmed, and suffered from scabs too. He also showed clear signs of ankylosing spondylitis, a condition that leads to rigidity of the spine and can cause inflammation of the eye. Interestingly, given Amenhotep II's apparent love of sport, regular exercise reduces the associated back pain. Thutmose IV died in his 30s, perhaps from a fatal illness, but suffered from a pelvic tilt, a condition that could have been caused by a pelvic fracture or simply bad posture while sitting. Amenhotep III was overweight and had abscesses in his teeth, while his grandson, Tutankhamun, contracted a severe form of malaria and had a club foot. He also fractured his left thigh bone shortly before his death.

The mummy thought to be Ramesses I displays a malformed ear, which was potentially connected to a severe ear infection that led to his death. Ramesses II, due to his advanced age at death, suffered from arthritis of the hips, arteriosclerosis of the arteries in his feet and abscesses in his jaw, and had lost teeth. His son Merenptah, who appears to have been quite overweight in life, also suffered from age-related ailments, including fractures in his femurs, arthritis of the vertebrae, bad teeth and arteriosclerosis. Siptah suffered from a clubbed left foot, either a result of polio or cerebral palsy early in his life, and died at a young age. Ramesses III was rather corpulent, while his son, Ramesses IV, who was around 50 at the time of death, had well-worn teeth – a frequent problem among aged ancient Egyptians – and was almost completely bald. Ramesses V appears to have

The mummy of King Seti I, one of the best preserved from the New Kingdom. Medical analyses have shown that he suffered from arteriosclerosis, a disorder also seen in the bodies of his son, Ramesses II, and grandson, Merenptah.

suffered from smallpox, but was possibly killed by a blow to the head during his early 30s rather than his illness. This unfortunate king may also have suffered from an inguinal hernia, as well as another illness – potentially bubonic plague, evidenced by a open bubo on the right groin.

Despite the health problems suffered by these New Kingdom kings, few of them show evidence of 'growth arrest lines', indicative of periods of malnutrition or illness, and they appear to have avoided many of the common diseases of their time. On the whole, then, they seem to have lived well-fed and healthy lives.

## Royal Banquets: 'Eating, Drinking and Making Holiday'

The king took his daily meals in a part of the palace called the Mansion of Life. There he was served by the master of the king's largesse, a man who oversaw the king's table, ensured that there were enough supplies and looked after the king's guests. He was the head of the king's personal provisions and thus in charge of a reasonably large organization. A royal meal could be quite lavish, though we are unaware of the precise recipes followed by the palace cooks. Bread was of course a staple food, and was produced for the palace in large bakeries. As shown in the tomb of Ramesses III, mentioned above, bread intended for royalty and nobles could be made in a variety of shapes, though normally the dough was placed in a conical mould. A wide range of vegetables was available, including garlic, onions, leeks, lettuce and cucumbers. Water melons were popular, as were olives from the Second Intermediate Period onwards, while dates were also eaten, sometimes in cakes. Honey was used as a sweetener, while butter, oils and fats were used to fry meats – 91 vessels of fat were found during excavations at Amenhotep III's palace at Malkata. The poor rarely ate meat, only the rich could afford to eat it regularly, and for them, cattle were frequently slaughtered and served up, as were ibexes, pigs, gazelles, antelope and deer. These could be boiled, stewed or roasted, while roasted duck and goose were also popular. Fish was widely eaten throughout the country, but the Victory Stele of Piye records how individuals that had eaten fish were barred from entering the royal palace, showing a taboo must have existed at that time. Beer was consumed by rich and poor alike, though wine was only available to the wealthy.

The king held large banquets in his formal audience hall and these were certainly large and riotous affairs. Papyrus Boulaq 18 records the presence of 60 people at one banquet, as well as the quantities of food served. At such events, food and pitchers of wine were brought by servants to people who had their own mats or little tables but no utensils – the servants poured water over the guests' hands to cleanse them, normally after the meals, but sometimes before too. After finishing their meals, royal guests washed out their mouths using water mixed with natron. The banqueters were entertained by musicians and dancing girls, and the court had resident musicians for daily entertainment. Papyrus Boulaq 18 refers to four musicians present at court: a flautist; a singer with a harp; a singer who used his hands to clap rhythm; and a female singer. King Amenhotep II and his favourite courtier, the high steward in Perunefer, Kenamun, are described in the

A limestone ostracon painted with the image of an elegant female dancer. Such entertainment was common at elite banquets, which could become riotous affairs.

latter's tomb as spending time together at the palace, watching the harem girls singing about Amenhotep's appearance. An Old Kingdom official, Ankhkhufu, who was the overseer of singers of the palace and overseer of flautists, is said to have been 'the delight of his lord daily'. Clearly the king enjoyed such musical performances on a regular basis.

Depictions of banquets from private New Kingdom tombs sometimes show scenes of drunkenness, including a female guest being sick, clearly having drunk too much, while in the 18th Dynasty tomb of Paheri a woman offers her cup to her servant, stating, 'bring me 18 goblets of wine. Can't you see I am trying to get drunk? My throat is dry as dust!' The pharaohs, like their courtiers, were also fond of a drink. Royal vineyards existed at Pi-Ramesses in the later New Kingdom, with one known as the 'Preserver of Egypt', and Tutankhamun took red wine to the afterlife with him, though no beer. Excavations at Malkata revealed a great number of pottery fragments inscribed with details of the original contents of the vessels. Many were for wine, and mention the year of production, quality ('good', 'very good', 'true' and 'blended') and origin. Other vessels contained ale.

Occasions on which the king himself was drunk are scarce. A letter sent from Amenhotep II to a childhood friend, Usersatet, now the viceroy of Kush, describes the king as 'eating, drinking and making holiday' when celebrating a festival with

Detail of a banquet scene from the tomb of Nebamun, showing a female flautist, two naked dancing girls and a rack of colourfully decorated vessels for wine.

his courtiers. The text is difficult to understand, leading some scholars to wonder whether the king was actually drunk when he wrote it, though this is purely speculative. Another more explicit example of royal drunkenness, albeit from a literary tale and so fictional, revolves around King Ahmose II of the 26th Dynasty. The tale, written in Demotic, presents the king announcing to his courtiers that he wishes to drink a vat of wine. The courtiers, understandably, suggest that this might not be a good idea, but the king – being Pharaoh after all – demands that they do not oppose him. And so, later that day the king and his wives drank together by the sea shore from a vat of wine, so that their faces were 'cheerful'. The festivities over, the king fell asleep on the sea shore, with the north wind cooling him. Unsurprisingly, he awoke the next morning with a headache of such severity that he was unable to get up or do any work. Stories regarding Ahmose's drinking are also recorded by Herodotus: 'He used to organize his working day on a regular principle', the Greek historian writes, 'from dawn till the time when the markets filled up, at mid-morning, he gave all his attention to such business as was brought to him, after which he spent the rest of

Occasionally guests could over-indulge themselves at banquets, as depicted in this detail from a Theban tomb of the 18th Dynasty.

Servants harvesting grapes from vines, a scene from the tomb of Nakht at Thebes.

the day in frivolous amusements, drinking and joking with friends.' Herodotus also records that King Menkaure of the 4th Dynasty, having been told by the oracle of Buto that he had only six more years to live (then dying in the seventh), decided to stay awake at day and night, enjoying every moment and drinking.

## Recitations

If banquets and musicians alone failed to provide enough amusement, the king could also be entertained by storytellers relating tales of magicians, visits to the underworld, ghosts, gods and adventure. It is probable that many of the literary tales that have survived from ancient Egypt were composed for the enjoyment of the royal court, and that they were actually performed rather than simply read. Tales were first written down in the Middle Kingdom, establishing a set form; however, their oral origins meant that they could still be adapted to individual circumstances and performances, with 'episodes' being extended or shortened according to the whim of the storyteller.

The introduction to *The Prophecy of Neferti* illustrates how a bored king might find his entertainment. It presents King Sneferu (4th Dynasty) meeting his royal council in the palace, just as he did each morning, but on this occasion, after the courtiers had left the audience chamber he summoned them back. The courtiers return, bowing in reverence, but the king speaks to them in an informal manner, asking them to find a person who can use choice phrases and fine words to divert him. The courtiers again bow and suggest a high priest of Bastet, a scribe 'skilled with his fingers' as an excellent candidate. The king agrees and Neferti is brought before the king. He offers to speak of future or past events, and the king chooses the former. Enthralled as the prophecy is related, the king writes down the scribe's words using his own writing roll and scribal palette.

*The Tales of Wonder*, recorded in Papyrus Westcar, recount how King Khufu (4th Dynasty) was entertained by stories told by his sons about the magical exploits of lector priests – men knowledgeable in the sacred texts, who read them aloud during religious ceremonies. Each prince takes his turn to describe events under previous kings. The first speaks of a magical crocodile made from wax by a lector priest to capture a man having an affair with his wife. The next prince relates a story set in the court of King Sneferu, telling how the king had searched through every chamber of the palace for a suitable amusement; unable to find anything of interest, Sneferu summons a lector priest for advice, who suggests that he go boating with 20 of the most beautiful women of the palace. Sneferu takes the priest's advice, but improves the plan by suggesting that the women wear nothing but nets while rowing. Later, out on the lake, one of the ladies drops a fish-shaped charm into the deep water and refuses to continue rowing until it is returned.

Desperate for help, the king again summons his lector priest, who uses his magic to place one half of the lake on top of the other, allowing him to find and retrieve the missing charm from the now dry lakebed. Another tale centres on a lector priest from the time of Khufu himself who could reattach the severed heads of animals, bringing them back to life.

Kings were frequently themselves the subject of literary tales, though, as in he above examples, they are rarely presented as untouchable gods. In *The Tale of Pepi II and General Sasenet* the king is said to go wandering each night alone. One night he is followed by a man named Tjeti, who wanted to know if the rumours about the king's nocturnal walks were true. Having secretly followed the king, Tjeti watches as Pepi reaches the house of General Sasenet and enters via a ladder, which is only lowered after the king throws a brick and stamps his foot. After the king had done 'that which he wanted' with the general, he heads back to the palace. It has been suggested that the tale relates to sexual exploits, though this is not made

## PHARAONIC PETS

The pharaohs enjoyed the company of pets, which can usually be distinguished from wild animals in depictions by the collars they wear. King Intef II of the 11th Dynasty is shown on a stele from his Theban funerary chapel accompanied by five dogs, some of which may have been imported from Libya as they were given foreign names. The greyhound Abutiu, who kept watch over an unidentified Old Kingdom king, was so loved by his royal master that he commanded a tomb be built for the dog at Giza, and that it be buried with a sarcophagus and other accoutrements normally reserved for humans.

Felines were also popular pets. Amenhotep II is depicted on a stele with a pet lion, while a son of Amenhotep III, Prince Thutmose, commissioned a sarcophagus for his cat emblazoned with the inscription 'the Osiris, the lady-cat'. As with Amenhotep II, both Ramesses II and III are sometimes depicted with a lion – a depiction of Ramesses II's war camp in Syria shows a lion being cared for by a keeper. In addition to his lion, Amenhotep II may have owned many other pets: three 'animal tombs' were found close to his royal tomb in the Valley of the Kings and among the mummified remains

were three monkeys and a dog. A 21st Dynasty God's Wife of Amun was buried with a mummified baboon.

Kings are first associated with horses in the 18th Dynasty. Thutmose I is shown with a horse on a scarab, while in a fragmentary literary tale Thutmose III talks of his horses being fed. Amenhotep II is also shown feeding horses on a scarab, and on his Sphinx Stele he speaks of a time when he trained them before he became king. On his own Sphinx Stele, Thutmose IV emphasizes the speed of his horses when riding his chariot, while Ramesses III talks of inspecting the horses of the royal stables, saying that he trained them with his own hands. Ramesses II relates how, because his horses had not deserted him during the battle of Kadesh, he would have them fed in his presence at the palace, and even had a ring made decorated with a pair of horses. The Nubian king Piye was especially fond of horses, having one depicted on his Victory Stele, where he describes his horror at his enemy's mistreatment of horses after taking the palace of King Nimlot during his campaign in Egypt: 'His Majesty then proceeded to the stable of the horses and the quarters of the foals. When he saw that they were starved, he said: "As I live, as Re loves me, as my nose is rejuvenated with life, how much more painful it is in my heart that my horses explicit. Still, the text does emphasize that it took the king four hours to walk to the house, he then spent four hours with the general, and took four hours to walk home – a total of 12 hours. The 12 hours of the night form an important element of royal Netherworld books, and so this reference may be a satirical allusion to the union of Re and Osiris in the middle of the night.

*The Tale of Setna and Si-Osire*, a Demotic text copied in the Roman Period, also shows little reverence for kingship. It describes the magician Si-Osire relating a tale of sorcery to King Ramesses II, set during the reign of Thutmose III of the 18th Dynasty. In the story, a Nubian sorcerer uses his magic to transport Thutmose to Nubia, where he is lashed in public with 500 blows of a whip. After six hours Thutmose is returned to Egypt, where he is described as lying down in the resting place of Horus 'with his buttocks badly beaten'. The courtiers then summon a sorcerer to protect the king from further Nubian magic, and he swears an oath on the king's 'rear-end' that the matter will be dealt with.

have been starved than any other crime that you (Nimlot) have committed at your discretion". The Nubian kings were also accompanied by the burials of horses close to their own small pyramids.

It was once thought that a royal zoo existed at Pi-Ramesses, based on the bones of hyenas, giraffes, antelopes and gazelles, ibexes and deer found there, as well as lions and elephants. However, it is more probable that the bones belonged to animals brought back as trophies from hunting trips for their skins.

The sarcophagus of the cat Ta-miat ('the cat'), beloved pet of crown prince Thutmose, son of Amenhotep III. The cat is seated before a table of offerings, while the inscriptions identify her with Osiris.

## Sports and Games

Outside the palace, the pharaohs enjoyed – or at least presented themselves as enjoying – many sporting activities. Since they lived on a river, it is not surprising that some of their activities involved water. The First Intermediate Period nomarch Kheti relates how, 'He (the king) allowed me to take swimming lessons together with his own children', while during the annual Opet Festival, Amenhotep II demonstrated his strength by steering a boat bearing 200 people with a 10-m (33-ft) long oar for just over 30 km (18 miles). Tutankhamun, too, is described at Luxor Temple as rowing during the Opet Festival, but again this was part of ritual ceremonies rather than for sport. Running is mentioned infrequently in the ancient sources, though the ever-boastful Amenhotep II does state that no one compared to him in running; it was also of course an important element of the *Sed* Festival, described above (pp. 97–98). A stele from the reign of King Taharqo provides the most detailed account of a running competition, relating how a select team of troops ran daily to keep fit. One day the king came to inspect these troops and asked them to demonstrate their fitness by running from the Faiyum Oasis to the palace at Memphis – a distance of roughly 50 km (31 miles) from the border of the Faiyum. During the race, the king inspired them by riding next to them on his chariot, and perhaps even ran alongside them for a short while. The winner was allowed to eat and drink with the royal bodyguard, and the runners up received gifts.

The common theme of kings demonstrating excellence in archery began in the 18th Dynasty, with both crown prince Amenmose, a son of Thutmose I, and Thutmose III described as enjoying themselves shooting. According to a stele from Armant, the latter is also said to have shot at a copper target three fingers thick with such strength that his arrows passed through it and emerged on the other side by three hands' breadths. It is, however, Amenhotep II who takes royal excellence in this sport to its greatest level. Amenhotep was taught archery in his youth by Min, the mayor of Thinis, and eventually equalled his father's achievement, shooting his arrow through a copper target three fingers thick for three hands' breadths. Not content with this, quite unusually, a stele from Medamud describes Amenhotep challenging his courtiers to an archery competition, and firing his arrows even deeper through copper targets, breaking his own (and his father's) record. On his Sphinx Stele he also boasts that he managed to pierce four copper plates stuck together. A broken reference to Tutankhamun performing similar feats no doubt took royal boastfulness even further. A fragment of gold leaf shows King Ay riding upon his chariot shooting arrows at a target. Interestingly, both this and a later cylinder seal of Ramesses II, which portrays this king standing shooting arrows, depict prisoners tied to the pole supporting the king's target – a symbolic motif of dominance, or cruel punishment? It is hard to say.

There is little evidence for kings fishing, though Amenemhat II does record that he made fishing nets with his courtiers, and a Ramesside ostracon (now in the Louvre) bears a sketch of a king seated on a stool making a net (although this was no doubt intended to be satirical). The pharaohs were, however, certainly fond of hunting. A cylinder seal from the reign of King Den (1st Dynasty) shows the king standing on a boat harpooning a hippopotamus, while scenes from the 5th Dynasty pyramid complex of Sahure depict a hunt in the desert, with the king shown standing holding his bow and arrows, aided by hunting dogs and servants with lassoes and a stick. Later Old Kingdom sun temples and pyramid complexes similarly included scenes of royal hunts, as did the 11th Dynasty mortuary temple of Montuhotep II. A Middle Kingdom text, *The Tale of the Sporting King*, describes an outing by the court and royal family under Amenemhat II to the Faiyum for a hunt. However, it was not until the New Kingdom that kings' hunting abilities were truly highlighted.

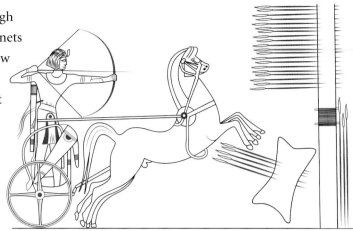

Drawing of a relief on a block from Karnak Temple depicting Amenhotep II shooting arrows through a copper target. Proclaiming excellence at archery was a standard royal boast in the New Kingdom.

Thutmose I hunted elephants by the lake of Niy when on campaign in Syria, as did his grandson Thutmose III, who 'slew seven lions by shooting arrows in the space of a moment. He captured a herd of 12 wild bulls in a single hour before breakfast time arrived, their tails being (draped) behind him. He dispatched 120 elephants in the foreign territory of Niy'. Thutmose also seems to have hunted a rhinoceros, as one is depicted on blocks from Armant, annotated with the animal's measurements. These hunts did not always proceed smoothly; it seems Thutmose was attacked by an elephant in Niy and was only saved thanks to the quick action of a soldier named Amenemhab, who cut off the animal's trunk. Amenhotep III proclaimed his hunting exploits on two sets of commemorative scarabs: one records that he killed 102 lions during his first 10 years as king; the other describes an occasion on which the king and court set out to hunt 170 wild cattle, spotted in the desert near the Faiyum Oasis. After the cattle had been herded into an enclosure with a ditch, the king killed 56 of them before allowing his horses to rest for four days. The archaeological remains of a hunting enclosure from the time of Amenhotep III were found at Soleb in Nubia, which, when combined with the depiction of a similar enclosure in the Middle Kingdom tomb of Senbi at Meir, provides a good impression of how a royal hunt was organized: essentially, the pharaoh shot at his prey from behind a barrier – the animals trapped within the enclosure – and was never in any serious danger of injury. Given these circumstances, it is not surprising that kings were successful hunters.

Bulls and lions were also popular prey for many kings: a Ramesside Period ostracon from Deir el-Medina shows a king in his Red Crown spearing a lion, aided by a faithful hunting dog, while at Medinet Habu, large, detailed scenes show Ramesses III engaged in bull and lion hunts. More unusually, Tutankhamun is shown hunting ostriches on a fan from his tomb. He is also depicted hunting various animals on his elaborate painted chest and on one of his bow cases. Hunting birds with throwsticks was an ever popular pastime among the ancient Egyptians, kings included; an actual example of a throwstick was found in Tutankhamun's tomb, and Amenhotep II went hunting in a place called Ta-She with the Mayor of the Faiyum, Sobekhotep, killing birds with his throwstick and spearing fish from his boat.

Sporting events could also form the entertainment at ceremonial occasions. At Amarna, a scene showing the king receiving tribute from Nubia includes wrestling matches, stick fighting and boxing; such events are described as occurring, 'in the presence of Pharaoh'. Similarly, before the Window of Appearance in the first court at Medinet Habu, where ceremonial rewards may have been presented, a scene depicts a referee warning a wrestler, 'Take care! You are in the presence of Pharaoh, Life! Prosperity! Health! Your [Lord!]'. Many of the scenes from Medinet Habu are copied from the Ramesseum, and so similar events may have occurred there.

Ramesses III prepares to spear a bull during a hunt, as two others lay wounded nearby; from Medinet Habu. Through portraying himself as a successful hunter, Ramesses was also showing himself as a powerful warrior and defender of Egypt from the forces of chaos.

A gilded wooden fan from the tomb of Tutankhamun showing the king on his chariot, accompanied by his hunting dog, in pursuit of two ostriches. One of the ostriches has been struck by two arrows.

Kings must have enjoyed board games from the earliest times, as shown by tower-shaped game piece found in a 1st Dynasty royal burial at Umm el-Qaab, Abydos. Four boards for the game *senet* were found in the tomb of Tutankhamun, one with its own playing table, as well as two astragals – dice made from bones from the hind legs of lambs. Queen Nefertari, wife of Ramesses II, is shown playing the same game against an unseen opponent in her tomb in the Valley of the Queens, and Ramesses III is depicted on the inner walls of the High Gate of his mortuary temple playing a board game, possibly *senet*, with a harem girl.

Queen Nefertari, Great Royal Wife of King Ramesses II, plays the board game *senet* in a scene from her tomb in the Valley of the Queens. Her opponent is absent because the scene represents her defeat of death, and thus her rebirth in the afterlife.

115

## CHAPTER 5

# THE PHARAOH ON CAMPAIGN

Riding into battle under the protection of the war god Montu, his enemies scattering in fright before him, the pharaoh symbolized Egypt's dominance in the world. Through his action, the forces of chaos, embodied by foreign enemies, were repelled, and the people of Egypt were kept safe. It was pharaoh's duty to secure divine sanction for a campaign, to muster and arm his forces and to lead them into foreign territory, but did he fight alongside his troops? Or was he nothing but a symbol, inspiring his troops on the day of battle, but ultimately protected from danger, too important to be risked?

## Early Warfare

Some of the earliest depictions of the Egyptian pharaoh to emerge with the unification of the state connected him with warfare. The Narmer Palette shows the king gripping an enemy by the hair, about to bring his mace down upon him, as well as a royal procession before two rows of decapitated enemies (see p. 18); other foes are shown fleeing or already slaughtered. The military emphasis in art was also mirrored in the names of the Early Dynastic rulers, such as Horus the Fighter (Hor Aha). Despite this, it seems the king played little role in early warfare. In the Old Kingdom there was no permanent military force – troops were called upon when needed by local leaders acting under the king's command. One such local leader was Weni, who led an army of Egyptians and Nubians against Asiatic Bedouin during the 6th Dynasty. Although Pepi I 'made' this military force, Weni states in his inscription at Abydos that the king ordered him to lead the army and that it was he who commanded the troops. Quite clearly Pepi did not accompany the mission. In this he was not being unusual – no other Old Kingdom monarch is known to have accompanied a campaign either.

With the Middle Kingdom, the king's role as war leader became more pronounced, developing out of the presentation of the provincial warlords

The Narmer Palette, discovered at Hierakonpolis and now in the Egyptian Museum, Cairo, displays the king in the White Crown gripping an enemy by the hair in one hand and about to bring a mace crashing down upon his head. Smiting scenes were symbolic of the king's defeat of chaos, as personified by Egypt's foreign enemies.

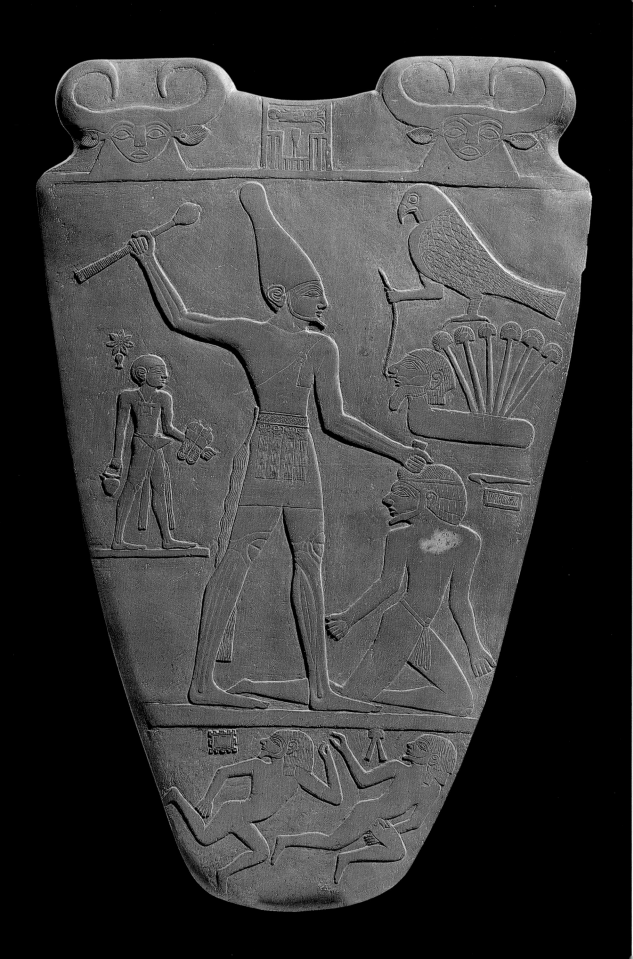

of the First Intermediate Period. From two fragments of a royal stele we learn that Montuhotep II led his army against foreign enemies and annexed an oasis, as well as part of Nubia. This inscription is notable because it records a dialogue between the king and his army in which he outlines a plan of attack, a form not found again until the late Second Intermediate Period. Subsequent kings did not follow Montuhotep's example, however, and in the 12th Dynasty royal sons may have led the army instead of the monarch. *The Tale of Sinuhe* describes Prince Senwosret – the future King Senwosret I – as being present during a campaign against the Libyans, and provides us with a eulogy to the king as warrior: 'Stout-hearted when he sees the mass, he lets not slackness fill his heart. Eager at the sight of combat, joyful when he works his bow. Clasping his shield he treads under foot, no second blow needed to kill. None can escape his arrow, none turn aside his bow.' Here we find a precursor to the standard form of bombastic eulogy associated with New Kingdom warrior kings.

Although as king, Senwosret I launched campaigns into Nubia and promoted himself as 'throat-slitter of Asia', there is no reason to believe that he personally accompanied his troops south; certainly, one of his campaigns was led by a military officer, a man named General Montuhotep. Later in the Middle Kingdom, on a stele erected at the fortress of Semna in Nubia, Senwosret III reflected on his military achievements and his abilities as king, proclaiming, 'I have made my boundary, out-southing my forefathers. I have exceeded what was handed down to me. I am a king, whose speaking is acting … one who is aggressive to capture, swift to success; who sleeps not with a matter (still) in his heart; who takes thought for dependents, and stands by mercy; who is unmerciful to the enemy that attacks him; who attacks when attacked, and is quiet when it is quiet; who responds to a matter as it happens … Aggression is bravery; retreat is vile.'

More detailed accounts of kings directly involving themselves in the art of war emerge in the Second Intermediate Period, a time when central authority had crumbled and the Asiatic Hyksos ruled the north. Both King Montuhotepi and King Ikhernofret (who is absent from king lists) speak of being beloved of their armies, defeating enemies, saving Thebes and being under the protection of Amun, while soldiers and courtiers of this time refer to following the king on campaign and the rewards they received. The first king seriously to threaten the Hyksos domination was Seqenenre Tao, known as 'the brave'. As his mummy shows that he died a violent death – either by assassination, fighting on the battlefield or execution following the loss of a battle – it is likely that he accompanied his troops on campaign. His successor Kamose led a naval campaign against the Hyksos and is presented in his inscriptions as taunting Apophis, the Hyksos ruler: 'Look, I am drinking of the wine of your vineyards,' he says, 'I am hacking up your dwelling place, cutting down your trees'. The king's role as war leader was born during these tumultuous and violent times and matured in the New Kingdom, when it became one of the monarch's primary aspects. The trauma of foreign control was damaging to the royal psyche – this was a clear violation of *maat*, an upset to the very order that the king vowed to uphold. To the New Kingdom kings, it was no longer enough simply to protect Egypt's borders; if the chaotic forces embodied by foreign enemies were to be effectively repelled, Egypt needed to expand its control.

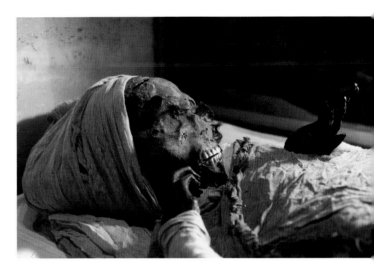

The mummy of Seqenenre Tao displays wounds that betray his violent death. He could have been killed fighting in battle or was executed after losing one, or was perhaps assassinated in the palace.

The Hyksos were chased out of Egypt into Palestine, but the Egyptians did not stop there. Thutmose I traversed the Levant, ultimately reaching the River Euphrates. These actions paved the way for the formation of an empire, with Nubia falling first. This was followed by parts of Syria-Palestine, the kings of its city-states submitting to the pharaoh, taking an oath of allegiance and sending tribute and their own children to Egypt as guarantees of loyalty. Once gained, this empire had to be maintained, so that over the course of the New Kingdom's 500 years, territory was won and lost, and great accounts of the pharaohs' wars were recorded, both pictorially and textually.

## Preparing for War

Many of the preserved accounts of New Kingdom military activity begin with a messenger arriving to inform the king of a foreign rebellion. Thutmose II was told of a Nubian uprising when sitting in his palace, while Thutmose IV is said to have been making offerings to the gods when his messenger interrupted him. This literary motif always presents a state of order being disrupted by unrest – order that the king now has to battle to restore. His typical response to the news is to express rage, and then to discuss matters with his closest advisers. King Kamose convened his courtiers to debate whether to go to war with the Hyksos, but failed to receive the positive response he desired; they were far more interested in preserving the status quo than becoming embroiled in a potentially long and bloody war. Angered, the king visited the god Amun to gain divine support, and having secured it war commenced. Similarly, after hearing of rebellion in Nubia, Thutmose IV consulted with Amun for guidance, seeking divine assurance that his campaign would be successful. Only then did he command his army to assemble.

Divine sanction was always required once the king and court had made their decision to go to war. This is made quite explicit in Ramesside war reliefs, in which

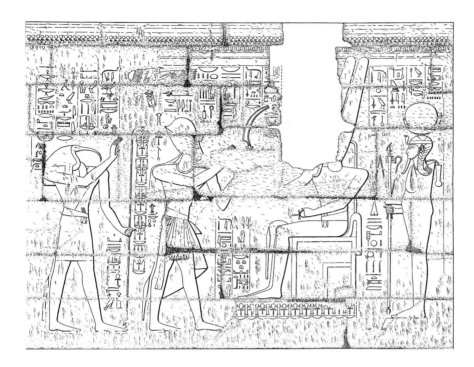

Amun is shown offering the king a sickle-sword, known as a *khepesh*. Other gods, typically Mut and Khonsu, watch as the sword – a symbol of Amun's endorsement of the campaign and thus the king's ultimate victory – is handed over. At Medinet Habu, the mortuary temple of Ramesses III, this sequence is particularly detailed. After receiving his *khepesh* from the god, Ramesses leaves the divine presence, now also holding a bow, and walks in procession accompanied by the war god Montu; priests carrying the standards of gods go before them. In the next scene the king mounts his chariot, while an official prepares his horse. The royal bodyguard and elite charioteers stand nearby watching, and a bugle is sounded as the king prepares himself for the coming campaign. The king is then shown riding in his chariot alongside his army. A chariot at the front bears the standard of the god Amun. These stylized reliefs no doubt reflect an actual visit by the king to the Temple of Amun to appear before the oracle of the god to ask for permission to initiate a war.

Once sanctioned, the king commanded his troops to be assembled. If he did not accompany them himself on the campaign he might send his commanders out with a simple royal decree – Thutmose II despatched his army to Nubia with a command not to let any of the male rebels live. This level of detachment was not always the case, however. Piye, on his Victory Stele, is unusual in being quite direct about his needs, managing his campaign from afar in some detail. After hearing of the activities of the expansionist ruler Tefnakht, the king wrote to his commanders saying 'Enter combat, engage in battle; surround [...], capture its people, its cattle, its ships on the river! Let not the farmers go to the field, let not the ploughmen plough. Beset the Hare nome; fight against it daily.' He then sets out explicitly the tactics to be used, ordering his commanders not to use stealth, or try to outwit the enemy in the manner of a man playing a board game, rather 'Challenge him to battle from afar. If he proposes to await the infantry and chariotry of another town, then sit still until his troops come. Fight when he proposes. Also if he has allies in another town, let them be awaited. The counts whom he brings to help him, and any trusted Libyan troops, let them be challenged to battle in advance, saying: "you whose name we do not know… Harness the best steeds of your stable, form your battle line, and know that Amun is the god who sent us!"' This shows that the location and time of a battle could be agreed in advance.

Piye also refers to being kept informed of battles and outcomes via correspondence with his commanders. He thus played quite a personal role in organizing his army, even though he was not with them. In contrast, Psamtik II of the 26th Dynasty spent time sightseeing around Elephantine Island near Aswan while awaiting news about a military force that he had sent into Nubia. On his victory stele he is described as roaming around the marshes and inundated land, and visiting the sycamore trees of the god's estate there. A messenger then arrives to tell him of the mission's success, and that 'one waded in their blood as in water'.

Unlike Psamtik II, many pharaohs did accompany their troops to war, apparently finding the idea quite alluring. Seti I, for example, upon hearing of an impending conflict with the Shasu, 'was happy at this. For, as for the Good God, he rejoices at engaging in battle, and he enjoys a transgression against him. His heart

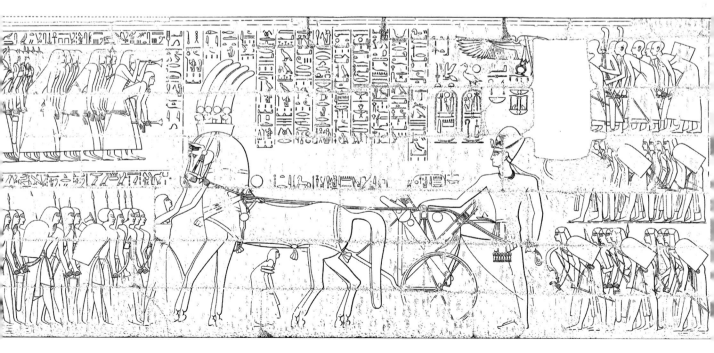

is satisfied with seeing blood when he chops off the heads of disaffected persons. He loves a moment of pounding more than a day of celebrating! His Majesty killed them all at once, he did not leave heirs among them. The one who escaped from his hand is a living captive, carried off to Egypt.'

## Mustering and Arming the Troops

Once war had been discussed and sanctioned, the troops were called up to service and assembled at a particular location in preparation for the march. Merenptah is said to have mustered his troops and chariots in the vicinity of the nome of *per-iru*, but capital cities, such as Memphis or Pi-Ramesses, being locations of the royal armoury, were no doubt also major assembly centres. Scenes from Medinet Habu show Ramesses III inspecting the horses in preparation for a campaign, as well as handing out equipment to his troops from a rostrum. The king then issues a command: 'Bring forth equipment! Send out troops to destroy the rebellious countries which know not Egypt, through the strength of my father Amun!' The crown prince, standing before the king, announces that every valiant soldier should pass by Pharaoh and receive his equipment. Among the items depicted are helmets, spears, bows, *khepesh*-swords, corslets, quivers and shields.

Further depictions of New Kingdom military equipment can be found in the tomb of Ramesses III in the Valley of the Kings, as well as in the tomb of Kenamun, an official who served under Amenhotep II. These include brightly coloured knee-length tunics with metal scales sewn on to their surfaces in bands of red, blue and yellow. Such scales were probably made of bronze, like the actual examples found

OPPOSITE **A 19th-century illustration of military equipment depicted in the tomb of Ramesses III, including brightly coloured body armour.**

Ramesses III inspects his horses before the start of a campaign, in a scene from Medinet Habu.

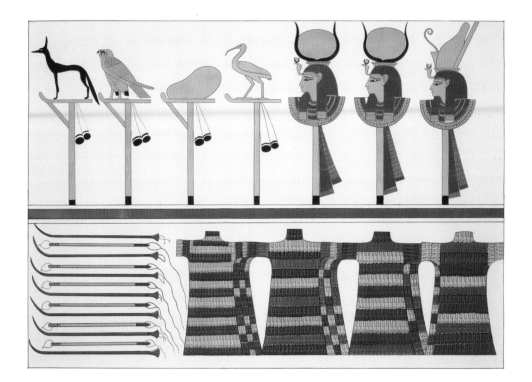

during excavations at Malkata. The fabric on to which they were sewn was either linen or leather; a booty list from the campaigns of Thutmose III mentions a 'fine bronze coat for fighting', followed by a leather determinative, indicating that bronze scales were fitted to a leather tunic. Tutankhamun was buried with a sleeveless cuirass made of thick leather scales attached to a linen shirt. Metal scales for armour have been found during excavations at Pi-Ramesses in an area of the site associated with chariotry, while a single bronze scale bearing the cartouche of Ramesses II was recently found on Salamina island, Greece – perhaps the souvenir of a Mycenaean veteran of the Egyptian army. Armour made from iron scales is known only from the reign of Shoshenq I on, though bronze scales continued to be used at the same time, as shown by scales of both materials excavated at the palace of Apries in Memphis, probably dating to the Persian Period.

BELOW LEFT **Scales of armour found at Pi-Ramesses (modern Qantir), made from a variety of materials, including bone, pottery and bronze.**

BELOW **A leather cuirass as it was discovered in the tomb of Tutankhamun.**

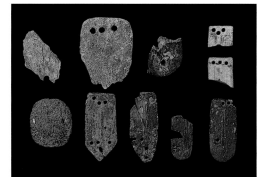

Helmets are also shown in the tombs of Ramesses III and Kenamun. Probably made of bronze, they are red or green with black stripes, and each bears two streamers emerging from their peaks. Although Sherden warriors (Mediterranean mercenaries) are typically depicted wearing horned helmets in Ramesside war reliefs, Egyptian soldiers are rarely shown wearing this form of protection. Sometimes, however, those attending to the king's horses are portrayed wearing helmets, emphasizing that, like body armour, they were connected to the chariotry. The king himself is never shown wearing a helmet of the kind depicted in the tombs of Ramesses III and Kenamun, though he is often represented fighting wearing the Blue Crown, which has erroneously been referred to as a form of war helmet. Sometimes he is seen fighting in a simple wig.

A particularly well-preserved scene at Medinet Habu, Ramesses III's mortuary temple, provides an insight into how the Egyptians wished to present the king on campaign, thanks to the survival of its painted detail. Over a transparent shirt he wears a tight-fitting tunic that terminates above the waist; tiny feather patterns adorning the tunic are probably decorative features rather than bronze scales. The tunic is held in place by two wide strips of striped material, with an upper band made to resemble feathers, each terminating in the form of falcon's wings at the king's arms; falcon heads are visible at either side of the king's chest – the whole would have given the appearance of two winged falcons embracing the king in an act of protection. A girdle is wrapped around the king's stomach and tied at the front, above the kilt. Elaborate armlets cover his biceps, two of which are in the form of rearing cobras, and he wears a wide beaded collar around his neck. On his head, his lappet wig falls at the front down to his chest in clearly divided stripes; he does not wear a helmet. The vast difference between this outfit and the typical chariotry equipment shown in the tombs of Ramesses III and Kenamun highlights the idealized nature of such reliefs, for although it is more than likely that the king's costume at war was more elaborate than that of his soldiers, would it truly have been this different? If indeed he did fight, surely he would have been as well protected as his soldiers, if not more so, and have worn a long leather tunic covered with bronze scales and a bronze helmet, like his charioteers.

Weapons were regarded as prestige items as well as implements of war. As early as the 3rd Dynasty, Sekhemkhet is depicted at Wadi Maghara in the Sinai with a dagger in his belt, while physical examples of ceremonial daggers have been found

Tasselled helmets, standard equipment for charioteers, as depicted in the tomb of Ramesses III in the Valley of the Kings. Though he is frequently portrayed on his chariot, the king is never shown wearing such a helmet.

Ramesses III dressed for war. The wings of two protective falcons cross the king's chest, securing his tunic in place. Beneath, he wears a transparent shirt.

ABOVE **A piece of chariot equipment made from leather, from the Egyptian Museum, Cairo.**

LEFT **Tutankhamun charging at Nubian enemies in his chariot, fanned by servants and assisted by his hunting dogs, depicted on a painted chest from his tomb.**

BELOW **A ceremonial dagger with a bronze blade and gilded pommel, found on the body of King Kamose.**

belonging to Ahmose and Kamose. Tutankhamun was buried with two daggers, one with a gold blade, the other of iron, and also with a full-size and a small *khepesh*-sword. His 14 self bows (there were also composite bows) included one that was much smaller than the others and so may have been used by him as a boy. When shooting arrows he wore a wrist guard; not only is he depicted wearing such an item, but a leather example was found in his tomb. A more ornate piece, made of gold and jewels, is known to have belonged to King Ahmose. Further weapons and equipment in Tutankhamun's tomb included two gilded wooden maces, as well as shields, one with a depiction of him as a sphinx trampling enemies.

Other military equipment, some quite elaborately decorated, is shown in the tomb of Kenamun, probably for use by Amenhotep II's personal guard as well as the king himself, providing a fascinating picture of Egyptian soldiery at war. The numerous items included four shields made of animal skins; bull's-hide shields; leather quivers, two of leopard skin; six leaf-shaped daggers of white metal; a bronze dagger; a dagger with a hawk's head as decoration on the handle; two sets of battle axes; two archers' wrist guards; horse trappings, such as ivory studs for the top of the yoke and a leather blinker; two sets of whips; a Syrian bow; a wrist guard bearing the king's name; a chariot; and a rare example of a sword.

All such weapons of war, as well as supplies for the march, needed to be gathered together in preparation for the campaign. Well-stocked and armed, battle orders given, and with the sanction of Amun, the army was finally ready to depart into hostile territory.

125

## The King and his Army

The main body of the army consisted of simple foot soldiers, who carried large leather shields with arched tops and were armed with spears, *khepesh*-swords or axes, though often wearing little but kilts and leather straps across their chests for protection. Other men were trained as archers, a role that required a great deal of strength. However, none in the army were as respected or admired as the charioteers. From the mid-18th Dynasty, chariotry formed an important wing of the army, with chariots deployed in formations and driven by charioteers who had their own ranking system, separate from the rest of the army. Although charioteers were set apart, soldiers could move up the ranks of the infantry, via newly created

> ‘When he (the king) was on the battlefield of his victories his strength caused (us) to be stout hearted.’
>
> The Soldier Amenemhab (18th Dynasty)

roles such as commander of bowmen or commander of forts, and one day join them. With their special status, charioteers were not unlike the knights of medieval Europe; they formed a highly trained elite of the fighting force, clad in leather corselets with bronze scales and protected by gleaming bronze helmets as they raced across the battlefield. It is no surprise that New Kingdom royal princes and kings wished to be seen as part of this highly prestigious group. Over time, the pharaohs became so linked with the chariotry that a poem was written, identifying each part of the chariot with an aspect of the king.

Also like medieval knights, charioteers were armed with various weapons and assisted by a team of followers. Each chariot was pulled by two horses and carried two men – one to steer the horses and shoot arrows, the other acting as his shield bearer for protection. There was also a runner, a man who followed the chariot armed with a javelin in order to protect the horses from enemies. The chariot cabin was equipped with two overlapping containers, one for the bow and the other for arrows. Javelins, identified in war reliefs by their orb-like peaks and tassels, were stored in a further case. Once on the field of combat, charioteers would aim to ride along the enemy front line, firing arrows as they moved, rather than charging them head on. The king is always shown carrying his quiver on his back, tied to his body. But the image of the king alone in his chariot, reins wound around his waist to steer and leave his hands free for his bow, riding directly at his enemies, is pure fiction.

Naval forces are known from the start of Egyptian history, but they were not a separate wing of the army; soldiers sailing on ships held the same titles as those fighting on land, while those on board were also involved in shipping cargo. Ships were simply used as a way of transporting troops in preparation for land-based

warfare. The Egyptian navy only came into its own during the 26th Dynasty, when warfare became more advanced as a result of a higher degree of foreign influence and technology. It is perhaps from this time, though possibly later, in the 30th Dynasty, that the Egyptians first used triremes – huge ramming galleys, propelled by three banks of oars. In this later phase of Egyptian history they also probably used triakontors – single-banked galleys with 30 oarsmen.

Foreigners were always an important element of the Egyptian army; even in the Old Kingdom Nubians, famed for their archery skills, and Libyans fought for the Egyptians. In the Ramesside period captured foreign warriors were frequently assigned to the army. Sherden warriors – Mediterranean mercenaries who wore horned helmets and carried swords and round shields – acted as bodyguard to Ramesses II at the battle of Kadesh. In the Late Period the Egyptian army became increasingly international. Psamtik I regained Egypt's independence from the Assyrians with the help of Gyges of Lydia; afterwards, Greek mercenaries became a regular fixture of the army, as did Carians, Jews and Phoenicians. According to Herodotus, King Necho II dedicated his armour to Apollo at Branchidae (modern Didim on the west coast of Turkey), indicating that a large number of Greeks served in his army. Foreign mercenaries were a constant source of friction with the Late Period Egyptian warrior class; the overthrow of King Apries by General Ahmose, who became Ahmose II, occurred as a result of the perceived unequal treatment between the two groups.

In addition to the troops, military scribes accompanied the pharaohs, noting down movements and activities on each day. Their records, called 'daybooks', which were ultimately stored in the palace archives, were used as the basis for the great poetic and

Detail from a scene of Ramesses III fighting the Sea Peoples: a charioteer stands behind the king, holding the reins of the royal horses. It is possible that this individual steered the king's chariot, though he is never shown when the king himself is in the chariot cabin.

Sherden warriors, with their distinctive horned helmets, swords and round shields, formed an important contingent in the Ramesside army.

commemorative inscriptions that promoted the kings' activities on temple walls and stelae. One such military scribe was Tjanuni, who died under Thutmose IV but had accompanied Thutmose III to the Levant and recorded his victories.

We can thus imagine a great army: the king, riding in his chariot, was followed by the royal princes, generalissimos, overseers of troops, viziers and chariot warriors. With them marched the foot soldiers, archers of various nationalities and the scribes, along with oxen and donkeys pulling carts of supplies. All were placed in divisions named after gods, each roughly 5000 men strong, including at least 50 charioteers and 'platoons' of 50 soldiers, forming companies of between 200 and 250 men (overseen by a commander), all marching or riding beneath their division's divine standard.

## Talking Tactics on Campaign

While marching, the king must have met with his commanders to discuss tactics and to decide on their overall war plan. Thutmose III was kept informed of the military situation in his tent each morning, just as in Egypt in his palace he was told of current events by his staff. When en route to the city of Megiddo in Palestine to face a coalition of rebellious princes, Thutmose III stopped at the town of Yehem to discuss the way forward with his commanders. Of the different roads available the most daring was the narrow Aruna pass because it forced the army to walk in single file, leaving them in significant danger if engaged. However, if they successfully navigated the route without meeting resistance, they would be at a great tactical advantage over the enemy. Thutmose asked his men their thoughts on his plan. Their response? 'May our victorious Lord proceed on (the road) that is preferable in his opinion; (but) do not make us go on this difficult road!' Despite their reluctance, the decision was made for them when a messenger arrived with new intelligence, confirming the king's suggestion as the correct course of action. The king then made an oath to lead his army on the difficult road, but gave each of his soldiers too afraid to follow him the option of taking a safer route – an offer that none are reported to have taken. Thutmose then led his troops safely through the pass and out to the other side, where they set up their camp in preparation for combat the next morning.

## Military Camps

Before the battle of Megiddo, Thutmose III pitched his camp at the Qina Brook. From there, he spoke to the entire army and gave provisions to his officers and attendants. Sentries were posted at the exits to the camp and told to be vigilant. Sadly, the 'annals' of this campaign provide no further details of the camp or the appearance of the interior of the royal tent, but the picture can be supplemented

OPPOSITE **The Egyptian military camp as shown in the Kadesh battle reliefs. The shield perimeter is a prominent feature, as is the royal tent in the centre.**

with information from both the battle reliefs of Ramesses II and a depiction of camp life from the Saqqara tomb of Horemheb. Taken together, these illustrations show that the overall perimeter of the camp was demarcated by shields pushed into the ground in tightly fitting lines. Within this area the space was divided into four quadrants by two roads that intersected at the royal tent, which stood at the centre of the camp. All around, men are depicted drinking wine, mock fighting or sleeping. Horses stand beside their chariots, while donkeys and oxen, still attached to their vehicles, receive a welcome rest from dragging their heavy loads; Ramesses' lion lies calmly outside the royal tent. Supplies are piled up in various places. The soldiers have no tents; possibly they simply slept on the ground.

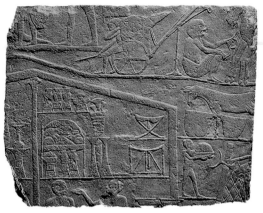

ABOVE **Relief from the Saqqara tomb of Horemheb, depicting the inside of the command tent. A central column holds up the tent and folding furniture is visible, as well as food supplies.**

The royal tent was set within its own rectangular enclosure; surrounding it were further small tents, perhaps for use by generals. Only two entrances gave access to this restricted zone, guarded by two stick-wielding soldiers. The royal tent itself was probably made of leather or cloth and was divided into two sections; one half was low, long and rectangular, the other square, with a high pointed roof – in the Horemheb camp reliefs, a large column stands at the centre of the command tent, creating this distinctive shape. These same reliefs also show an array of furniture within the tent, including a folding stool, as well as provisions. Similar items of folding furniture were found in the tomb of Tutankhamun, among them a collapsible 'campaign' bed. Ramesses II's reliefs depict the king seated in his royal tent upon a gilded throne; he wears the Blue Crown and holds a long staff in his hand, his feet rest on a footstool. Clearly, the pharaohs did not leave luxury behind in Egypt.

## The Battle

Before the battle of Megiddo, Thutmose III addressed his troops, saying 'Prepare yourselves, sharpen your weapons, because one is to engage in battle with that impotent enemy in the morning'. The 'annals' of his wars, inscribed on the walls around the barque shrine of Amun at Karnak Temple, then dramatically introduce the battle, 'His Majesty set out on a chariot of fine gold/electrum, equipped with his equipment of war like strong-armed Horus, lord of action, like Theban Montu, his father [Amun] strengthening his arms'. The position of the Egyptian army is described, with the southern wing on a hill south of the Qina brook and the northern wing to the northwest of Megiddo, 'while His Majesty was in their midst, Amun protecting his body (in) the melee'. Despite this build up, the battle itself is summed up in a single sentence, 'Then His Majesty prevailed over them at the front of his army.' Apparently, the enemy fled at the sight of the king and hid within the walls of Megiddo, initiating a siege that would last seven months.

Texts are rarely detailed in their accounts of battles (though see 'The Battle of Kadesh', pp. 134–35); Merenptah, however, relates that his archers spent six hours 'utterly destroying' invading Libyans and Sea Peoples, with the survivors put to the sword. Ramesses III describes his readiness for the naval battle against the Sea Peoples in the eighth year of his reign, saying that he 'caused the Nile mouth to be prepared like a strong wall with warships, galleys and coasters, equipped, for they were manned completely from bow to stern with valiant warriors, with their weapons; the militia consisting of every picked man of Egypt, were like lions roaring upon the mountain tops. The chariotry consisted of runners, of picked men, of every good and capable chariot-warrior.' He then recounts in detail how the enemy were engaged in fierce fighting, dragged ashore and surrounded and slain, their bodies heaped up in piles. Although not present on the field of battle, Piye, on his Victory Stele, relates the commands that he gave to his troops attacking Memphis, 'Forward against it! Mount the walls! Enter the houses over the river! When one of you enters the wall, no one shall stand in his vicinity, no troops shall repulse you! To pause is vile.'

War reliefs, mainly of the Ramesside period, also provide an idealized insight into the activities of kings at war. When shown fighting in battle, the king is always the largest warrior in the scene, riding valiantly in his chariot against chaotically falling foes. Often he fights alone against his enemies, though royal princes may be present; if his charioteers and foot soldiers are depicted, they are on a smaller scale. As noted above, he typically wears either his Blue Crown or a simple wig, and steers his horses by means of reins tied around his waist so that his hands are free to fire his arrows, which of course never miss their target, and he is armed also with his *khepesh*-sword. Although conventional in appearance, each such scene can be very vivid in its detail, especially in depictions of the foreign soldiers, thus providing a great deal of information on the wider world in which the New Kingdom pharaohs lived and fought.

Occasionally, more innovative scenes are included on temple walls, which show the king performing specific acts on the battlefield. At Medinet Habu, Ramesses III is depicted dismounting from his chariot, trampling on the bodies of fallen enemies as he does so; another scene shows him standing on corpses while firing arrows at the invading Sea Peoples in their boats, aided by royal princes. Behind the king, a fan-bearer keeps him cool as he shoots, and another man holds the reins

## DIPLOMACY

Egypt enjoyed good trading relations with its neighbours, especially Mesopotamia, from Predynastic times, while in the Old Kingdom wood was imported from Lebanon and luxury goods were brought from the land of Punt (somewhere along the Red Sea coast). In the Middle Kingdom, fortresses were built in Nubia and along the eastern Delta (called the 'Walls of the Ruler') to control the flow of goods and immigrants, to the extent that under Senwosret III, Nubian traders could only enter Egypt under special circumstances. The growth of the Egyptian empire in the New Kingdom forced the pharaohs into increasing contact with the kings of equally powerful neighbouring states, and in this new political reality, foreigners could no longer be regarded as worthless symbols of chaos but had to be dealt with either through diplomacy or warfare.

It is no surprise then that envoys from as far away as Crete are shown in New Kingdom tomb scenes bringing gifts to the royal court, and that the pharaohs frequently married the daughters of foreign kings – often Hittite or Mitanni – cementing relations between their royal families. A formal treaty may have existed between the Egyptians and the Hittites from as early as the reigns of Thutmose III or Amenhotep II, while Ramesses II signed a major peace treaty with the Hittites in the 21st year of his reign, a copy of which was inscribed on the walls of Karnak Temple and the Ramesseum, while a further one was kept in Hatti (see p. 38). Treaties were not signed with vassal kings, instead these were forced to swear an oath of loyalty to the pharaoh.

The Amarna Letters – clay tablets from Tell el-Amarna, inscribed in cuneiform – are a major source of information for late 18th Dynasty diplomacy, recording correspondence between Egypt and its vassal kings in the Levant and also with the great kings of Near Eastern 'superpowers', such as Babylon and Mitanni. With this latter group, the topics discussed mainly include diplomatic marriages and the exchange of luxury goods, though mutual assistance pacts are also mentioned. Although an office existed at Amarna to manage correspondence (the 'Bureau for the Correspondence of Pharaoh'), this should not be regarded as a true foreign office, established to deal exclusively with international diplomacy. Foreign ambassadors were not permanently based in Egypt, though foreign messengers, despatched on specific business, often had to wait for years in Egypt to receive responses to their kings' requests.

The Amarna Letters, such as this example, are clay tablets inscribed with Akkadian cuneiform. They provide an insight into international diplomacy in the late 18th Dynasty.

of the royal horses; as this individual wears a helmet, it is likely he is Ramesses' chariot shield-bearer – someone never depicted when the king himself is riding in his chariot (see p. 127). In another episode in the reliefs, Ramesses III is seen dragging a chief on to his chariot. Scenes of Seti I at war are also innovative in content. One depicts him striding on the battlefield, trampling over fallen enemies as he moves and about to spear a chief with his javelin; another shows him carrying prisoners under each arm, taking them back to his chariot. He is also portrayed, armed with a bow and *khepesh*-sword, binding Asiatic prisoners who are described as 'the spoil which His Majesty brought back on his own two feet'.

In addition to scenes of kings engaged in the heat of battles on land and at sea, they are also represented besieging towns. On the walls of the temple at Beit el-Wali, Ramesses II is shown on a scale larger than a Syrian fortress, holding its chief by the hair as he emerges from the building's roof. Syrians on the rampart beneath him plead for peace, while one offers a brazier as a symbol of surrender. Below, a young prince hacks at the walls with his axe. In a depiction carved on the walls of Medinet Habu showing Ramesses III's siege at Tunip, also in Syria, Egyptian soldiers are shown scaling ladders, hacking down a doorway and cutting down trees. As at Beit el-Wali, a Syrian chief offers a brazier to the king in the hope of ending the violence.

## Did the Pharaohs Fight?

Given the bombast and exaggerated nature of royal battle reliefs and inscriptions, it is legitimate to ask what evidence there is that the pharaohs actually fought alongside their troops. All court-produced material concerning the king must be treated with caution: it presents him in a particular manner intended to aggrandize his achievements (see also p. 18). As defender of *maat* and Egypt, the king was the only individual who could kill anyone; in battle scenes, all arrows originate from his bow, and he often fights alone, riding at his enemy without his army. Both pictorial and textual sources are interconnected, in that they each reinforce the same motifs, emphasizing again and again the king's supreme abilities as warrior. The textual sources may use the scribal 'daybook' records as their basis, providing accurate dates and accounts of troop movements, but any action by the king is adapted to fit his perfect image. Consequently, it is impossible to use textual sources alone to answer the question of whether or not kings fought, they are simply too idealized at the key moments of combat. At best they can be regarded as neutral sources – the king may have fought as described, or he may not.

To challenge this idealization, however, it is possible to approach the question from other angles, examine other types of evidence and then try to make a judgment based on probability. Looking at the royal mummies, for instance, none show any sign of having been killed or wounded on the battlefield – except for Seqenenre Tao, and it is just as possible that he received his fatal blows in a ceremonial execution following the loss of a battle or that he was assassinated in the palace as that he received them fighting on the battlefield. It seems more than likely that Egypt's great liberator, Ahmose, was too frail to fight in actual combat, while the 'warrior pharaohs' Thutmose III, Amenhotep II and Ramesses II, who all glorified their campaigns in the Levant, betray no signs of cuts or broken bones – nothing to indicate a life spent fighting enemies on the front line. This fact, and the evident requirement to keep the king as safe as possible, as evidenced by his extensive personal bodyguard both inside and outside Egypt, suggests that Egyptian kings may not have been as daring as their official texts would have us believe. If they were on the battlefield, they were no doubt far from the action.

Our understanding of whether a king led a campaign in person is also complicated by a Ramesside literary tale known as *The Taking of Joppa*. Here, the royal sceptre of Thutmose III is said to stand in for the king, and is spoken of as if the king himself were actually there. Other portrayals describe the royal *bau* – the king's fiery manifest wrath at the loss of order – as leading the army to victory. This was a way for scribes to present the king as leading the army abroad when in fact he did not leave Egypt. Army commanders are never named in royal texts; however, in their own inscriptions these commanders do refer to their military roles, often stating that they led the army, and leaving it unclear as to whether the king himself was present or not during the campaigns they describe.

Given the ambiguous and idealized nature of all the different kinds of evidence, it is not possible to ascertain whether the kings fought or not, or even to be absolutely certain that they accompanied each of the campaigns they are said to have won.

## THE BATTLE OF KADESH

The battle of Kadesh was fought between the Egyptians, under the command of Ramesses II, and the Hittites and their allies, led by Muwatallis II. Depictions of the battle were carved on the walls of Luxor Temple, Karnak Temple, the Ramesseum, Abu Simbel and Ramesses' temple at Abydos, providing a particularly detailed visual representation of events. These can be combined with two surviving written accounts – known as the Bulletin and the Poem – to reconstruct the battle.

In his fifth year as king, Ramesses II and his army marched into the Levant, setting out from the fortress of Sile with the aim of taking the city of Kadesh, which had recently switched allegiance from the Egyptians to the Hittites. Ramesses' army was split into five separate divisions: those of Amun, Re, Ptah and Seth were to march overland, while a support force sailed along the Phoenician coast with the intention of joining the rest of the army at Kadesh. While on the march, the king and the division of Amun pressed on ahead of the other divisions, and at the town of Shabtuna they met two Shasu Bedouin; these had been allied with the Hittites, but now wanted to defect to the Egyptian side. To prove their allegiance, they informed Ramesses that the Hittite army was in Aleppo, 193 km (120 miles) away, too fearful to fight Pharaoh and leaving Kadesh an easy target.

Having released the Shasu, Ramesses continued on his journey and set up camp northwest of Kadesh, planning to besiege the town the next day. But, just as all seemed to be going well, the Egyptian scouts captured two Hittite spies and interrogated them, only to learn that the Hittites had deceived them and were in fact camped at the northeast of Kadesh, waiting for the Egyptians. In response, the king summoned and berated his officers, and sent his vizier to speed up the arrival of his other divisions. Before the vizier could reach them, however, the division of Re came under attack. The survivors fled to join the king and the division of Amun, but by the time they arrived the Egyptian camp had already been overrun by the Hittites and their chariotry.

2 The Hittites camp nearby, hidden from the Egyptians

4 The Hittites surprise the Re division before they can reach camp; the Ptah and Seth divisions are too far behind to be of assistance

7 Ramesses attacks the enemy, but finding himself alone prays to Amun

Lake Katina

Muwatallis

Ramesses

KADESH

Orontes

1 Ramesses sets up camp with the division of Amun

6 The Egyptian camp is overrun by the Hittites and their chariotry

8 The Hittites incur casualties

Lake Shabtuna

5 Survivors of the Re division flee to join the king and the division of Amun

**Reconstruction diagram of the battle of Kadesh, showing the different phases.**

The king took to his chariot and tried to rally his troops to fight back. Driving at a gallop, he charged the enemy forces. Finding himself alone, completely surrounded by Hittite chariots, the king prayed to Amun for help and reproached his soldiers for abandoning him: 'How faint are your hearts, O my charioteers, none among you is worthy of trust!' Nevertheless, the king had not been entirely deserted in his moment of need. His shield-bearer Menena was still with him, but in great fear the man begged the king to flee to safety. However, the king replied 'Stand firm, steady your heart, my shield-bearer! I will charge them as a falcon pounces, I will slaughter, butcher, fling to the ground; why do you fear these weaklings whose multitudes I disregard?'

Ramesses then rode into his enemy six times, fighting them off, until help finally came in the form of his support troops from the coast. The Hittites, now in danger of being surrounded, fell back, giving the Egyptians time to regroup and push them back further. The enemy fled, swimming across the Orontes river to safety. We are told that the prince of Aleppo became so wet during his escape that he was hung upside down to drain the water from his body.

The remains of the Egyptian divisions now regrouped and praised the king for his success, but Ramesses forcefully expressed his anger at their cowardice: 'Have I not done good to any of you, that you should leave me alone in the midst of battle? You are lucky to be alive at all … I crushed a million countries by myself on Victory-in-Thebes, and Mut-is-Content, my great horses; it was they who I found supporting me, when I alone fought many lands. They shall henceforth be fed in my presence, whenever I reside in my palace; it was they whom I found in the midst of battle, and charioteer Menena, my shield-bearer.'

Both the Hittites and Egyptians faced one another again the next morning, but the battle ended as a stalemate. The Egyptians then record that Muwatallis sent an envoy to their camp offering a diplomatic end to the fighting, to which Ramesses agreed. Many years later, the Hittites and Egyptians signed a major peace treaty, ending hostilities between them indefinitely, copies of which are preserved in both hieroglyphs and cuneiform.

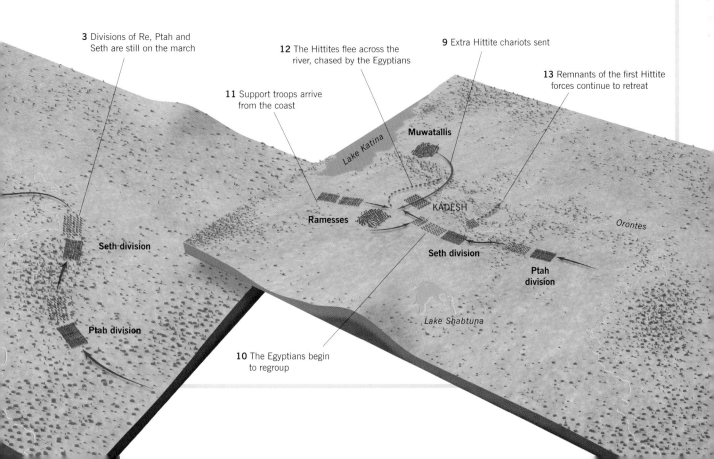

3 Divisions of Re, Ptah and Seth are still on the march

12 The Hittites flee across the river, chased by the Egyptians

9 Extra Hittite chariots sent

13 Remnants of the first Hittite forces continue to retreat

11 Support troops arrive from the coast

Muwatallis

Lake Katina

KADESH

Ramesses

Orontes

Seth division

Seth division

Ptah division

Ptah division

Lake Shabtuna

10 The Egyptians begin to regroup

## After the Battle

Following a battle, the booty was collected and redistributed by the king, and the defeated chiefs were made to pledge allegiance to the pharaoh. Soldiers cut hands or phalli from the dead to prove that they had made kills and so receive rewards for their efforts. These severed limbs and members were passed on to the royal herald and heaped into large piles to be counted by scribes; a scene dramatically illustrated at Medinet Habu. Any captives taken were branded with the royal cartouche on their arms and assigned to work gangs. They were then brought before the pharaoh in long processions, sometimes led by the crown prince and viziers. An even worse fate befell some. At Medinet Habu we are told that all the Libyan chiefs were burned, their hearts having been removed. Some captives even remark, 'We have begged for ourselves our own death of our own volition, our legs are carrying us off to the fire ourselves'. A text from the reign of Merenptah, inscribed at Amada, speaks of survivors having their hands cut off for their crimes and others having their ears and eyes removed. They were then taken to Kush where 'they were made into heaps in their settlements'.

After the royal review of captives, the long journey back to Egypt began. The army marched, 'driving donkeys before them, laden with uncircumcised phalli of the country of Libya (Libu), together with the hands of [every?] foreign country which had accompanied them, like fish by the basketful…'. At Karnak, Seti I is shown riding back to Egypt with captured Libyans on his chariot, a scene first found under Amenhotep II. Again, not all captives had such a (comparatively) easy time; the soldier Ahmose Son of Ibana relates how Thutmose I sailed back to Karnak with a Nubian, perhaps an enemy chief, hanging down head first at the prow of his ship. Amenhotep II treated his prisoners with equal disdain, returning to Egypt 'with the joy of his father [Amun], (after) he had killed the seven chiefs with his own club … who were placed upside down at the bow of the falcon ship of His Majesty … And so the six men from these enemies were hung in front of the rampart of Thebes and the hands likewise.' Another was taken to Nubia and hung from the rampart at Napata, to serve as a warning and reminder of the power of pharaoh.

Eventually, the army reached the border of Egypt, a scene depicted under Seti I at Karnak, which shows the king arriving at a canal populated by crocodiles; on the Egyptian side, the priests and officials greet the triumphant monarch. Soon after returning to Egypt a grand celebration was held in which certain soldiers who had distinguished themselves on the campaign

Golden flies, such as these belonging to Ahhotep found in her tomb at western Thebes, were awarded to soldiers for valour, like medals of honour after a campaign. Sometimes they could be strung together and worn as a necklace.

Detail of a scene from Medinet Habu: military scribes count the hands severed from fallen enemies to estimate the number slain. Severed limbs and phalli were taken back to Egypt and perhaps displayed before the god Amun at Karnak.

Seti I smites enemies before the god Amun at Karnak. It is possible that real prisoners were killed at the temple as a symbol of the triumph of order over chaos.

lined up before the king at his Window of Appearance and received golden flies – awarded like modern medals for valour and special achievements. Land and slaves were also bestowed on soldiers who had exhibited particular courage and ability. As the soldier Ahmose Son of Ibana records, after King Ahmose despoiled the city of Sharuhen: 'I brought spoil from it: two women and a hand. Then the gold of valour was given to me, and my captives were given to me as slaves.' Following his involvement in the defeat of the rebel Teti-an, he notes that he was given more slaves and land. The close proximity to the king, and so the opportunity to distinguish oneself in his eyes, meant that military service provided potential for a great deal of social mobility. Over the course of the New Kingdom, many men of reasonably low status received not only awards and land, but also positions of importance at court.

The king gave much of his spoils to the temples, with Amun in particular benefiting. The munificent gifts Thutmose III made following his campaigns are detailed on the walls of Karnak Temple, while Ramesside war reliefs show the king bringing long lines of captives before the Theban triad. In such scenes, the king typically stands holding a rope tied around the necks of his prisoners, each additionally shackled in a different excruciating position. The final act before Amun may have been the ritual execution of some of the prisoners, a symbol of the king's dominance over all foreign countries. At Karnak, Seti I is depicted in the Red Crown of Lower Egypt, standing before Amun, who offers him a *khepesh*-sword, and the goddess of Thebes. In front of him, numerous prisoners of various nationalities are tied to a stake, fearfully awaiting the king's mace to come crashing down on their heads. A similar scene at Beit el-Wali depicts Ramesses II smiting a Libyan, while Pharaoh's dog bites his helpless prisoner.

## CHAPTER 6

# ROYAL CITIES

The great cities of Egypt were renowned throughout the ancient world. These were major centres of trade and habitation, dwarfing the villages by their sheer size and spectacle. Focal points of government, with vast offices, treasuries and granaries, they also contained magnificent state-sponsored temples that served as homes to Egypt's national gods, and grand palaces for the pharaohs – sometimes several of differing function in the same city – which signalled the presence of royal power. Today, however, these once great cities are less well known. Thousands of years of construction have been focused on the same terrain, burying any remains deep below modern villages, towns and cities, and there is therefore a lack of archaeological data on Egypt's ancient settlements. In the Delta, the combination of damp conditions, the use of ancient mud-bricks as fertilizer and the frequent reuse of stone have led to the complete obliteration of most settlements. Our understanding of Egyptian cities is therefore reliant on a small number of excavated settlement remains and the accounts of classical authors.

## Temple, Palace and Cosmos

Because the king and his entourage travelled frequently between residences, and because various cities could be important for different reasons simultaneously, we cannot really speak in terms of a single 'capital' city – though Memphis in most periods came closest to the meaning of this word. Rather, there were royal cities – locations that served as a major residence for the king, with significant offices of government and a major temple dedicated to a state god. Both palace and temple served as the city's main architectural focus.

If the king decided to visit a city's major temple complex, he would be flanked by a heavy military escort and carried in his kiosk or carrying-chair along the narrow city streets between his residence and the temple. These streets would

The imposing pylon entrance of Luxor Temple, with a glimpse of the first court beyond.

normally be bustling with activity – noisy, crowded, dusty and hot – but during royal processions the atmosphere was no doubt more restrained, the local people gazing in awe at the spectacle unfolding before them, held back by a long line of soldiers. Catching tantalizing glimpses of the king's entourage between jostling shoulders, an onlooker might be rewarded with a splendid sight: on a long platform held aloft by 12 men, its carrying poles resting on their shoulders, stood a tall kiosk; within, the king sat on his throne flanked by carvings of strolling lions and protected by images of goddesses. Retainers in front and behind waved ostrich-plume fans set atop tall poles, ensuring a constant flow of cool air, while priests, walking ahead yet twisting their torsos backwards to face the royal presence, wafted incense towards the king, purifying the air and creating a pleasant smell in the less than aromatic city streets.

From his elevated vantage point, rocked gently from side to side by the rhythmic steps of his porters, the king watched city life – men and women visiting markets, conducting business and selling their wares, families walking along dusty streets, children playing. All around him were mud-brick houses, some several storeys high, which had grown organically; built by local people wherever there was space, they created an uneven miscellany of ad hoc architecture. Discarded pots lay smashed on the ground mixed with the scattered remains of meals –

When travelling, the king was carried in his chair by servants. The royal throne is normally depicted flanked by lions, as seen in the drawing on this ostracon.

A bustling market scene from the 5th Dynasty tomb of Niankhkhnum and Khnumhotep at Saqqara. Vendors sit beside their wares, including baskets full of vegetables, fish and figs. At the bottom right a long piece of cloth has been unrolled to entice a buyer, and in the top register manicurists, pedicurists and barbers are hard at work.

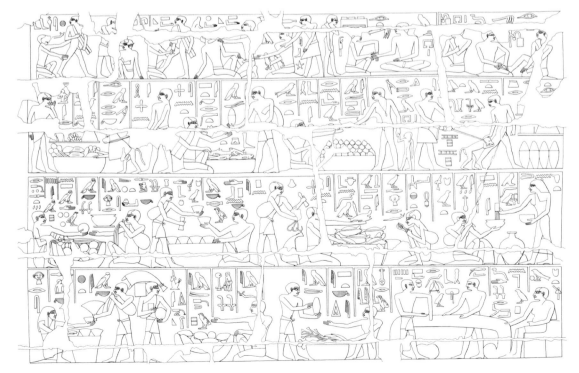

bones, decaying bread and rotting vegetables – picked at by scrawny feral dogs. It was an alien world to the pharaoh.

The king was the first to catch sight of the approaching temple in the distance. Built and rebuilt over the centuries on the same sacred ground, temples were often higher than the surrounding town but barred from view by an imposing trapezoidal mud-brick enclosure wall. On the king's impending arrival, the great wooden doors were swung open, and pilgrims and priests bowed their heads in adoration. The royal entourage passed through this outer gateway and continued towards two great stone towers, both lined with tall flagpoles flying pennants and brightly decorated with painted reliefs showing scenes of the king offering to the gods and smiting his enemies. These two towers, and the grand doorway between them that served as a connection to both sides, marked the monumental entrance to the temple proper; Egyptologists today refer to this structure by its Greek name – pylon. Here, the king would descend from his throne and enter the temple, leaving most of his entourage behind.

The Temple of Amun at Karnak. The king passed along the avenue of ram-headed sphinxes in the right foreground, through the pylon, or gateway, and continued along the temple's main axis to reach the god's sanctuary in the innermost part of the temple, a place that few were allowed to enter.

As the king progressed beyond the pylon gateway towards the rear of the temple he first walked through the open space of the courtyard, bathed in dazzling sunlight. He passed statues dedicated by Egypt's elite, each serving as a connection between the dedicatee and the gods and an eternal reminder of his piety. Then the king entered the gloom of the hypostyle hall, a forest of tall stone columns supporting a lofty roof. In this shadowy, enclosed space, ever-moving shafts of light cast from grilles high up near the ceiling threw spotlights on carved and painted reliefs: here the king offering before a god, there a hymn, carved in deep hieroglyphs and painted in vivid colours. Following the scent of slowly dissipating incense from the morning rites, the king finally reached the great wooden doors that separated him from the darkest and most exclusive part of the temple – the god's barque shrine and sanctuary, a place that only he and specific priests were allowed to enter. The rest of Egypt's population were forbidden from progressing beyond the temple's first courtyard – if even allowed that far. Within the sanctuary, amid its claustrophobic perpetual night, where the ceiling was low and the floor level raised, the king performed his rituals, ensuring the continued favour of the gods for Egypt and its people.

This set plan, consisting of pylon gateway, courtyard, hypostyle hall and sanctuary, was common to state temples from the New Kingdom onwards. Of these standard elements, the first three could be repeated several times, so that any given

Majestic columns within Karnak Temple's Great Hypostyle Hall, representing the first papyrus plants that emerged from the primeval swamp at the beginning of time. The hall was originally roofed, with the only light entering through high clerestory windows.

temple could have more than one courtyard or pylon. And just as each of the king's acts within the temple was imbued with meaning, every element of a temple's design also held a particular significance: for example, the divine sanctuary represented the primeval mound from which the world emerged at creation, while the hypostyle hall's tall columns were the primeval plants that grew at the beginning of time. The pylon was built in imitation of the hieroglyph for 'horizon', from which the sun rose each morning; after rising it was as if it travelled along the temple's axis and set beneath the divine sanctuary. The temple, through its design, emanated orderliness and mimicked the workings of the cosmos.

Leaving the temple, again carried in his palanquin or perhaps riding on his chariot, the pharaoh might travel to a nearby palace to prepare himself for his next duties. Depending on his needs, he might visit a small palace set within the temple grounds, constructed mainly for ceremonies, or another dedicated to the conducting of business, close to the city's administrative centre. Both forms of palace contained only limited royal suites, with bedrooms and dining rooms, among other essentials, designed in an abbreviated form for short-term use. If the king wished to retire for the evening, he might travel back to his main local residence, perhaps in an exclusively royal district, far from the central hub of the city.

In most cases, the king's palace complex was set within a monumental enclosure wall, embellished with niched towers, recesses and dummy doorways draped with matting. This distinctive appearance became a symbol of royal power from the beginning of Egyptian history (see p. 16); Egyptologists refer to it as 'palace façade' decoration. As the design for the frame surrounding the royal Horus name, 'palace façade' acted as a perch for the divine Horus falcon. It was also used for the exterior decoration of private tombs, false doors and sarcophagi during parts of the Old and Middle Kingdoms.

The great outer gateways of the palace were protected by guard-posts, and before the main gateway was an area known as the *arreyet*, overseen by the vizier. This

The standard plan of an Egyptian temple from the New Kingdom onwards. Darkness increased, the ceiling lowered and the floor level rose the closer one approached towards the god in his sanctuary, situated at the furthest point from the pylon and the daylight outside.

## THE LOST CITY OF ITJ-TAWY

The walled city of Amenemhat-Itj-Tawy ('Amenemhat-seizes-possession-of-the-Two-Lands'), or Itj-Tawy in its shortened form, was founded by King Amenemhat I and served as the major royal residence into the Second Intermediate Period. The city's association with the 12th Dynasty was so strong that the Turin Canon king list refers to this royal line as being 'of Itj-Tawy'.

The city has not been located archaeologically and so little can be said of its layout and principal buildings. It was, however, regarded as a centre for artisans and craftsmen, and Amenemhat I, in *The Teachings of Amenemhat*, possibly describes one of the city's royal palaces: 'I have raised for myself a palace adorned with gold, its portals of lapis lazuli, its walls of silver, its doors of copper with bolts of bronze'. As Amenemhat I's pyramid was built at Lisht, just north of the Faiyum, it is very probable that this 'lost city' lies beneath the fields on the west bank of the Nile nearby.

One of the last references to Itj-Tawy is inscribed on the Victory Stele of Piye, from the Third Intermediate Period, in which it is mentioned among the cities that surrendered to Piye during his march northwards to face the Delta kinglets: 'Then His Majesty sailed north to Itj-Tawy, and he found the stronghold closed and the walls filled with valiant troops of Lower Egypt. Then they opened the fortifications and they threw themselves on their bellies …. His Majesty then proceeded to have a great offering presented to the gods who are in this city, consisting of long-horned cattle, short-horned cattle, fowl, and everything good and pure. Then its treasury was assigned to the treasury and its granaries to the endowment of his father Amun-[Re, Lord of the Thrones of the Two Lands.]'

functioned as a waiting area, where those without permission to enter the palace relayed information to the authorities within and awaited a response. It was also a place where people heard official judgments that had been decided on by those within the palace, and where commodities were received and officials were punished. Once within the palace enclosure, the visitor was met with numerous storage buildings and offices (perhaps including one for the vizier), as well as a treasury, all spread over a large area. Overall, this was the part of the palace dedicated to royal business and palace operations, which was called the *per-nesu*, 'King's House'. Encompassed by the *per-nesu*, or perhaps next to it, but still within the great outer enclosure wall, the residential part of the complex was known as the *per-aa*, 'Great House'. This was entered through a great double gateway, which was lined with flagstaffs in the manner of temples and perhaps decorated with images of defeated foreigners, forming a magical barrier to the chaos beyond its perimeter.

Unlike temples, many of the palace's interior chambers were decorated with scenes of nature, but there were other structural similarities between the two institutions. Typically, palaces were rectangular, their ceilings were sometimes painted to represent the sky, and their floor levels rose gradually towards the rear of the building, where, in place of the divine sanctuary, there was a throne dais (see p. 81), representing the primeval mound on which the creator god initiated creation – the royal throne on the dais took the place of the god's shrine. A columned hall was a central feature, located just before the exclusive private suite at the rear of the building, into which access was severely limited. Such parallels allowed government business conducted within the palace to be elevated to divine status; both temple and palace worked together to maintain cosmic order.

## Memphis

The earliest of Egypt's great royal cities was Memphis, described in a Ramesside love poem as 'a chalice of fruits, set before (Ptah) of the pleasant face'. It was founded, according to tradition by Egypt's great unifier, King Menes, at the point where the Nile Valley opens out to the Delta, and thus architecturally united the north and south as a physical symbol of Menes' momentous achievement. In this way, the city acted as 'the Balance of the Two Lands', as it was later known. According to Herodotus, Menes built the city on land reclaimed when he diverted the Nile and built dykes to stop it from flooding. By the Roman Period these dykes were named after the various sectors of the city that lay nearby. In the three thousand years that separated Menes from the Romans, Memphis grew into a major centre of commerce, royal display, religion, military strength and learning.

Memphis was originally known as White Walls (*Ineb Hedj*), perhaps a reference to the monumental whitewashed fortified walls that surrounded the city or the royal palace. Over the following centuries, as the city grew it merged with other towns in the vicinity, one of which was Pepi I's pyramid town Men-Nefer, which later became Hellenized as Memphis. And because of the gradual eastward movement of the Nile, if the city wished to retain its river links it too had to expand east in pursuit.

In the time of King Piye, during the Third Intermediate Period, the city was still surrounded by a massive fortified wall, and could be sealed off from the outside world in case of attack. Piye's Victory Stele relates, 'His Majesty saw that it was strong, the walls were high with new construction, and the battlements manned in strength. No way of attacking it was found.' This was undoubtedly a different city wall from the early Old Kingdom one – the city had grown and shifted, in part as a result of the changing course of the Nile – but it shows that great settlements like Memphis were heavily protected and fortified.

'The like of Memphis has never been seen ... her granaries are full of barley and emmer, her lakes are full of lotus-buds ... and with lotus-blossoms; oil is sweet and fat abundant ... The Asiatics of Memphis sit at ease, confident ... lotus-buds about their necks ... The noble ladies of Memphis sit at leisure, hands bowed down with (festive) foliage and greenery.'

Papyrus Sallier IV, Ramesside Period

Pre-New Kingdom Memphis cannot be reconstructed, and even its New Kingdom appearance is not well known, though the limited information available can be supplemented by the writings of classical authors. The city's major focal point was the Temple of Ptah, built in the New Kingdom on virgin land east of the old centre of 'White Walls'. Herodotus describes visiting this temple and writes of its various entrances and the great colossi erected there. In the late 1st century BC, Strabo commented on the stall that housed the sacred Apis bull, located in the temple area, and told how this divine incarnation of the god Ptah was released once a day to be seen by tourists. The bull's mother, also worshipped, was kept in a stall nearby. Interestingly, given the sacred nature of these animals, bull fights were held in front of the temple.

According to one reconstruction of New Kingdom Memphis, suggested by the Egyptologist Kenneth Kitchen, to the east of the Ptah Temple lay the 'Fine District of Pharaoh', an area of palaces and vast royal estates. On the basis of the location of the excavated palace of Merenptah east of the Ptah Temple, Kitchen has suggested that a string of New Kingdom palaces existed on the river bank here, stretching from north to south. The palace of Thutmose I, referred to in various sources, probably stood at the northern end, northeast of the Temple of Ptah, with Merenptah's palace at the southern end and others in between. However, as only Merenptah's palace has been found archaeologically, it is possible that this area was instead occupied by offices, magazines and houses – essential features of the city that needed to be close to the river. Another Egyptologist, David O'Connor, for example, has suggested that Thutmose I's palace lay immediately north of the Ptah Temple, where the palace of Apries was later built, rather than in the location suggested by Kitchen.

South of the Ptah Temple was the South District, which included a series of 'wards', perhaps as many as 12, each overseen by a district officer. Ramesside papyri detailing timber accounts provide the names of houses in this sector, as well as street names and chapels. In addition to the royal estates of Horemheb, Ramesses I and Seti I (among others), there were over 70 elite villas, with properties belonging to a vizier, a chief lector priest and administrator, a steward of property, a deputy of pharaoh's granary, and military men. Lower-ranking bureaucrats also lived in this area,

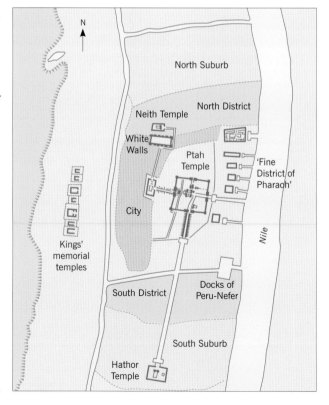

Imaginative reconstruction of New Kingdom Memphis, with the temple precinct of Ptah at the centre and the 'Fine District of Pharaoh' to its right.

including men connected to royal establishments such as standard-bearers and stable masters, as well as merchants and a chief builder. These houses may have been state-owned and came with the job.

The 'docks of Peru-Nefer' may have been situated on the river close to another suburb with housing for the nobility. The city's Nile waterfront was lined with storehouses and docks, which handled goods from all over the known world. In Ptolemaic times a toll-house on the river controlled the port. East of the Ptah Temple, again in Ptolemaic times, there was a market, as well as housing and a hippodrome.

Memphis also had a North District and a North Suburb, but little can be said about them in the New Kingdom. In the Late Period, King Apries built a palace in the north, on a large mud-brick platform which raised it above the surrounding city; the Ptolemaic palace was probably nearby, perhaps a little further to the east. In Strabo's day, these palaces were already nothing more than ruins. From at least as early as the Persian occupation, this northern part of Memphis acted as an administrative centre, while further north again was an area of gardens. In addition to the Ptah Temple, there were smaller cult centres across the city, such as that of Hathor-of-the-Southern-Sycamore, south of the Ptah Temple, and a Temple of Neith-North-of-the-Wall. In the New Kingdom a series of royal mortuary temples also existed on the edge of the cultivable land and desert, in an area called Ankh-Tawy – 'The Life of the Two Lands'.

There is practically no information on the bazaars, streets and squares of New Kingdom Memphis. It is clear, though, that most houses occupied by average Egyptians were of more than one storey and had flat roofs, and that richer Egyptians enjoyed life within their own personal compounds, complete with refreshing pools of water and private gardens. Across the city, there was a tendency for both trades and also foreign populations to cluster together, each housed within separate walled enclosures – their thick dividing walls of mud-brick pierced with gates – of which eight have so far been physically located. Generally, the different trade quarters had their own specialized markets. The streets within were on a grid pattern and were very unsanitary, as refuse and waste from the houses were simply thrown into the public space.

## Thebes – Luxor

Although disparate villages existed at Thebes from the Early Dynastic Period, it was only with the success of the 11th Dynasty, who originated in the area, that the city rose to prominence. Amun, the local god, also reaped the benefits of their dynastic success, as it is to the Middle Kingdom that the earliest phase of the great Temple of Amun at Karnak dates. Excavations have revealed that Thebes' east bank settlement was built on a grid system during the Middle Kingdom, indicative of state planning, and covered an area of roughly 1000 by 500 m (3280 × 1640 ft). But this Middle Kingdom incarnation of the town was completely razed when the New Kingdom pharaohs decided to build their grandiose temple to Amun on the site of the old settlement.

During the New Kingdom the Temple of Amun expanded significantly and the surrounding population moved accordingly, living around its perimeter on lower ground. Within the divine space encompassed by the temple's enclosure wall a number of royal palaces were constructed, most probably used for ceremonial purposes and as rest-houses for kings when performing rituals at the temple.

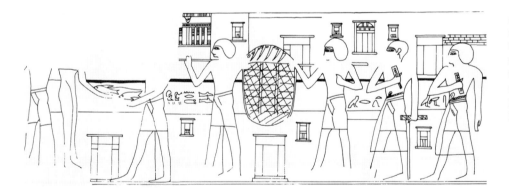

A rare depiction of a row of houses at Thebes, from the tomb of Wensu (above), and a painting from the tomb of Minnakht (below), showing a Theban villa in plan form, surrounded by its garden.

Undoubtedly, further palaces existed on the east bank near the temple, as kings required sumptuous residences to live in and conduct business, as well as simple rest-houses. There must also have been offices, magazines, bakeries and workshops, around which Thebes' estimated population of roughly 90,000 people (under Amenhotep III) lived their lives and built their homes wherever they could find space. As a scene from the Theban tomb of Wensu (now lost) shows, houses were built in tightly fitting rows on either side of the city's roads, all abutting one another and of different heights. This world has today disappeared beneath the modern city of Luxor, but the ancient state's grand design for the 'holy city' can still be seen in the great processional route, lined with sphinxes, that connected Karnak and Luxor temples, and which played a key role in the annual Opet Festival of royal renewal (see p. 95).

A reconstruction of the Theban east bank, with the processional route that connects Luxor Temple (in the foreground) to Karnak Temple (in the distance). Housing built up in the available space between and surrounding the two temple precincts on the riverside.

‘Stronger is Thebes than any other city, she has given the land one master by her victories. She who took the bow and grasped the arrow, none can fight near her, through the greatness of her power.’

Papyrus Leiden I, Ramesside Period

The west bank of the Nile occupied an equally important place in this grand processional scheme. The area closest to the Nile was predominantly used for its agricultural land, but further away, on the edge of the desert to the west, the 11th Dynasty kings built their tombs, later followed by those of the 17th Dynasty. Shortly afterwards, Egypt's New Kingdom pharaohs built their large mortuary temples – places where priests served their royal cults and honoured Amun – on the great plain below the Theban hills, where their actual tombs were hidden in the Valley of the Kings. During the Beautiful Festival of the Valley the divine Theban triad – Amun, Mut and Khonsu – left Karnak Temple on the east bank and visited these royal temples on the opposite side as part of a great processional circuit. Each mortuary temple had an associated palace attached to its first court; these no doubt served a symbolic purpose, acting as ritual rest-houses for the royal *ka*-spirit. It was on the west bank too, that Amenhotep III built his palace complex, today known as Malkata, and, beside it, the great Birket Habu – a monumental artificial lake. Little is known about the west bank's rural population, but Papyrus 10068 in the British Museum describes housing for about 1000 people between the mortuary temples of Seti I and Ramesses II in the 20th Dynasty, many being priests or administrators.

Amenhotep III, father of Akhenaten, wearing the Blue Crown.

BELOW **Aerial view of Tell el-Amarna, ancient Akhetaten. The Royal Road cuts horizontally through part of the city's Central Quarter, separating the Great Palace on its far side from the King's House (right) and the Mansion of the Aten (left). The Great Palace and King's House were connected by a bridge spanning the road.**

## Akhetaten – Tell el-Amarna

The royal city for which we have most evidence is Akhetaten ('Horizon of the Aten'), modern Tell el-Amarna in Middle Egypt. As it was only occupied for a short span of time, it provides us with a snapshot of city life towards the end of the 18th Dynasty. It was founded by Akhenaten to be a completely new royal residence city

and cult centre for the god Aten; as a virgin site, unconnected to any previous god, it was perfect for his needs. The king's first step was to delineate the city's perimeter, which he marked with a series of boundary stelae. The area thus defined, 16 by 13 km (10 × 8 miles) in size, comprises a vast expanse of farmland on the Nile's west bank, with space set aside for the city proper on the east.

The city was constructed quickly and with the minimum of planning. It was divided into three main quarters – the North Suburb, Central Quarter and South Suburb – all connected by the 'Royal Road' leading from north to south. At the far north was the North Riverside Palace. This was Akhenaten's main residence, surrounded by a large fortified wall. Numerous supply and administrative buildings were built next to it, including a granary, and so it appears that the palace had a food supply independent of the rest of the city. A short distance away were villas for courtiers. Along the royal road to the south was another royal palace, called the North Palace; this was for the eldest princess, Meritaten, and her household, and perhaps served as her main residence; as such it can be classed as a harem palace. Further south was the North Suburb, where officials lived.

The Central Quarter was the principal administrative and religious hub of the city. Consequently, it received the most planning. Along the riverfront was Akhenaten's Great Palace, comprising several large courts and colossal royal statues; it may have provided a grand setting for receptions and ceremonies. The Great Palace was connected to the nearby King's House by a bridge spanning the Royal Road. The King's House consisted of a small palace, a courtyard and a large set of storerooms and magazines; it may have been more than one storey high, and incorporated a number of robing rooms. Here Akhenaten held meetings with his courtiers,

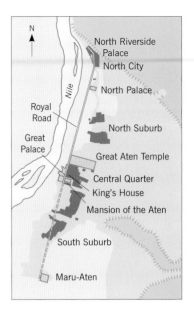

Simplified plan of Akhetaten, showing the major features.

A model of the North Palace at Amarna. This probably served as Princess Meritaten's main residence.

but also appeared at its Window of Appearance to distribute rewards and rations to crowds gathered in the courtyard below. Such interactions emphasized and symbolized the population's dependence on the royal family. The King's House was thus mainly administrative in function – a form of 'office' for the pharaoh, set among other governmental buildings. This was Akhetaten's business district, where the Bureau for the Correspondence of Pharaoh and the House of Life (an archive and centre of scribal learning) were located. There were also long storage magazines, only accessible through their attached offices, and barracks for the military and police, as well as many other support buildings, perhaps even complete with their own housing for the official in charge.

Two temples to the Aten (the solar disc and focus of cult during the reign of Akhenaten) were constructed in the Central Quarter – the Great Temple to the Aten and the Mansion of the Aten. The latter was close to the King's House and included a robing room and Window of Appearance. To the south was another temple, called the Maru-Aten; this was a royal retreat among greenery and pools. Most of the government's highest officials who worked in the Central Quarter lived in large, single-storey villas in the South Suburb, far from the king's residence in the north. These villas were set within compounds, complete with their own gardens, pools, granaries and wells; some even had shrines dedicated to the king and royal family. One such compound belonged to the sculptor Thutmose, and was where the famous bust of Nefertiti, now in Berlin, was found. Most of Amarna's population, however, lived in smaller housing, erected wherever space was available, but often following a remarkably similar overall plan to the larger villas.

At Amarna, the royal family led a life segregated from the rest of the population, spending most of their time hidden behind the monumental walls of the North

Kings often rewarded courtiers from their Window of Appearance during grand ceremonies. Here, Akhenaten, Nefertiti and three of their daughters can be seen handing out collars, cups, gloves, rings and armlets to the courtier (and future king) Ay and his wife Tiye, while high officials look on in adoration and servants dance in celebration.

Riverside Palace. On occasion though, they rode in their chariots along the Royal Road to the Central Quarter, performed various rituals and ceremonies, saw to business, and then returned to their seclusion. Depicted within the Amarna tombs of the nobles, these great events replaced the magnificent processions of the gods that had become popular during the earlier 18th Dynasty, especially at Thebes.

Akhenaten also intended that Akhetaten would be the burial site for himself and his courtiers. Rock-cut tombs were dug into the hills at the northern and southeastern sides of the city, while Akhenaten's family tomb was dug into a wadi, east of the central city (see also p. 177). The artisans who excavated and decorated these tombs lived in their own village east of the South Suburb.

Akhetaten did not survive much longer than its founder. Akhenaten's son, Tutankhamun, may have spent his early childhood there, but after only a few years as king he and the court moved back to Memphis, and it is from there, in the old palace of Thutmose I, that we find him issuing decrees to reinstate the old ways. Now despised, any trace of Akhenaten's heresy was actively pursued and eradicated and his grand city was systematically deconstructed brick by brick until only the foundations remained, left to be covered by the ever-shifting sands before being revealed again by archaeologists centuries later.

## Pi-Ramesses – Qantir

Founded in the 19th Dynasty, Pi-Ramesses was built on the site of the ancestral town of the Ramesside dynasty in the northeast Delta, close to the Hyksos centre of Avaris (Tell el-Daba). Seti I constructed a palace and a military barracks, but it was only under Ramesses II that it was significantly developed. Recent geophysical work has suggested that the main city was built on an oval island in the Nile and

"His Majesty has built himself a Residence whose name is "Great-of-Victories". It lies between Syria and Egypt, full of food and provisions. It follows the model of Upper Egyptian Thebes, its duration like that of Memphis. The Sun arises in its horizon, and even sets within it."

Papyrus Anastasi II, Ramesside Period.

that a large temple was situated just across the river at its northern edge, surrounded by an enclosure wall. As in other royal cities, state-organized and industrial areas were built on a grid pattern, while most housing grew up around them organically. The survey has also revealed a district of large villas in the West City, perhaps for housing the elite, and an area of smaller housing in the East City. A further temple also existed in the East City, surrounded by rows of mud-brick storage magazines.

As a new royal city, Pi-Ramesses became a popular place to live, as one ancient scribe wrote: 'Everyone has forsaken his own town and settled in its neighbourhood'. Virtually nothing of its architectural glories can be seen today, however, though there are references to them in the ancient texts. Scribes present Pi-Ramesses as dazzling with lapis lazuli and a place of great balconies, as home to temples dedicated to Seth, Ptah, Re and Amun, and as a place where the military mustered and from where the navy sailed north to the Mediterranean or south to Memphis. The city's military focus is evident from recent excavations. In the southern part of the city, remains were found of a chariot garrison from the time of Seti I and Ramesses II, including a wide, pillared exercise court and extensive stables for horses. Objects associated with chariotry were also discovered, including daggers and arrowheads, and, more unusually, moulds for producing Hittite-style shields.

The city was also a centre of production and trade, as shown by the discovery of workshops for both glass and bronze manufacture, and the presence of Mycenaean, Cypriote and Levantine pottery. In addition to foreign traders, who by necessity came and went, there was a strong permanent foreign presence at Pi-Ramesses, giving the city a cosmopolitan flavour. Not only were there foreign sanctuaries, such as one dedicated to Astarte, but foreign dignitaries owned residences within the city, including a chief of Sidon.

Pi-Ramesses' glories were short-lived, however. Towards the end of the New Kingdom, the great Nile tributaries that fed and supplied the city began to dry up, leaving the court and elite no choice but to abandon the settlement. Much of the stonework was moved to nearby Tanis, which became the new major royal centre in the Nile Delta (see p. 156).

Excavations of the stables at Pi-Ramesses (below left), uncovered arrowheads, lance tips and short-swords, the weapons of charioteers (below right).

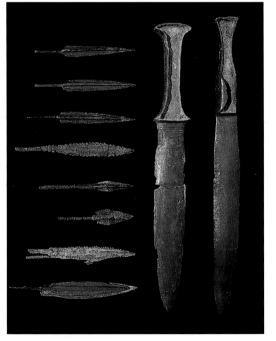

## The King on the Move

The pharaohs travelled around Egypt regularly, sailing up and down the Nile between cities and towns for various purposes, such as attending festivals and seeing to local affairs. In preparation for these journeys, it was the vizier's duty to assemble the army contingent that escorted the king and to give instructions to the captain of the royal boat and other army staff before their departure. Further courtiers were also involved in organizing the king's journey. The royal herald Intef describes travelling ahead of the king in order to set up his living quarters in the field; according to him, a temporary palace might be 'embellished more than the palace of Egypt – purified, cleansed, secret, sacred of their temples'. A golden cubit rod found in the tomb of the architect Kha details another royal camp: 'His Majesty came, his heart being joyful, from the house of his noble father Amun with his army before him like locusts. His Majesty moored at Hermopolis and in two days built his residence (called) Fortress of Aakheperure, of one *schoenus* in length and one *schoenus* in width.' This was an enormous size, and should best be understood as the overall ground covered by the encampment. As well as such temporary accommodation, the king owned 'mooring places of Pharaoh' around the country. These were small but permanent lodgings for the king and his entourage as they travelled, probably similar to the small palaces attached to New Kingdom mortuary temples, or the King's House at Amarna. He might also stay in the various harem palaces (see p. 92).

The king's arrival at a city was a major event, requiring much preparation. 'Get on with having everything ready for Pharaoh's arrival', one official commanded an underling, and proceeded to list a huge range of required items, in large quantities, including bouquets of flowers, loaves of various kinds, cakes, dried meat, milk,

The sons of Ramesses III carry their father, seated on his throne, during the festival of Min, in a scene from Medinet Habu. The king's throne is flanked by lions and rests within an elaborate kiosk, itself flanked by further lions and surmounted by uraei.

## ROYAL CITIES AFTER THE NEW KINGDOM

### TANIS – SAN EL-HAGAR

Only a few poor burials attest to activity at Tanis during the Late Ramesside Period, but, with the start of the Third Intermediate Period, this small trading port was transformed into a major royal city, constructed from stonework dragged from Pi-Ramesses (p. 153). Amid tensions between the north and Thebes, the pharaohs, from Psusennes I on, built their own temple complex here dedicated to Amun. This became a copy of the god's complex at Karnak, complete with its own temples to Mut and Khonsu. The kings were buried within stone-lined subterranean chambers constructed inside the temple precinct, beginning a new royal trend that would last until the end of the Late Period. Their tombs were discovered by Pierre Montet in 1939, still containing much of their burial equipment, including the gold mask of Psusennes I. This king was buried in a sarcophagus belonging to the 19th Dynasty pharaoh Merenptah, re-carved for his use. With the exception of

work conducted under the 26th and 30th Dynasties, little major construction was carried out at Tanis after the 22nd Dynasty. The city saw a brief resurgence under the Ptolemies, but then declined under Roman rule. Nothing is known of Tanis' administrative or housing quarters – they still lie beneath the two great archaeological mounds that dominate the site, awaiting excavation.

### BUBASTIS – TELL BASTA

Located in the eastern Delta, beside the now extinct Tanitic branch of the Nile, Bubastis was occupied from the Early Dynastic Period but only became prominent under the 22nd Dynasty. The city was the cult centre of the cat- or lion-headed goddess Bastet. Her temple, which stood at the centre of the city, is described by Herodotus as being more attractive than any other in Egypt and as almost entirely encircled by two canals, something confirmed by the discovery of an ancient canal during recent fieldwork. Each year, a great festival

held in honour of Bastet was attended by hundreds of thousands of pilgrims, who, according to Herodotus, drank a year's worth of wine over the course of the event. Pilgrims also honoured Bastet by dedicating cat mummies to her, all of which were interred in a vast cemetery to the northwest of the site. Close to this cemetery an industrial area produced faience and bronze votive objects for pilgrims. Herodotus also describes a stone-paved road, lined with trees, leading eastwards from the temple to a marketplace. Although this area has not been explored archaeologically, it was probably the city's main area of habitation. Further settlement zones of the Late Period and Graeco-Roman Period also existed south of the temple.

### SAIS – SA EL-HAGAR

The ruins of Sais are located in the western Delta, on the eastern bank of the Rosetta branch of the Nile. As a family of rulers from Sais, the 26th Dynasty instigated the main period of construction at the city, building directly on top of the earlier, smaller settlement. Further work was undertaken during the 30th Dynasty and under the Ptolemies, and as a result of their patronage Sais became a centre of great palaces, temples and administrative buildings, though these have not survived the passage of time. Still, it is probable that, like Memphis, the city was divided into zones, including a temple area, housing and an administrative quarter. Herodotus mentions a 'great and splendid palace of Apries' and a temple dedicated

to the goddess Neith, where the tombs of the 26th Dynasty kings were located. There were also temples to Atum, Re and Osiris Hemag, a form of the god depicted wrapped in bandages decorated with semi-precious stones – probably carnelian. The 'Festival of the Lamps', the passion play of Osiris and a festival of Neith were all major events in the city.

Based on the textual and archaeological evidence, two possible reconstructions of ancient Sais have been proposed. In one, the site's great Northern Enclosure may have contained the Temple of Neith, along with the tombs of the kings in its courtyard (as at Tanis). The temple to Osiris Hemag may have been to the north of the Neith temple, beside a sacred lake, while to its east, on a casemate foundation, was the royal palace. Outside the Northern Enclosure, and to its northeast, was a cemetery. The city suburbs and industrial area may have been to the south, in an area now known as the 'Great Pit'. It is probable that further temples existed there too and perhaps a large mausoleum. A second interpretation is that the Temple of Neith existed on the site of the 'Great Pit', and that the temple to Osiris Hemag lay south of it. A processional way led north from the temple, flanked by the royal tombs, to the Northern Enclosure, where a second temple to Neith had been built beside a 'tomb' for Osiris; the royal palace was perhaps located next to this temple. In this reconstruction, the main town of Sais developed around the southern temple's enclosure, and included centres of faience and pottery production.

cream, carob beans, grapes, pomegranates and figs. When staying in a particular nome, the king lived at the expense of his nomarchs, and they might have to commandeer extra supplies from local institutions. This practice of requisitioning supplies from local mayors was banned under Horemheb at the end of the 18th Dynasty – it seems the needs of the court may have become excessive over time.

The 'royal progress' – a circuit of the country by the royal court – was a standard element of kingship from the earliest days of the unified state. The Palermo Stone, dated to the 5th Dynasty, refers to the 'Following of Horus', a biennial circuit of the country. The aim may have been a census for taxation purposes, but it also emphasized the king's dominance to local rulers, ensuring that they remained in check. It is possible that the king also took part in legal hearings at such times. Travels by later kings are also documented: records from the time of Seti I describe the king as being in the palace of Thutmose I at Memphis on one day, then in the eastern Delta region, and then in Luxor for the Opet Festival; Ramesses II attended the Opet Festival shortly after his coronation, and then stopped at Abydos to inspect the work on his father's mortuary temple (see below) and inform a local priest of his appointment to the cult of Amun at Karnak, before continuing north; while on his way from Thebes to Nubia, Thutmose IV stopped at Edfu to attend a festival; and records from Lahun make reference to a royal progress to the Lake of Sobek, perhaps to perform a ceremony.

Although the king's movements are mentioned infrequently in the Late Middle Kingdom Papyrus Boulaq 18, we do learn that he (it is uncertain which one) was present at the palace during a visit of the *medjay* (a people of Nubia), and spent periods of time at Medamud. More distant places could be visited too. Seti I claims to have visited the gold mines east of Edfu, and Ramesses IV personally made a preliminary survey at Wadi Hammamat in his third year in preparation for an expedition. An Old Kingdom inscription at the First Cataract in Nubia records two visits by King Merenre to the area, and provides specific dates, while the Palermo Stone refers to the visit of a king to Elephantine.

In the Old Kingdom kings made visits to review progress on the construction of their pyramid, as recorded in tombs of officials of the period. At such times the king was carried on his palanquin attended by fan-bearers and under military escort. 'With regard to this tomb of mine', the courtier Debehen states, 'it was the King of Upper and Lower Egypt Menkaure [may he live forever] who gave me its place, while he happened to be on the way to the pyramid plateau to inspect the work being done on the pyramid of Menkaure'. The king later went to inspect the construction of Debehen's tomb. The vizier Washptah is said to have collapsed during a royal inspection of King Neferirkare's pyramid at Abu Sir (see also p. 90). Pharaohs also inspected

The inscriptions on the 5th Dynasty Palermo Stone refer to a biennial 'Following of Horus', in which the king and court travelled around the country, perhaps to collect taxes.

construction work at temples: the Karnak Flood Stele of Sobekhotep VIII, a Second Intermediate Period king, refers to a royal progress to the broad court of the Temple of Amun to witness damage caused by a flood; while the 13th Dynasty priest Amenyseneb records King Khendjer's inspection of restoration work at the 'Temple of Abydos'. Kings frequently say that they found temples fallen into a state of ruin, a situation they rectify by ordering restorations – thereby re-establishing *maat* after chaos. Such references tend to be brief and conventional, but Ramesses II is particularly detailed concerning the sorry state of affairs he discovered during his visit to Abydos: 'he found the buildings in the cemetery belonging of former kings, their tombs in Abydos, falling gradually into ruins, and part(s) still under construction … walls lying (unfinished), one brick not even touching the next … Indeed, the Temple of Menmaare (Seti I, Ramesses' father) had its front and rear still under construction when he went to heaven. Its monuments were unfinished, its pillars not set up on the terracing, its statue lay on the ground.' Ramesses commanded that these temples be repaired.

## The Pharaoh and his People

The pharaohs were not like Roman emperors – they did not build lavish theatres, baths and venues for sporting events to appease the population. Their relationship with their subjects was quite different. The king's main duty was to please the gods and ensure order, objectives he achieved by making offerings, building temples and securing Egypt's borders. As long as the country was stable and prosperous, the king was performing his function and the people had no cause to complain.

Nevertheless, in the Old Kingdom the state played little role in supporting temples, and it was left to local people to construct and maintain them. The king's main concern at this time was his own funerary complex of tomb and temples, and it is there that state building power was focused. The religious cults within these temples operated as a mirror of palace life, with servants – the priests – washing and dressing the king in the form of statues and providing his meals. From the Middle Kingdom, kings did make gifts of stone elements and other donations to the temples, but the main focus was still on the king's own needs. It is only in the New Kingdom that temples became fully state run and the priesthood professional. From this time onwards, the king played a major role as builder of temples and donor to all the gods; images showing him before the gods become ubiquitous on temple walls.

In the New Kingdom, then, temples were the main way in which the king made an impact on a community's landscape; they were monumental, visible symbols that he was fulfilling his responsibilities. When standing before a temple's pylon entrance, local people gazed up at colossal statues, tall obelisks and imposing,

garishly painted scenes of the king smiting enemies before the gods. They must surely have felt awe at such an epic spectacle, but simultaneously been reassured that in the ongoing cosmic war against chaos, the king was on their side, fighting on their behalf. Such striking emanations of royal power were not strictly state propaganda, however. The king had no need to convince the general public of his worthiness to rule – good king or bad king, he was as much a part of the world as the soil or sky, and news of his personal aptitude as ruler would hardly have filtered down to Egypt's villages. Rather, these were works for eternity, intended both to please the gods and to aggrandize the king's acts in the eyes of those to come. As Senwosret I remarks: 'A king who is evoked by his works is not doomed'. Although the public was excluded from the interiors of temples, their construction was a necessary act for the population's continued well being, and was no doubt recognized as such.

Paradoxically, given the importance of temple building, the state paid little attention to their maintenance. Many pyramid complexes were already dilapidated by the end of the Old Kingdom – priests at Neferirkare's pyramid complex at Abu Sir had to perform their own repairs when wooden columns and the roofing began to collapse. The valley temple of Menkaure was hurriedly finished in brick after the king's death, only to be engulfed by his expanding pyramid town. As previously mentioned (see above), kings are frequently said to find temples 'in a ruinous condition' and command repairs; state-funded restoration efforts at temples across Egypt must have been sporadic at best.

By building magnificent temples and erecting colossal statues – here at Luxor Temple – the pharaohs changed Egypt's landscape and left eternal symbols of their pious acts for the gods.

From the Old Kingdom, Egypt's population was subjected to a great deal of interference from the state. For taxation purposes, information was stored in state archives on land use, canals, trees, lakes and wells; while from the Middle Kingdom there were household census lists and records of household possessions too. People could be required to perform military service or other governmental labour, and if they fled to avoid it they were sent to state farms and labour camps to toil away their lives. Taxation supported society's 'non-producers', including bureaucrats, soldiers and police, and enabled the pharaohs to perform their divinely ordained functions and fund their great works; by paying his tax, the average Egyptian was contributing to the pharaoh's cosmic duties. In return, state granaries ensured a surplus for times of bad harvest, with everyone receiving a form of 'minimum wage' in rations. To guarantee the best crop yield possible, irrigation was promoted by the state from the beginning of Egyptian history. King Scorpion of Dynasty 0 is perhaps depicted cutting an irrigation canal on his macehead from Hierakonpolis (see p. 17), while Senwosret II began a project of irrigation in the Faiyum. Shipping routes were also a concern of the state: a canal was dug at the First Cataract during the Old Kingdom and was repaired in both the Middle and New Kingdoms to allow ships to pass through. Those working for the government sometimes received housing, either in villas in city suburbs for those of a higher rank, or in small houses in purpose-built settlements, as was the case at Deir el-Medina for the artisans working on the royal tombs in the Valley of the Kings, who also received rations and slaves.

Although it was not the pharaoh's duty to provide entertainment for the masses, it could be a by-product of his acts. Major religious festivals were attended by the local population and these were no doubt jubilant affairs; even if not specifically organized for the benefit of the people they might be accompanied by wrestling, stick-fighting and boxing. However, there was no major annual sporting event in the style of the Olympic Games until the Ptolemaic Period, when Ptolemy II instituted the 'Ptolemaieia' in honour of his father, to be held every four years.

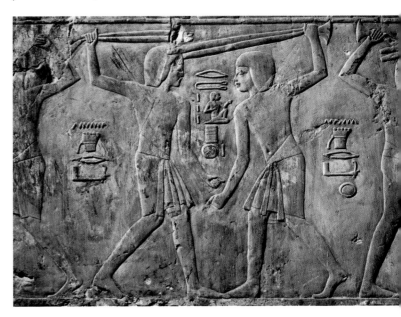

Stick-fighting and other sporting activities were popular events during Egypt's many annual festivals.

## CHAPTER 7

# THE PHARAOH IN DEATH

Each pharaoh marshalled the extensive resources at his command to build a suitable tomb for himself. This was his palace of eternity, where his body was placed, secure under the watchful eyes of the gods, surrounded by his possessions – some used in life, some commissioned especially for his burial. Given the amount of time required to construct and decorate a royal tomb, and also to manufacture its vast array of grave goods, it was normal for a king to initiate this process soon after ascending the throne, perhaps within a matter of months. From pit tombs covered by mounds, to pyramids, to the rock-cut shaft tombs of the Valley of the Kings and the subsequent burials within temple enclosures, the form of pharaoh's tomb changed over the centuries, marking an evolution in royal afterlife beliefs as much as in architectural fashion.

## The First Royal Tombs

Constructed on the desolate plains of Abydos, the tombs of kings of Egypt's Dynasty 0 were similar in overall size and layout to those of the contemporary elite, making them difficult to distinguish. Essentially, they were subterranean, rectangular, brick-lined and large. However, though lacking any form of identification, Abydos Tomb U-j (see p. 16) was almost certainly built for an early king, since it was particularly sizeable and well stocked with food and drink, while tombs in Abydos Cemetery B included burial goods made for kings Narmer, Iry-Hor and Ka of Dynasty 0, and Hor-Aha of the 1st Dynasty, securely identifying them as royal. Each subsequent king of the 1st Dynasty was also interred at Abydos.

These 1st Dynasty tombs consisted of two main components that were completely separate: the burial itself and a massive rectangular enclosure made of mud-brick and encompassing a small chapel. The enclosure was built about 1.5 km (almost 1 mile) north of the burial proper and served an uncertain purpose, although it was certainly connected to the burial rites. The actual tombs were set

The burial chamber and granite sarcophagus of Ramesses IV in the Valley of the Kings (KV 2). The chamber's walls are decorated with excerpts from the *Amduat* and *The Book of Gates*, while the ceiling displays dual arched figures of the goddess Nut, along with excerpts from *The Book of Nut* and *The Book of the Night*, which together describe the sun god's journey through the day and night hours.

within large pits lined with mud-bricks to form chambers. At the centre of each was the burial chamber, but further rooms for storage could surround it – even at this early time kings entered the afterlife with luxurious items, including stone vessels, jewelry and objects of ivory and wood. The burial chamber was constructed as a wooden shrine, most probably made from cedar, its walls hung with reed matting in imitation of the royal palace, allowing the king to sleep for eternity in a representation of his earthly bedchamber.

In the early 1st Dynasty, once the royal corpse had been lowered into the burial chamber from ground level a roof was set in place over it and a low mound, plastered and whitewashed, was built above the tomb. This was probably then encased (and so completely hidden) by a further mound, which marked the tomb's location, as did stelae bearing the king's Horus name. Given this building sequence, work could not be completed on the tomb until after the funeral. From the time of King Den, however, stairways descending to the substructure were incorporated into the design, allowing the builders to complete the superstructure in advance of the burial. David O'Connor, who has excavated extensively at Abydos, has suggested that a small brick chapel was connected to the mound, perhaps a precursor to the later royal mortuary temples – places where priests fed and worshipped the dead king's soul.

Both the tomb and the separate enclosure were each surrounded by subsidiary burials – small square tombs sealed at the time of the royal funeral. These appear to have belonged to sacrificed retainers: courtiers and servants killed either by strangulation or by having their throats slit so that they could continue to serve their lord in the afterlife. King Djer, second king of the 1st Dynasty, was buried with 326 such retainers, but the practice had virtually ceased by the end of the dynasty and it is not found at all under the 2nd Dynasty, except for three possible examples associated with Khasekhemwy's burial.

For reasons that remain elusive, though perhaps connected to the growing importance of nearby Memphis, kings of the 2nd Dynasty preferred to be buried at Saqqara rather than Abydos. Because of the nature of the local bedrock, these Saqqara tombs took a different form, being rock-cut tunnels rather than mud-brick structures sunk into pits. At the bottom of a staircase, the artisans excavated a long central underground gallery running from north to south and flanked at regular intervals by storage magazines, themselves sometimes flanked by further magazines, together creating a vast subterranean labyrinth. The burial suite was cut at the southern end of the gallery and consisted of a series of rooms of differing shape and size, made in imitation of the palace's private apartments and perhaps even including a model latrine. To date, only two 2nd Dynasty royal tombs have been identified at Saqqara, generally assigned to Hetepsekhemwy and Ninetjer,

though further rock-cut tombs of this period may lie undiscovered in the vicinity of the 3rd Dynasty Step Pyramid of Djoser. The superstructures of these tombs have been completely obliterated, though it is possible that both funerary enclosure and burial, separate at Abydos, were combined, with the enclosure situated above the subterranean passages. It is also possible that a mound and a stele identifying the pharaoh interred beneath were positioned directly above the burial chamber. Peribsen and Khasekhemwy, the final two kings of the 2nd Dynasty, returned to Abydos for their burials, building tombs in the style of the early 1st Dynasty, though Khasekhemwy's had an unusual elongated plan and a limestone burial chamber.

## The Pyramid Age

The developments in royal funerary architecture that occurred over the Early Dynastic Period culminated with the creation of Djoser's Step Pyramid at Saqqara (3rd Dynasty) – the first monumental stone building in history and a massive leap forward in world architecture. Its designer, Imhotep, who was later deified, combined previous traditions, fusing the great enclosure and burial together, while adding his own innovations. The burial mound now became a pyramid, built as a series of steps rising up to the heavens, which dwarfed any contemporary structure on earth. As high priest of Heliopolis – cult centre of Re – Imhotep may have intended his creation to represent the solidified rays of the sun, though it could equally have been a stairway for the king's soul to ascend to heaven or the

ABOVE **The 2nd Dynasty tomb of Khasekhemwy at Abydos, with multiple chambers in a long linear arrangement.**

OPPOSITE ABOVE **An ivory figurine of an Early Dynastic pharaoh wrapped in his** Sed **Festival cloak and wearing the White Crown of Upper Egypt.**

OPPOSITE BELOW **A granite stele, one of a pair, that originally marked the tomb of Peribsen at Saqqara. The king's name can be seen within the rectangular** serekh**, representing the royal palace. Although the god Horus is typically shown perched on top of the** serekh**, here Seth is carved instead.**

original mound of creation that emerged from the chaotic waters of Nun; perhaps it even symbolized all three. Directly below the pyramid is a deep, wide pit, cut vertically into the bedrock like a giant lift-shaft, that terminates in a dark space with a sarcophagus chamber (also referred to as a burial vault) at its centre. This overall arrangement can be regarded as inspired by the great pits and mounds of the tombs at Abydos. At the bottom of the pit, doorways lead to a network of rock-cut passages, many of them for storing thousands of large calcite vessels magically intended to supply Djoser with nourishment in the afterlife – an evolution of the extensive magazines associated with 2nd Dynasty royal tombs. One doorway, however, leads to a corridor decorated with three panels, each depicting Djoser performing *Sed* Festival rituals. Around the panels are elaborate dummy doorways with blue faience tiles imitating the reed matting within Early Dynastic burials, while lintels and jambs display the king's name and epithets. Egyptologists refer to this part of Djoser's underworld as the 'king's apartments', in the belief that they may represent royal palace quarters.

Such innovations – in fact adaptations of past traditions – are common in Djoser's complex. In the large space encompassed by his outer rectangular niched enclosure wall are buildings for an eternal *Sed* Festival, one that would be carried out by Djoser's spirit in the afterlife. Imhotep had dummy stone pavilions erected, copies of those made from perishable materials to house the gods' statues during the real *Sed* Festival, while in the vast courtyard to the pyramid's south he placed markers representing the limits of the kingdom for Djoser's spirit to run

The Step Pyramid of Djoser at Saqqara, the first pyramid ever built. Much of the space within the king's great funerary enclosure is dedicated to his eternal *Sed* Festival.

laps around and display his authority over Egypt for eternity. A further unusual addition is the so-called South Tomb, constructed at the southern limit of the complex, which takes the form of a deep, rock-cut burial – a copy in many ways of the arrangement under the Step Pyramid itself, even including a miniature sarcophagus chamber. It is uncertain what its purpose was, and there has been much speculation as to what might have been 'buried' there: it may have been a statue of the king, protected below ground so that his soul could inhabit it if his body were damaged, or perhaps it was the royal viscera, which were stored separately from the mummy. Whatever the explanation, some subsequent pyramids continued this tradition by including a smaller pyramid to the south.

Djoser's is the only step pyramid to have been completed. His successors began similar pyramids but were unable to finish them, no doubt because of their short reigns. The next innovation in funerary architecture occurred at the start of the 4th Dynasty with King Sneferu, who built three pyramids – two at Dahshur and one at Meidum. There was much experimentation in pyramid building during this time, with Sneferu's architects perfecting the angles of slope and base size, and they also created the first true, smooth-sided pyramid. This would become the model for future pyramid complexes, with the massive pyramids of Khufu and Khafre at Giza marking the zenith of pyramid building, both in terms of size and style of construction. But it was Khufu's pyramid that became known as the Great Pyramid, and rightly so. To the elderly farmer, standing in his small patch of land, watching

The Giza pyramids: the Great Pyramid of Khufu is in the foreground, with that of Khafre behind and Menkaure's in the distance. The three small pyramids in the foreground belong to Khufu's queens.

as an observer from a distance, this imposing structure would surely have inspired respect and fear. For years he would have watched it rise slowly skyward, built stone by stone, level by level by gangs of men, many local villagers who returned home each season with their hands calloused and their backs aching from the cruel physical toll of hauling limestone blocks of unimaginable weight up increasingly steep ramps. Now, in place of the empty desert of the farmer's youth, the pharaoh had created a mountain, dominating the skyline for miles around, its peak piercing the heavens, its white casing dazzling and shimmering in the midday heat.

Royal afterlife beliefs had changed by the 4th Dynasty, most probably related to the increased importance of the sun cult. The interior chambers of these pyramids no longer represented a recreation of the royal palace, though certain features may have persisted, and there was no need for vast storage galleries. It seems the king relied on his role as son of the sun god to ensure his afterlife, and connected himself firmly with the sun's movements across the sky, enjoying a rebirth each day at dawn. A standard plan also emerged at this time for the pyramid complex, consisting of a valley temple (a form of ceremonial entrance to the whole complex, with a still debated cultic role) next to an artificial bay and canal, which allowed access for river boats; a long, narrow causeway, which ran eastwards from the valley temple; and, at the opposite, upper end of the causeway, a mortuary temple, where the king's soul was worshipped and nourished, built immediately to the east of the pyramid. The pyramid's entrance was on its northern face.

During the 5th Dynasty less emphasis was placed on the pyramid itself, which became smaller and had a simple subterranean plan. Instead, the builders focused their attention on the surrounding complex, with the mortuary temple, for example, becoming much more extensive. Papyri found at the 5th Dynasty pyramid site of Abu Sir reveal that the organization of Old Kingdom pyramid temples was much like that of the palace. Every day, the king's *ka*-spirit rose from his sleep in his pyramid's burial chamber, called the House of the Morning, and took up residence in his statues in the mortuary temple, where he was met by the priests. They served him food and attended to his dress, while burning incense for purification. This daily interaction with his priests was just one aspect of the king's afterlife. The Egyptians did not believe in a singular soul, rather they saw a person as composed of various parts that became separated at the time of death. In the Old Kingdom, the king differed from the rest of society in possessing a *ba*-spirit in addition to his *ka*-spirit. The *ba* left the tomb during the day and could travel anywhere, though it had to return at night to sleep within the corpse.

From the Pyramid Texts, first inscribed on the interior walls of the 5th Dynasty Pyramid of Unas, we learn that the afterlife was divided

A fragment of the Pyramid Texts from the pyramid of Pepi I. These inscriptions, first found on the interior walls of the 5th Dynasty pyramid of King Unas at Saqqara, ensured the king's safe arrival in the afterlife and describe his afterlife expectations.

## PYRAMID DECORATION IN THE 4TH AND 5TH DYNASTIES

Until the Pyramid Texts were inscribed on the walls of King Unas' pyramid at Saqqara at the end of the 5th Dynasty, the interior walls of royal tombs had typically been left bare. King Djoser included his name and epithets on door lintels and jambs below his pyramid and had panels of blue faience tiles made to resemble hanging reed matting, as well as relief panels depicting him performing ritual acts, but subsequent kings did not follow suit.

Despite their apparent lack of decoration, it is possible that 4th and 5th Dynasty pyramid chambers originally contained wooden frames adorned with hangings, similar to that found packed away in the Giza shaft tomb of Queen Hetepheres. Her wooden frame fits almost perfectly within the burial chambers of the three queens' pyramids (GIa, b, c) to the east of the Great Pyramid, and could originally have been intended for any one of them. Furthermore, the granite ceiling beams of the King's Chamber in the Great Pyramid display dark rectangular stains at their edges, seemingly left by a wooden frame that once stood within; although this construction may

have primarily served as a structural support, it does not preclude an additional religious, decorative role. Such a feature would have harked back to the Early Dynastic burials of Egypt's first kings, in which the burial chamber was essentially a wooden shrine built within the tomb pit and hung with reed matting – a symbol of the royal palace.

The continued importance of this motif can be seen in Unas' pyramid, as well as those of the 6th Dynasty kings, where the walls surrounding the royal sarcophagus are etched and painted to look like a large frame hung with reed matting. Thus it seems plausible that the undecorated walls of the 4th and 5th Dynasty royal burial chambers were left plain simply because any carvings or paintings would have been obscured by traditional hanging mats, long since stolen or decomposed, leaving only the blank, silent stones we see today.

The walls surrounding King Unas' sarcophagus within his pyramid at Saqqara are etched and colourfully painted with images of reed matting, made in imitation of actual reed mats that lined the walls of 1st Dynasty royal burials.

into sky, abyss, *Duat* (Netherworld) and horizon, and that the king existed in various forms: he simultaneously took his place among the circumpolar stars and travelled across the sky with the sun god in his boat. The king is also said to jump into the sky as a grasshopper or to fly there as a falcon or goose. Other contradictory ideas abound: the king is chief of the gods yet protected by them; and he might be present in the sky with Orion or in the *Duat* with Osiris, with whom the king was identical in death. By utilizing the power conferred by the Pyramid Texts, the royal *ba* rose from the tomb, passed through the *Duat* and was transformed at the horizon into an effective spirit (*akh*) in the sky. The king's *akh* co-existed with his *ka* and *ba*, but was also a fusion of both.

## The Middle Kingdom

We have little information concerning the royal burials of the First Intermediate Period, though a king named Ibi built his pyramid near that of Pepi II at Saqqara, and a Herakleopolitan king, perhaps Merikare, built his close to that of Teti. The 11th Dynasty King Intef I excavated a rock-cut tomb at El-Tarif in Thebes, today known as *Saff el-Dawaba*, consisting of a large court with an entrance chapel followed by two rows of pillars and three chapels – one for the king, the others probably for queens. His successors, Intef II and III, built similar tombs, also at El-Tarif.

Montuhotep II, Egypt's second great unifier, constructed his tomb at Deir el-Bahri in Thebes. At the end of a long causeway, this burial complex took the

OPPOSITE ABOVE **The *ka*-statue of King Wahibre Hor, still within its shrine, was discovered in his shaft tomb at Dahshur. The upraised arms on the king's head form the hieroglyph for *ka*. The statue was originally adorned with a necklace covered with gold leaf, and wrapped with a kilt or loincloth around the waist.**

The upper terrace of Montuhotep II's mortuary temple at Deir el-Bahri. The square space surrounded by columns may once have supported a small pyramid. The mortuary temple of Hatshepsut, built roughly 500 years later, can be seen in the foreground.

form of a T-shaped terrace, reached by ramp. On the upper level an ambulatory surrounded a square central edifice, which may have once supported a pyramid. Behind the ambulatory was a colonnaded court and then a hypostyle hall, at the rear of which a statue of the king was placed within a rock-hewn niche; before it was an altar for offerings. Beneath the colonnaded court the burial chamber lay at the end of a long rock-cut tunnel, which originally contained wooden models of scenes from daily life placed in niches along its walls.

Kings of the 12th Dynasty emulated the great Old Kingdom rulers by building pyramids, though these were inferior to their predecessors' in both construction and size, and were not decorated with the Pyramid Texts. They were built at traditional sites, including Dahshur and Saqqara, but also at newly important centres near and within the Faiyum, such as Lisht, Lahun and Hawara. Amenemhat I built a pyramid of stone at Lisht, in a manner similar to late Old Kingdom pyramids. His successor, Senwosret I, did likewise, building a pyramid of roughly the same size as Menkaure's and surrounding it with nine queens' pyramids. From Amenemhat II onwards, however, pyramids were built of mud-brick cased with stone slabs, and their entrances were moved from the traditional northern face to other locations for reasons of security; Senwosret II built his pyramid's entrance beneath an unused tomb close to his pyramid. Interior passages also became more complex, with sliding blocks hiding rooms, again for security. These later Middle Kingdom kings were clearly concerned for their eternal safety and wished to ensure that neither they nor their treasures were disturbed, perhaps indicating that the tombs of their Old Kingdom forebears had already been robbed.

## Transition: The Second Intermediate Period

Only 10 royal burials of the 13th Dynasty have so far been identified, all at Dahshur. Of the six that have been excavated, five were pyramids, while one, that of King Wahibre Hor, was a shaft tomb. This proved to be virtually intact. In the king's antechamber was a ka-statue, still standing within its naos (shrine), two calcite stelae, a case for staves, pottery and wooden dummy vessels. A sarcophagus contained a rectangular coffin in which lay the body of a 45-year-old man – undoubtedly the king himself. On his body were two falcon collars and a dagger, and a stave had been placed beside him, as well as two long sceptres, an inlaid flail, two small calcite vases and a wooden mallet. His wooden canopic chest contained four human-headed canopic jars.

No royal burials are known from the mid-13th Dynasty to the start of the 17th Dynasty. However, pyramidions – capstones placed at the peaks of pyramids – have been found from this period, including one

BELOW **The pyramidion, or capstone, of Amenemhat III's pyramid at Dahshur, now in the Egyptian Museum, Cairo.**

of Merneferre Ay of the mid-13th Dynasty, discovered near Faqus in the Delta, and another from Tell el-Daba. This is perhaps evidence either that later kings constructed pyramids in their own zones of power once central authority had broken down, or that the Hyksos (or other individuals) later moved these pyramidions from their original locations (probably Dahshur).

The 17th Dynasty rulers built their tombs at Dra abu el-Naga at Thebes, in the form of small, steep-sided pyramids, each fronted by a little chapel and forecourt with two obelisks, with burial chambers beneath. From the description of the tomb of Sobekemsaf II, as narrated by one of its robbers and recorded in a 20th Dynasty text known as the Abbott Papyrus, we get a rare insight into how a royal tomb of this period appeared: 'We took our copper tools and forced a way into the pyramid of this king through its innermost part. We located the underground chambers and, taking lighted candles in our hands, went down … [we] found the god lying at the back of his burial place. And we found the burial place of Queen Nubkhaas, his consort, beside him, it being protected and guarded by plaster and covered with rubble.' They then recount how they opened the sarcophagi and coffins, and discovered the king's mummy still equipped with his sword and jewels. 'The noble mummy of the king was completely covered in gold and his coffins were decorated with gold and with silver inside and out, and inlaid with various precious stones.' A gold-mounted heart scarab of Sobekemsaf II, perhaps one of the items stolen from his body in antiquity, is now in the British Museum; it is the earliest known example of such an item being used by royalty.

The Abbott Papyrus also refers to an inspection of the tomb of King Kamose, relating that it had not been broken into. Sometime afterwards, however, the king's body was removed and hidden in a pit at Dra abu el-Naga, where it was discovered in 1857 contained in a simple, ungilded coffin. Various items were found on the king's badly disintegrated body, including a bronze dagger with a silver handle and gilded pommel (see p. 125), a bracelet with two figures of lions, a mirror, a scarab and amulets. Kamose's nephew, King Ahmose, who united Egypt and initiated the 18th Dynasty, built the last royal Egyptian pyramid at Abydos. It is unclear whether he was ever buried there, however, and his true final resting place may still await discovery or identification among those at Dra abu el-Naga at Thebes.

## The Valley of the Kings

The kings of the New Kingdom selected a new burial place, hidden in the hills below the peak of El-Qurn on the West Bank of the Nile at Thebes. For these kings, their innovation was to separate the royal mortuary temple from their place of burial, which was to be kept secret in the Valley of the Kings. They had learnt from the mistakes of the past, having seen the great tombs of their predecessors

Unlike other organs, which were removed during mummification, the heart was left inside the body to be weighed by Osiris against the feather of *maat* in the Hall of Judgment. Without the heart, the deceased had no hope of entering the afterlife and so a heart scarab would be placed in the mummy wrappings above it to ensure its safety. This gold and green jasper heart scarab of Sobekemsaf II is the earliest known example made for a king.

robbed. The New Kingdom mortuary temples, constructed in the plains below the Valley, are now increasingly referred to by Egyptologists as 'memorial temples' because they were not simply locations for the worship and nourishment of the dead king's spirit, but were each the focal point of three divine cults: of the king (fused with Amun); of a form of Amun specific to the temple's location (the main focus of cult in the temple); and of the sun god Re. Mut, the wife of Amun, and their child Khonsu were also honoured, as was the king's father (or royal ancestors) and other gods.

The royal tombs in the Valley of the Kings were excavated from the rock of the mountain, following a mortuary tradition long in use at Thebes. And although they were no longer topped by pyramids, the naturally pyramid-shaped peak of El-Qurn may have been regarded as a more than adequate alternative to a man-made construction. Ineni, the overseer of works commissioned by Thutmose I to build his tomb, records: 'I saw (to) the excavation of the rock-tomb of His Majesty, none seeing, none hearing'. Based on this inscription, Thutmose I is regarded as the first king definitely to have been buried in the Valley of the Kings, though it is possible that his predecessor, Amenhotep I, started this trend. Amenhotep's tomb has never been firmly identified, but he was worshipped at Deir el-Medina, the village that housed the workmen who cut and decorated the tombs in the Valley of the Kings, and it would seem unusual for the villagers to worship Amenhotep without having some connection to him.

The courtyard of the Ramesseum, the mortuary (or memorial) temple of Ramesses II at Thebes. Unlike in the Old and Middle Kingdoms, when the royal tomb and mortuary temple were side by side, in the New Kingdom they were kept separate.

Until the latter half of the period, except for the burial chamber, 18th Dynasty royal tombs were generally undecorated. A passage descended steeply into the cliff face, taking one or two right-angled turns before reaching the burial chamber. This twisting layout was perhaps inspired by the equally tortuous nature of the Netherworld as the Egyptians conceived it, a design earlier followed by the substructures of Middle Kingdom pyramids. Unlike the pyramids, however, with their clear solar connection, these New Kingdom royal tombs emphasized the king's connection to Osiris, as well as Re; each was a copy of the god's tomb as the Egyptians envisioned it.

The burial chamber was also a representation of the cosmos, with the sarcophagus as the primeval mound, a starry sky above and walls decorated with the *Amduat* – commonly known as *The Book of What is in the Netherworld* – which details the nightly voyage of the sun through the 12 hours of the night in the Netherworld (the *Duat*). The fate of the sun god and the dead king (who in death was Osiris) were intertwined: both faced the dangers of the Netherworld during the hours of darkness, were rejuvenated after uniting in the middle of the night (an event that symbolically occurred in the burial chamber) and were eventually reborn at dawn. Along the way they interacted with various Netherworld denizens, both helpful and aggressive. Their main enemy was the serpent Apophis, who was defeated each night. The inscriptions of the *Amduat* magically provided the deceased king with the requisite knowledge to navigate successfully through this dangerous territory.

The burial chamber of Thutmose III in his tomb in the Valley of the Kings. The *Amduat* (or *The Book of What is in the Netherworld*) decorates the walls, as if a long papyrus roll has been unfurled around the room.

Although blocks decorated with the *Amduat* were discovered in the tomb of Hatshepsut, the earliest fully preserved copy is on the walls of Thutmose III's burial chamber. It is rather schematic, consisting of simple stick-figures and cursive hieroglyphs, all copied in imitation of an unfurled papyrus roll. Amenhotep II's *Amduat* was equally restrained, though his artisans decided also to include fully realized figures on the columns within his burial chamber.

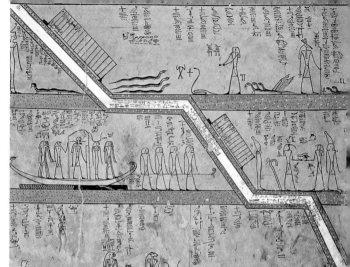

The fourth hour of the *Amduat*, as depicted in the tomb of Thutmose III. In this hour the solar barque travels through the realm of Sokar, where it is dragged along the 'path of fire' in the form of a snake.

Under the 19th Dynasty, the use of carved and painted decoration expanded throughout the tomb, and the right-angled turns were abandoned in favour of a long, straight plan descending into the cliff face. More chambers and side-chambers were also added to the overall tomb layout. This extra wall space allowed the artisans to employ additional 'books', such as *The Litany of Re* or *The Book of Gates*, in their decorative schemes, though all essentially charted the solar progress in the manner of the *Amduat*. Effectively, the first half of the tomb became associated with the movement of the sun, while the second half was associated with Osiris. The straightening of the axis also appears to have been motivated by solar themes: the tomb's long linear descent was regarded as aligned symbolically from east to west (irrespective of reality), in imitation of the sun's journey across the sky.

Generally, royal tombs in the Valley followed a basic standard plan, with individual elements sometimes repeated in larger tombs and different sections given specific designations. The initial corridor was known as the 'First God's Passage of the Sun's Path', which could be followed by a 'Second God's Passage'. A third 'God's Passage' was lined with niches – those on the right were called the 'Sanctuaries in which the Gods of the East Rest' and those on the left were the sanctuaries for the

Seti I's 19th Dynasty tomb follows a long straight axis, and would have been the first tomb in the Valley of the Kings to be decorated throughout in painted raised relief if work had been completed before the king's funeral.

entrance

pillared hall

well shaft

side chamber

burial chamber

175

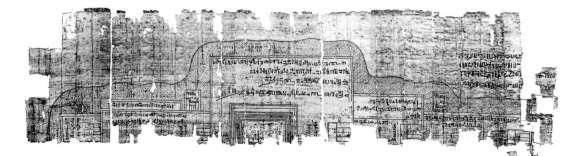

gods of the west. A further 'God's Passage' included niches called 'door-keeper's rooms'. From the reign of Thutmose III, the next chamber incorporated a deep well shaft and was called the 'Hall of Waiting'. The meaning behind this curious feature is unclear – it was perhaps to catch floodwater from the occasional heavy downpours that afflicted the Theban region or it may have been a way of thwarting would-be tomb robbers. Despite such a possible functional origin, as time progressed the well came to be regarded as a symbolic burial place for the god Sokar and perhaps an entrance into the Netherworld. Even when, from the reign of Ramesses III, the well was no longer excavated, the basic chamber continued to be included, highlighting its symbolic importance. A pillared hall, called the 'Chariot Hall', followed the 'Hall of Waiting'; then came the burial chamber, known as the 'House of Gold (in which one rests)'. This name could be a reference to the eternal nature of gold or to the skin of the gods, which was made from gold, or perhaps simply to the treasures stored there. A papyrus in Turin records the names of additional sectors for Ramesses IV's tomb, including the 'God's Passage which is the *Shabti* Place', located behind the burial chamber, and two 'treasuries'.

A papyrus, now in Turin, bearing a plan of the tomb of Ramesses IV. Details of chamber and corridor dimensions and decoration are given in hieratic. The tomb was evidently complete when the plan was drawn, as the tomb's doors are said to be 'fastened' throughout.

## After the New Kingdom

With the abandonment of the Valley of the Kings at the end of the New Kingdom, no single royal burial place was favoured; kings of the Third Intermediate Period through to the end of the Late Period were interred at various sites, mainly across the Delta. It became the custom for pharaohs to be buried within the grounds of the major temple at their ancestral home or centre of power, in small tombs sunk into the ground near the enclosure wall. Accessible via vertical shafts, these were perhaps topped by small chapel superstructures. The kings of the 21st and 22nd Dynasties were predominantly buried at Tanis, though for a brief time Bubastis may have served as the preferred burial site until it was abandoned due to flooding. As with the city of Tanis itself, much of the stonework used to construct the royal tombs was brought from Pi-Ramesses. Once set in place to line the tomb, these blocks were decorated with scenes typical of New Kingdom royal Netherworld books. Since not all royal burials of this period have been discovered at Tanis, scholars have suggested that some may still await discovery at the city, but in a different place from the known royal tombs, or that perhaps some of the kings were buried at Memphis or Ehnasya el-Medina.

King Harsiese of the 23rd Dynasty, who ruled from Thebes as the founder of a separate royal line concurrent with the reign of Osorkon II, was buried within the enclosure of Medinet Habu in a simple burial chamber reached by a stairway, perhaps once surmounted by a chapel. No other royal burial of the 23rd Dynasty is known. As many royal lines existed in the later Third Intermediate Period, various sites may have been home to 'royal' tombs; the burial of a queen called Kamama, for example, was discovered at Leontopolis (Tell Moqdam), though most of the contents were destroyed by water. The 24th Dynasty, who ruled their territory from their home town of Sais, were probably buried in that city.

Rulers of the 25th Dynasty were buried in Nubia, beneath steep-sided miniature pyramids, first at el-Kurru and then further downstream at Nuri (both in modern

## AKHENATEN'S FINAL RESTING PLACE

During the Amarna Period, Akhenaten ordered that his royal tomb be excavated in the cliffs far along a large wadi (a dry riverbed), east of his new city of Akhetaten (Tell el-Amarna; see p. 150), to receive his body in death. His burial chamber lay at the end of a long straight axis, interrupted only by two subsidiary corridors that led northwards to further suites, most probably for the burial of family members including Princess Meketaten and his mother, Queen Tiye.

Although apparently interred in his tomb as planned, Akhenaten did not remain buried at Amarna for long. When the court abandoned the city, it appears that his remains, along with those of Queen Tiye, were returned to Thebes (perhaps by Tutankhamun) and buried in a tomb in the Valley of the Kings, now designated KV 55, which was discovered in 1907. Numerous fragments of burial equipment were found in this tomb, including four calcite canopic jars, inscribed for a queen called Kiya; the fragments of a gilded wooden shrine for Queen Tiye; and a beautiful though much damaged wooden coffin (now restored), the names deliberately erased from its surface and its gilded face removed. When opened, the coffin was found to contain skeletal remains with a golden vulture pectoral wrapped around the skull. Although the identity of these remains was debated for many years, recent scientific analyses, involving DNA tests and CT-scanning, have suggested that they are almost certainly those of Akhenaten, reinterred in the Valley of the Kings and reunited with his ancestors in death.

The elaborate coffin that contained the remains thought to be of Akhenaten. The face has been removed and the cartouche excised, destroying the occupant's chances of entering the afterlife.

Sudan), the largest of which belonged to King Taharqo. Each pyramid had a chapel at its east side and a stairway that led to a substructure consisting of a single room with a rock-cut bench at its centre; here the king was laid to rest. Though only traces remain, from the reign of Shabaqo the Nubian royal burial chambers were painted with scenes of the king and the solar disc in the style of earlier Egyptian royal tombs.

The 26th Dynasty kings were buried at Sais, within the temple enclosure of the goddess Neith, though nothing remains today. A pink granite fragment (now in the Louvre), bearing the name of Psamtik II and thought to come from his tomb in Sais, displays a bas-relief scene from the *Amduat*, providing an indication of the decoration present. Herodotus, who visited Sais, says that King Apries was buried 'in the family tomb in the temple of Athene (Neith), nearest the shrine on the left-hand side as one goes in'. He then provides further description of the royal tombs: 'The people of Sais buried all the kings who came from the province inside this precinct – the tomb of Amasis (Ahmose II), too … is in the temple court, a great cloistered building of stone, decorated with pillars carved in imitation of palm-trees, and other costly ornaments. Within the cloister is a chamber with double doors, and behind the doors stands the sepulchre.'

The great Persian rulers – Cambyses and Darius – of the 27th Dynasty were buried in their homeland, at or near Persepolis, but it is uncertain where Amyrtaeus of Sais, sole king of the 28th Dynasty, who liberated Egypt, was interred. The 29th Dynasty royal cemetery was at Mendes (Tell el-Rub'a) in the Delta. In 1992 the tomb of Nepherites I was discovered here, in the vicinity of the Temple of Banebdjed, in an area of existing Third Intermediate Period and 26th Dynasty burials. A limestone mastaba was set above the burial chamber and the king

King Taharqo of the 25th Dynasty was buried beneath a pyramid at Nuri in modern Sudan, seen below. The other kings of the 25th Dynasty were also buried under steep-sided pyramids, but at nearby el-Kurru.

possibly used existing blocks and stelae in its construction. Its remains show that the tomb was decorated in a traditional manner, including floral patterns, a dado of cartouches and scenes from the *Amduat*. The tomb was destroyed sometime between the reign of Nectanebo I of the 30th Dynasty and the Ptolemaic Period, with the most likely culprits being the Persian 31st Dynasty. Classical sources relate that the sacred Ram of Mendes was killed by the Persian Artaxerxes III, and it is not unreasonable to assume that further damage was caused at Mendes under his rule.

It is unclear where the 30th Dynasty royal tombs were situated, though Samannud (Sebennytos), Mendes and Behbeit el-Hagar (just north of Samannud) have all been suggested, as has Saqqara. Given that Herodotus states that this dynasty originated at Samannud and that other Late Period dynasties, such as the 26th and 29th, were buried in their birth places as recorded by Manetho, it is likely that they intended their burial place to be within the grounds of the Temple of Onuris-Shu in that city. Although it has not been located and thus never excavated, it is possible that this burial site was plundered in antiquity and its contents dispersed, as objects from these royal tombs have come to light: Nectanebo I's sarcophagus (now in Cairo) was found in pieces, re-used in modern buildings, and Nectanebo II's sarcophagus had been re-used in an Alexandrian mosque before it was moved to the British Museum. *Shabti*s are also known for both kings. But as both Nectanebo II and his predecessor, Teos, fled Egypt before their deaths, it is probable that neither were buried in their tombs.

Persian royal tombs at Naqsh-e Rustam, Iran. The tomb at the far right belongs to Darius I, while the central tomb is believed to belong to Xerxes I, and that at the far left to Artaxerxes I; all were kings of Egypt of the 27th Dynasty.

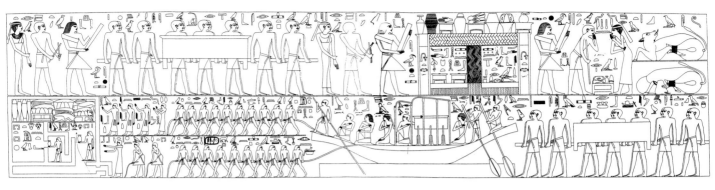

## Mummification and the Royal Funeral

Traditionally, there was a 70-day period between death and burial. This number was chosen for ritual rather than practical significance, as it was the length of time that the star Sirius vanished from view each year. Its return was regarded as a rebirth and it thus became connected with the funeral rites. In reality, the length of time that a body spent with the embalmers fluctuated; Queen Merysankh of the 4th Dynasty was buried 273 days after her death, for example.

When the king died his body was drawn on a bier or ritual boat in a procession from his place of death to the riverside. This procession, accompanied by mourning and lamentation, included a man identified as the embalmer, a lector priest (responsible for reading the sacred texts), a *sem* priest (who performed the burial rituals) and two women known as the Great and Little Kite, who were associated with Isis and Nephthys respectively. The mourners then loaded the body on to a boat and ritually crossed a waterway – usually the Nile – westwards, thus symbolically entering the realm of the dead. In the Old Kingdom they next sailed up a canal to the valley temple of the pyramid complex, and in the New Kingdom to the west bank of the Nile at Thebes.

Their first stop was the *seh-netjer*, the 'divine booth' (the *Ibu en Waab* or 'Tent of Purification' for non-royals), where the mummification process began with the body being ritually washed in natron, a naturally occurring dehydrating agent consisting of sodium carbonate, sodium bicarbonate, salt and sodium sulphate. This 'divine booth' was apparently a temporary wooden and reed-mat structure – a sort of tent – erected before the valley temple in the Old Kingdom and perhaps near the royal mortuary temple in the New Kingdom. Attempts at mummification had been made from the early days of Egyptian civilization, though very few royal mummies have survived from that time. A mummified arm, wearing elaborate jewelry, was found by the British Egyptologist Flinders Petrie during his excavations at the 1st Dynasty royal tomb of Djer at Abydos; it may have belonged to the king or perhaps to one of his queens. Fragments of bodies were found

Drawing of a relief from the tomb of Qar at Giza, showing the funerary procession from the *Ibu* (upper register, right), where the body was ritually purified, to the *Wabet* (lower register, left), where the embalming took place.

Ahmose I's mummy was found in the Deir el-Bahri cache in 1881, though the precise location of the tomb of this king, who expelled the Hyksos from Egypt and reunited the country, is still unknown.

in Old Kingdom pyramids, but it is unclear whether these are the remains of the original kings or of later intrusive interments. A well-preserved mummy, sometimes cited as being that of King Merenre, was found near the royal sarcophagus in that pharaoh's pyramid at South Saqqara, while a single canopic jar in the burial chamber of Pepi I still contained the king's tightly wrapped internal organs.

Royal mummies have survived from the New Kingdom, however. Two caches were discovered at Thebes, one in a tomb at Deir el-Bahri (DB 320), the other in the tomb of Amenhotep II – both used as hiding places for important mummies moved from their original resting places by 21st Dynasty Theban priests. Consequently, only Tutankhamun and Amenhotep II were found in their own tombs. No mummy of a post-New Kingdom pharaoh is known, though the bones of kings Psusennes I, Amenemopet and Shoshenq II were found at Tanis, their flesh having completely rotted away in the damp conditions of the Delta. Following an examination of these remains by Douglas Derry, Psusennes I was shown to be quite aged at death and suffered from severe arthritis of the vertebrae and abscesses of the teeth. Amenemopet's remains were in a particularly bad condition, while Shoshenq II appears to have died from an infected head wound.

After having been ritually cleansed, the king's body was taken from the *seh-netjer* to the *Wabet*, the 'Pure Place', also referred to as the *Per Nefer*, 'House of Beauty'. In this building (perhaps the valley temple in the Old Kingdom pyramid complex) the main process of mummification was carried out by a team of specialists, overseen by a man called the master of secrets. Once the body had again been cleansed and all the hair had been shaved off, the brain was removed through the nose, torn and ripped apart by a hooked instrument; any remaining matter was then washed out. The embalmer next made an oblique incision on the left side of the king's abdomen, just large enough for him to place his hand within the body and empty the torso of its organs. The embalmer washed the removed viscera with natron and covered them in resin before placing each organ in its own separate compartment within the canopic chest or individual canopic jars. The heart, however, always remained within the body. It was regarded as 'the seat of the mind' and was required for the afterlife judgment before Osiris, when it was weighed against a *maat* feather; if the heart proved too heavy, the deceased could not enter the afterlife. The kidneys often remained in place too, by virtue of being difficult to reach rather than having any particular religious significance. Resin helped to ensure the skin was preserved.

Next, the embalmers filled the king's body with packets of natron and placed further packets around him. For between 30 and 40 days, the king lay on the embalming table, the moisture draining from his corpse. During this process of desiccation, the king's toenails and fingernails were kept in place, either by binding

This canopic jar from the tomb of Psusennes I at Tanis contained the king's embalmed stomach. Its lid is made in the form of the jackal-headed god Duamutef, one of the Four Sons of Horus. Each of these four gods protected a particular organ, removed from the body and placed in its own jar during mummification. Animal-headed canopic jars only came into use late in the 18th Dynasty.

or fingerstalls, as there was a danger otherwise that they would simply fall off. Afterwards, once the natron had been removed, the body was rubbed with oils, and resin was poured into the brain cavity; sometimes linen was also placed within. The body cavity was then filled with cloth or other packing materials, such as sawdust. In the later New Kingdom the embalmers also tried to make the mummy more life-like; Ramesses III, for example, was the first king to have artificial eyes placed in his eye sockets. Then the wrapping process began, involving alternately wrapping and oiling for a period of 17 days, during which the embalmers crossed the king's arms over his chest in the manner of Osiris holding the crook and flail. As each limb was wrapped, a variety of spells was read aloud. This was not the only supernatural protection the king received – magical jewelry and amulets were placed among the wrappings to help protect his body from harm. The heart scarab (see p. 172), for example, was placed above the chest to protect the true heart and ensure that it would not testify against the deceased in the afterlife. Once the body was wrapped, the king's golden mask was placed on his head, signalling that he was ready for burial in the tomb. Before leaving the *Wabet*, however, a ritual called the Hour Vigil was performed, in which Seth, as a malevolent force, was warded off during the hours of the night.

When the time of the funeral arrived, priests offered food to the royal mummy before escorting it from the *Wabet*. It may then have been taken on a ritual boat journey to Egypt's ancient holy cities – Sais, Buto, Heliopolis and Abydos. As time progressed, this may have been done symbolically during the procession from the *Wabet* to the necropolis, or during the funerary rituals at the tomb, rather than physically. Certainly, for private burials of the New Kingdom, the *muu*-dancers, individuals regarded as incarnations of the ancient gods of Buto and who played an important part in these rituals, performed their dance at the entrance to the tomb.

Returning to the pyramid or Theban west bank (depending on the period), the royal corpse continued its journey to the tomb on its sledge, still accompanied by the Kites and other members of the procession, as well as porters carrying the royal funerary objects. In the New Kingdom, various funerary ceremonies were conducted on the processional route from the royal mortuary temple to the tomb in the Valley of the Kings: men

The tomb of Psusennes I was found largely intact at Tanis. A gold plaque (above) was placed over the incision in the king's abdomen made by embalmers to remove his internal organs, preventing malevolent forces from entering his body, and his golden death mask (below) was placed over his head.

poured libations of milk on to the ground and burned incense, while professional mourners wailed and lamented, some heaping dust on their heads in an age-old gesture of grief. The cries of sorrow must have echoed around the Valley. Small kiosks were set up along the route, containing offerings of bread, meat, fowl, beer, wine and water, and rituals were conducted around the statues of the deceased. Afterwards, all the pots associated with the food and drink offerings were smashed. Communal meals may also have been held at this time.

In the burial chamber of Tutankhamun, one painted scene depicts 12 men leading the deceased king's funerary cortege, including two viziers (identified by their particular clothing) and high officials, all wearing white linen robes and white headbands. These men pull the royal funerary sledge, though private tomb scenes show the deceased's sledge being dragged by four oxen, with a second sledge following closely behind carrying the canopic chest. Tutankhamun's scene also shows his coffin as visible upon the sledge, within a tall shrine decorated with garlands and topped by rearing uraei; however, the royal coffin may in fact have been hidden from view by an elaborate painted leather funerary tent, similar to the 21st Dynasty example of Queen Istemkheb, discovered in the Deir el-Bahri cache and now in the Egyptian Museum, Cairo. An enigmatic object, the *tekenu*, was also typically dragged along behind the deceased – perhaps a representation of the dead body, wrapped in linen, its meaning is still much debated.

Tutankhamun's funeral, as depicted on the east wall of his burial chamber. Twelve high officials, including two viziers, drag the royal funerary sledge, upon which a shrine containing the royal mummy rests.

The painted leather funerary tent of Queen Istemkheb. Such tents probably hid the coffin from view during the funeral.

## BURIAL EQUIPMENT

In addition to the largely intact funerary assemblage of Tutankhamun, the royal tombs in the Valley of the Kings have provided us with many fragments of royal burial equipment, making it possible to gain an idea of the lavish content of a typical New Kingdom royal tomb.

The royal mummy lay within a series of nested coffins and sarcophagi, themselves within a series of gilded wooden shrines decorated with texts and scenes from Netherworld books. Fragments of shrines similar to those belonging to Tutankhamun have been found in other royal tombs, while a plan of Ramesses IV's tomb, on a papyrus now in Turin (see p. 176), shows the original location of his shrines.

The canopic chest, storing the king's preserved liver, lungs, stomach and intestines, was located close to the sarcophagus, again within further nested shrines, each upon a sledge. Tutankhamun's canopic chest has four compartments, each containing its own miniature coffin for the royal viscera and covered with a human-headed stopper. Such chests were popular until the end of the 19th Dynasty when individual canopic jars became more fashionable.

Royal tombs also contained many ritual statues, some of gods, others depicting the king in various acts. The walls of Seti II's well-shaft room in his tomb are painted with images of such ritual statues, while fragmentary three-dimensional equivalents were found in the tombs of Thutmose III, Amenhotep II, Thutmose IV, Amenhotep III, Horemheb, Ramesses I, Seti I and Ramesses IX. Intact versions were discovered in Tutankhamun's tomb. Taken together, it appears that these statues were a typical feature of any New Kingdom royal tomb. Those from Tutankhamun's tomb, all found within their own shrines, show the young king in different poses, wearing either the Red Crown or White Crown; they were wrapped in linen shawls and set on a wooden base. Two depict him standing on a feline, while two show him harpooning and three are of him striding. Many gods are also represented, including Atum, Ptah, Geb and Isis. Worker statues, known as *shabti*s, were placed in tombs to magically carry out agricultural work in place of the deceased in the afterlife. A total of 413 were found in Tutankhamun's tomb, made to resemble the king holding the crook and flail and wearing different forms of headdresses and crowns; they were also provided with miniature tools to perform their work in the next world.

Many other items that might be of use to the king in the afterlife could be placed in the royal tomb, some made specifically for the burial, others taken from daily life. Tutankhamun's included chariots, model boats, calcite lamps, guardian statues, animal-headed ritual beds, thrones, jewelry boxes, weaponry, clothing, wine, meat and bread, even family heirlooms and locks of hair. As with the ritual statues, fragments of similar objects have been found during excavations in other royal tombs in the Valley, indicating that the content of Tutankhamun's tomb was not atypical. A large amount of elaborate jewelry could also accompany the king, including lavish pectorals with winged scarabs and falcons, all picked out with precious stones, golden pendants and beaded collars. In addition to the great treasures of Tutankhamun's tomb, silver bracelets, rings, a silver sandal, intricate golden earrings and a pair of silver gloves were found in KV 56, an undecorated tomb in the Valley of the Kings from the time of Seti II, which may have belonged to a prince.

A wooden *shabti* figurine of Tutankhamun, wearing the Red Crown of Lower Egypt and holding the crook and flail. Placed in the tomb, sometimes in great numbers, *shabti*s performed work for the deceased in the afterlife; Tutankhamun had 413 *shabti*s of different materials and various sizes.

OPPOSITE BELOW **Kings were buried with elaborate and precious jewelry. Seen here are a bracelet from the tomb of Psusennes I at Tanis (left); a pectoral of Tutankhamun (centre); and earrings inscribed for Seti II found in KV 56, the so-called 'gold tomb' of the Valley of the Kings, where a child of Seti II and Tawosret may have been interred (right).**

The unusual decoration in the well-shaft room of Seti II's tomb in the Valley of the Kings (KV 15) includes representations of funerary objects, such as ritual statuettes of gods and kings. The images of the king standing on a feline resemble an actual figurine found in the tomb of Tutankhamun, as well as fragmentary examples from other royal tombs. It appears that each royal tomb contained a standard array of ritual objects.

The largely intact Third Intermediate Period burials of Psusennes I, Amenemopet and Shoshenq II at Tanis all contained many spectacular grave goods, though any organic matter, such as leather, had long since rotted away in the damp conditions in the Delta. Psusennes I's remains, discovered wearing a stunning golden mask (see p. 182), jewelry and golden finger and toe stalls, had been laid to rest within a silver mummiform coffin. This had been placed within a mummiform sarcophagus of black granite, adapted from a private example of the New Kingdom, which had in turn been placed in a pink granite sarcophagus originally belonging to Merenptah.

Psusennes' associated grave goods included two pectorals, four scarabs, 36 rings, bracelets, weapons and sceptres, three necklaces composed of golden discs, *shabti*s, sandals and golden vessels. His son, Amenemopet, was also found to be wearing a golden mask, though few of his other burial goods were present. Shoshenq II too was adorned with a golden face mask, but had been placed within an unusual hawk-headed mummiform coffin made from silver. He was also buried with four miniature silver sarcophagi for his internal organs, though unlike his full-size coffin these were human-headed. Among Shoshenq II's other equipment were pectorals and seven elegant bracelets, formed from gold and inlaid with semiprecious stones, all bearing Shoshenq I's cartouches.

Some of King Osorkon II's burial goods were also found at Tanis, though since his tomb had been plundered in antiquity few of his original treasures remained, beyond fragments of his hawk-headed coffin, *shabti*s, calcite vessels and a sarcophagus for his son. He also had a canopic chest that had apparently been reused from the Middle Kingdom.

An ostracon describing the transport of funerary objects to the tomb of Merenptah notes that the treasurer and chief steward could also be present during a royal funerary procession.

In the late 18th Dynasty, it is possible that the royal funeral lasted four days and three nights, though this is by no means certain. Four shrines, nested one inside another, were found in the tomb of Tutankhamun, leading the German Egyptologist Horst Beinlich to suggest that the smallest may have been used in the procession to the tomb and that the others were used over the course of the funeral rituals, perhaps at the mortuary temple. In his view, they acted as a form of protection for the royal body before it was placed in the tomb, a different one being used on each of the three nights of the funeral and containing a different ritual bed. Three ritual beds were found in Tutankhamun's tomb – one hippo-headed, one lion-headed and the third cow-headed. According to Beinlich, on the first night the hippo metaphorically ate the dead king, on the second the lion rejuvenated him, and on the third the cow gave birth to him in the Netherworld.

In the Old Kingdom, the final rituals took place at the pyramid itself, while in the New Kingdom it was no doubt at the entrance to the tomb in the Valley of the Kings. At this point, the procession was met by the ceremonial *muu*-dancers, and censings, libations and offerings of clothing and food took place (as well as the reading of the Pyramid Texts in the Old Kingdom). The mummy was stood

The mummy of Osiris lies on a funerary bed, flanked by Nephthys on the left and Isis on the right, both in the form of kites; from the tomb of Nefertari in the Valley of the Queens.

upright to face the sun. The most important ritual was now the 'opening of the mouth', in which the *sem* priest used a special adze, among other ritual implements, to touch the mummy's face-mask (or a statue representing the deceased), enabling the deceased to breathe, see, hear, eat and speak in the afterlife. In its fullest form, this ritual consisted of 75 episodes. The role of the *sem* priest in private funerals was played by the heir to the deceased's estate; in royal burials it was the king's successor. In the tomb of Tutankhamun, the official Ay is shown performing this function, legitimizing his role as successor despite not being of royal blood. One of the final elements of the 'opening of the mouth' was the slaughtering of a calf before its mother; its bloody foreleg was then offered to the mummy.

The royal sarcophagus was almost certainly already in the tomb during the funeral; Merenptah's, for example, was moved into his tomb during the seventh year of his reign. Tutankhamun's three coffins, however, were perhaps kept in a tent near the tomb entrance or within the antechamber during the final rituals. The workmen then carried them to the burial chamber and placed them within the sarcophagus, lying open and awaiting the royal mummy. At the same time other objects could be placed in the tomb, many carefully positioned for ritual significance. Once all the necessary equipment and furnishings had been deposited, the nested coffins and sarcophagus sealed with the royal mummy inside, and the funerary shrines erected, the burial chamber could be blocked off from the rest of the tomb with a hastily constructed wall, sealing it – so it was hoped – for eternity. The artisans then plastered the wall, leaving a wet surface for the high officials to stamp their seals into, sometimes repeatedly. One by one, each additional room could then be filled with objects and sealed off in turn, until the burial was complete and the last mourner had ascended the steps back into the sunlight. The funeral was officially over. Pharaoh now rested in darkness.

On the north wall of Tutankhamun's burial chamber Ay, on the far right, wearing the Blue Crown and a leopard skin, performs the 'opening of the mouth' ceremony on the mummy of Tutankhamun (in the form of Osiris); in doing so, Ay legitimized his claim to the throne. In the central scene Tutankhamun meets the goddess Nut, while on the far left he embraces Osiris, followed by his *ka*-spirit.

# CHAPTER 8

## THE LAST PHARAOHS

With the invasion of Egypt by Alexander the Great of Macedon in
332 BC, historians cease to count the great dynasties compiled by
Manetho and instead refer first to a very brief Macedonian Dynasty
comprising Alexander himself, his half-brother Philip Arrhidaeus
and son Alexander IV, followed by the longer Ptolemaic Period and
finally the Roman Period. These last two phases are often referred
to collectively as the Graeco-Roman Period, and constitute the
final incarnation of ancient Egyptian civilization. Egyptian tradition
now fused with that of the Greek-Macedonian regime, creating a
unique hybrid, centred at the newly founded city of Alexandria.
Pomp, excess, rebellion, intrigue, murder – the Ptolemies reigned
through it all, their decadent dynasty culminating in the suicide of
Cleopatra VII and the absorption of Egypt into the Roman Empire,
when the divine office of pharaoh passed into the hands of a long
line of absentee pharaohs.

### Alexander and the First Ptolemies

After his bloodless invasion, Alexander remained in Egypt only for a single winter,
but long enough to visit Heliopolis, Memphis and the Serapeum – burial place
of the sacred Apis bulls at Saqqara – and to travel to Siwa Oasis, where he was
proclaimed a god by the renowned oracle of Amun. 'He put his question to the
oracle', the chronicler Arrian relates, 'and received (or so he said) the answer which
his heart desired'. This event affected Alexander deeply, and from this time on he is
often depicted with ram's horns – a symbol of Amun. Following his return across
the desert, Arrian continues, Alexander founded Alexandria on the Mediterranean
coast by first laying out its city limits with grain. He was then crowned at Memphis
in the style of a traditional pharaoh and received the full five-fold titulary,
according to *The Alexander Romance*, composed around the 2nd century AD.
Alexander's name could now be seen written in hieroglyphs and enclosed by royal

The Roman emperor
Trajan offers a boat to
the goddess Hathor at
Dendera. The emperor
wears the traditional Red
Crown of Lower Egypt, a
uraeus is at his brow, a
bull's tail hangs from his
kilt, and he stands below
two cartouches containing
his name in hieroglyphs.
Irrespective of his origins,
Trajan was presented as a
true pharaoh.

cartouches in such sacred places as Luxor Temple, alongside depictions of him offering to Egypt's gods in the age-old manner, with the uraeus at his brow and crown upon his head. To further reinforce his legitimacy, stories began to be circulated identifying him as the physical son of Nectanebo II, the last native Egyptian pharaoh, who had fled Egypt in the face of Persian aggression. Despite his clear love for Egypt, emphasized by his wish that one day he be buried at Siwa, in 331 BC Alexander continued his campaign eastwards, expanding his empire towards India. In his place, he left an Egyptian called Doloaspis to manage the country, two military men to lead the army and a further individual to gather tribute.

Alexander died in Babylon in 323 BC and was subsequently laid to rest in Memphis before his body was moved to Alexandria. His empire was carved up between his generals, but remained under the control of a triumvirate based in Macedonia and acting under the overall authority of his half-brother Philip Arrhidaeus and his son Alexander IV – both ultimately murdered. Initially, Ptolemy, one of Alexander's generals, ruled as satrap of Egypt, overseeing a series of wars in which territory was won and lost. However, once another of Alexander's

A coin depicting Alexander the Great wearing ram's horns, a symbol of the god Amun, whose oracle proclaimed Alexander a god at Siwa Oasis.

A depiction of Alexander the Great, wearing the Blue Crown and offering before Amun-Min at Luxor Temple. Alexander only spent a single winter in Egypt, but his experiences profoundly affected him for the rest of his life.

## ALEXANDER'S LOST TOMBS

Alexander rested in three separate tombs over the course of his eventful afterlife. After hijacking the dead king's ornate funeral carriage, Ptolemy I brought the body to the Memphis region, perhaps Saqqara, where it remained for the burial rites. These were conducted in the Macedonian tradition in 321 BC. This tomb was only temporary, however, nothing more than a place for the royal mummy to rest while Ptolemy had a splendid mausoleum constructed in Alexandria.

It is not known when Alexander's corpse was moved to this new tomb, or even where in Alexandria it was built, though it probably stood in the Alpha zone at the centre of the city (see p. 192). Despite the expense and time spent preparing this monumental final resting place, within a century Alexander was on the move again. Ptolemy IV took Alexander's body and the remains of the earlier Ptolemies and placed them together in a new mausoleum, creating a dynastic crypt with Alexander as its founder. This was the famous *Sema* (or *Soma*), located within the city's palace district; most probably in an area that is today mainly below sea level around the Silsileh promontory.

Although no clear depiction or description of the *Sema* exists, evidence suggests that it was built as a circular tower filled with columns, and had a conical roof topped by a pyramid and a sculpture. Given the architectural similarities, and the emperor's apparent love of all things related to Alexander, it may have inspired Hadrian's mausoleum in Rome – the modern Castel Sant'Angelo. Alexander's burial chamber was cut into the rock below the *Sema*. There, the great men of the day could pay their respects to the dead king.

Not all were reverential, however. Strabo records that Ptolemy X melted down Alexander's original golden sarcophagus and replaced it with one made of 'glass'. Furthermore, according to Flavius Josephus, Cleopatra VII stole gold from the tomb; Caligula took Alexander's breastplate back to Rome, and even wore it on one occasion; and, reputedly, Septimius Severus had the tomb locked so that no one else might view the body.

The Castel Sant'Angelo in Rome, Emperor Hadrian's mausoleum, may have been constructed in imitation of Alexander's final resting place in Alexandria. Hadrian was an admirer of all things Egyptian, having visited the country in AD 130–31.

When Caracalla visited, he left behind his purple cloak, belts and rings of precious stones to honour the dead Alexander, but took the king's goblets to drink his wine from. Augustus was more respectful. He had Alexander's body brought from his tomb's 'inner sanctum' so that he could place flowers and a golden crown upon it.

By the 4th century AD, references to Alexander's tomb cease in the classical sources. Around this time, riots caused much destruction across Alexandria, as did earthquakes, and the *Sema* was certainly ruined, its stonework ultimately finding its way into new constructions. Though occasional references by later commentators and travellers refer to seeing a tomb of Alexander among the ruins of Alexandria up to the 16th century AD, the ultimate fate of Alexander's body remains a mystery, and none of his tombs has so far been identified.

## ALEXANDRIA

Alexandria, founded on 7 April 331 BC, was 'the crossroads of the whole world' according to Dio Chrysostom of Prusa, and 'the first city of the civilized world' in Diodorus' opinion.

A reconstruction of Alexandria. Today much of the ancient city is either buried beneath the modern one or lies submerged under the sea.

Strabo, who visited at the beginning of the Roman Period declared: 'The city has magnificent public precincts and the royal palaces which cover a fourth or even a third of the entire city. For just as each of the kings would for love of splendour add some ornament to the public monuments, so he would provide himself at his own expense with a residence in addition to those already standing so that now, to quote Homer, "there is building after building"'. He adds, 'The so-called *Sema* is also part of the royal palaces; this was an enclosure in which were the tombs of the kings and of Alexander.'

The city was divided into five quarters, each identified by a Greek letter. It gradually became densely populated, with thriving markets and guilds for all types of crafts and trades. People from all over the known world came and settled there, though it remained primarily Greek in culture. The remains of much of the city and its monuments now lie buried beneath

generals, Antigonus, who controlled land stretching from Greece to Gaza, declared himself (and his son, Demetrius) king of his domain, Ptolemy did likewise. In 304 BC he crowned himself King Ptolemy I of the newly founded Ptolemaic Dynasty, the first of 15 kings to bear that name. After further fighting, Alexander's hard-won empire settled into three major territories – Macedonian, Seleucid and Ptolemaic – each vying with the others for more influence. After an influx of Greek settlers, Alexandria slowly began to build its reputation as the premier trading port of the Mediterranean and became Egypt's first city, with ancient Memphis relegated to second place.

the modern city, inaccessible, or are submerged under the sea, a result of subsidence and seismic activity, where they are gradually being explored and revealed by underwater archaeologists.

Alexandria was the jewel in the Ptolemies' crown – it formed a showcase for their wealth and splendour from which they could display their success to the world. Not only was Alexander's tomb (see p. 191) a major tourist draw, but the Mouseion, which included the famous library of Alexandria, perhaps founded under Ptolemy I, was also the world's premier centre of learning, attracting scholars from across the Mediterranean world. Another major attraction was the Pharos lighthouse, one of the Seven Wonders of the Ancient World, which could safely guide ships to port from far out at sea, ensuring the steady flow of trade goods. Alexandria even boasted its own equivalent of the Olympic games, held every four years and initiated by Ptolemy II in honour of his dynasty, while great festivals and theatrical performances were also a frequent pleasure of Alexandrian life. On the other hand, the city was also infamous for its riotous inhabitants – the notorious 'Alexandrian mob', whose not infrequent involvement in politics could be to the benefit or detriment of the Ptolemaic kings. The mob ensured the accession of Ptolemy V; was incited to murder Ptolemy VI, but did not carry it out; and showed clear hostility to Ptolemy XII because of his pro-Roman sympathies.

A tomb at Taposiris Magna built in imitation of the famous Pharos lighthouse of Alexandria.

The Ptolemaic Dynasty remained in power for roughly 300 years, and manifested itself through a mixture of Egyptian and Greek-Macedonian traditions. Understanding that the security of their rule rested on appeasing the overall population, the Ptolemies patronized the great temples and encouraged the traditional religion by giving funds to the priesthoods. As with Alexander before them, depictions of the Ptolemies were carved on the walls of Egypt's temples; shown ever youthful, ever dutiful to their obligations to the gods, they wear the traditional crowns, uraei, false beards and kilts of a Ramesses II or Thutmose III and stand beside titularies spelling out their names in hieroglyphs. Royal statues were also produced in the traditional style, with muscular bodies, short kilts and the *Nemes*-headdress falling over their shoulders. To the casual observer, nothing had changed – until he looked into his purse. There, coins of silver and bronze displayed the profiles of royalty, Alexander and Zeus-Ammon with a very Greek realism, heads adorned with curling locks and unfamiliar diadems, while their reverse sides were emblazoned with the Ptolemaic eagle perched on a lightning bolt.

Egypt's administration continued to operate on traditional lines – the country remained divided into nomes and all land belonged to the crown. Detailed bureaucratic records were kept and taxes were collected with apparently great efficiency, providing funds for the extravagances of the Ptolemaic court. In the early Ptolemaic Period, the old Egyptian elite remained active too, including members of the 30th Dynasty royal family. The eldest son of Nectanebo II returned to Egypt under Alexander or the early Ptolemies and commissioned a statue, indicating his continued affluence and importance, while a great-nephew of Nectanebo I, also called Nectanebo, acted as mayor of Sile in the eastern Delta and served as a generalissimo under Ptolemy I.

Nevertheless, despite the Ptolemies' promotion of Egyptian tradition, Greek-Macedonian influence was strong. Anyone wishing to enter government administration was required to read and write Greek, while in the early Ptolemaic Period top bureaucrats were all chosen from the Greek elite. High-level officials bearing Egyptian names did continue to operate in the provincial administration under Ptolemy II, however. But Ptolemy V was the first to be crowned according to Egyptian custom at Memphis, and apparently only Cleopatra VII learnt to speak Egyptian. Furthermore, in addition to portraying themselves as true pharaohs, the Ptolemies also had to follow Macedonian royal traditions. To be regarded as a legitimate Macedonian king (a *basileus*), Ptolemy I required the army's support – which he could count on – and had to be a member of the Argead (Alexander's) bloodline; to this end, he spread the story that his father was not in fact Lagus, but Philip II, Alexander's father. Each Ptolemy also had to prove himself as the ideal citizen of a Greek *polis*. He had to be a saviour and protector to his people, a man of exceptional character who made donations to the great cities and their temples, and a source of wisdom, encouraging learning throughout his territory.

One curious feature of Ptolemaic kingship was the frequent marriage of true brothers and sisters, beginning with that of Ptolemy II and Queen Arsinoe II.

A basalt statue of Ptolemy I, now in the British Museum, London, which presents the Greek-Macedonian king in the manner of a traditional pharaoh.

A coin bearing the image of Ptolemy II and Arsinoe II. Coins of the Ptolemaic Period display a level of portraiture absent in the earlier phases of Egyptian history, and are strongly influenced by Greek styles.

This has often been explained as inspired by ancient Egyptian practice, but the pharaohs did not marry their true siblings, only half-brothers and half-sisters. The Ptolemies may have misunderstood this or were perhaps directly copying the mythical union of Osiris and his sister Isis. They may equally have been acting in imitation of the marriage between Zeus, who was claimed as a direct ancestor by Ptolemy II, and Hera. Ptolemaic queens frequently served as full co-regents, wielding tremendous power and sometimes instigating civil wars.

Ptolemy I inherited an empire that stretched westwards from Egypt across North Africa, and northeast into Palestine, and the military exploits and territorial expansionism of the Ptolemies would have pleased even Ramesses II. Displays of military strength, and the respect they gained, were of great importance to these kings, so that from the very beginning they set out to conquer further territory in the northern Levant and among the Aegean islands. Ptolemy I took Cyprus and lent his support to fighting in Macedon; Ptolemy II invaded parts of modern Turkey and some of the Aegean islands; Ptolemy III extended his territory into Syria, parts of the Aegean and northern Nubia. Throughout these campaigns, the Ptolemies' military tactics derived from those of Alexander, to the extent that they even used African elephants and excluded the Egyptian warrior class. Only under Ptolemy IV, when Antiochus III attempted to regain Syrian territory, did a Ptolemaic king for the first time include these respected native Egyptian warriors in his army.

## The Fall of the Ptolemies

Despite initial success at ensuring Egypt's continuing unity, in the 2nd century BC the Ptolemaic Dynasty began to implode, collapsing under the weight of dynastic infighting, Egyptian rebellion and the increasing influence of Rome. The rot set in under Ptolemy IV, who lived a life of excess, obsessed with festivities and neglectful of his administrative duties, and constantly under the sway of powerful advisers. He was, however, a talented diplomat and warrior, leading Egypt successfully in arbitrating in squabbles between its allies and defeating the Seleucid king Antiochus III at the battle of Raphia (modern Rafah, south of Gaza) to secure the country's northeastern border. Ptolemy IV died in 205 BC, aged around 40. Shortly afterwards his wife, Arsinoe III, was murdered, falling victim to a palace coup, and the Ptolemaic Dynasty continued on its bloody descent.

Ptolemy IV was succeeded by his eldest son, Ptolemy V, who was only six years old at the time. On 26 March 196 BC, the child was crowned at Memphis following ancient tradition, no doubt in an attempt to gain favour with the priesthood in this most tumultuous of times. As Ptolemy sat on his throne, surely mesmerized by the ancient rites being conducted around him, curious and perhaps a little

A statue of Arsinoe II, the first Ptolemaic queen to marry her own brother (Ptolemy II). This began a tradition of brother-sister marriage that lasted until the end of the Ptolemaic Dynasty, ensuring that royal power was confined to a small number of people.

frightened, he could not have known what his future would hold. This pomp and ceremony, so reassuring in its re-enactments of age-old rites – the same words, the same movements, timeless in their performance – may have given him the impression that his reign would be just as eternal, blessed by the gods, a continuation of those of his royal predecessors – opulent, powerful, successful. But it was not to be. He spent his youth manipulated by influential advisers, and, by the age of 16, was married off to a 10-year-old Syrian princess for the sake of diplomacy. To make matters worse, rebellion was in the air.

The Theban region had been in revolt since 206 BC, first led by a 'pharaoh' named Harwennefer and then under Ankhwennefer, both assisted by Nubian military support. Another revolt, this time in the Delta, only ended in 185 BC. In the eyes of the rebels, the Ptolemaic Dynasty failed to rule according to *maat*, and had done nothing but exploit Egypt's resources and people. Thebes remained independent, with its influence stretching as far north as Abydos, until 186 BC, when the Ptolemaic regime restored control and brought the rebel leaders to Memphis to be punished. Though no doubt invigorated by his success over his enemies, Ptolemy V had little time to celebrate; in 180 BC, before reaching his 30th birthday, he was dead, probably poisoned.

The throne then passed to the five- or six-year-old Ptolemy VI, who ruled alongside his mother until her death in 176 BC and later shared power with Cleopatra II – his sister-wife – and their younger brother Ptolemy VIII (nicknamed 'potbelly') between 169 and 164 BC. In 170 BC Egypt was invaded by the Seleucid king Antiochus IV, followed by a further invasion in 168 BC, when Antiochus had himself crowned in the traditional Egyptian manner and appointed a governor to rule in his name. Angered by the treatment of their Ptolemaic allies, the Romans intervened, entering Egypt and commanding Antiochus to leave; he duly departed, never to return. Though at this time the Romans acted only as national protectors, in the coming years Egypt would fall increasingly under their control. In 163 BC, when Ptolemy VIII declared himself sole ruler of Egypt, Rome interceded again, swiftly returning Ptolemy VI and Cleopatra II to power and sending Ptolemy VIII to rule in Libya after his expulsion by the Alexandrian mob. Nevertheless, Ptolemy VIII did eventually succeed to the throne in 145 BC, returning to Egypt after Ptolemy VI fell from his horse in battle and fractured his skull, dying five days later. The results were disastrous – civil war erupted, with Alexandria supporting Cleopatra II as sole ruler and the provinces supporting Ptolemy VIII.

A calcite head of Ptolemy V or VI, now in Berlin; he wears a Greek cloth diadem below his Double Crown, thereby emphasizing his legitimacy as a traditional pharaoh and as a Greek-Macedonian king.

Perhaps taking advantage of the situation, in 131 BC a rebel 'pharaoh' named Harsiese took control of Thebes for a few months. In 130 BC, after the Alexandrian mob tried to set fire to his royal palace, Ptolemy fled to Cyprus for a brief time. There, he murdered his own son by Cleopatra II, apparently sending the dismembered body to Cleopatra as a birthday present. It is probable that this tragic young prince should be equated with the ephemeral Ptolemy VII. Despite this horrific event, as well as continued infighting, reconciliation between the warring siblings occurred in around 124 BC, and Ptolemy VIII continued his oppressive rule until his death in 116 BC, at the age of about 65.

Further dynastic squabbling marred the reign of his son and successor, Ptolemy IX, who fled to Cyprus in 107 BC, accused of attempting to murder his mother, Cleopatra III. Ptolemy X, a younger son of Ptolemy VIII, was crowned in his place. Allegedly monstrously fat, and extremely unpopular with the people of Alexandria, Ptolemy X was himself driven out of Egypt in 88 BC and was apparently killed on the way to Cyprus by the Alexandrian admiral Chaereas. Ptolemy IX then returned to Egypt and ruled until his death in 80 BC, leaving his daughter Berenice III to rule for six months as an extremely beloved queen. For the last 19 days of this period

Ptolemy VIII followed by Cleopatra II and III, both of whom he married, in a scene from the Temple of Sobek at Kom Ombo. The three royals shared power, but had an increasingly tumultuous relationship.

she reigned as co-regent with her new husband Ptolemy XI; at the end of the 19th day he had her murdered. In retaliation for this heinous act, the Alexandrian mob dragged Ptolemy from his palace and executed him in the gymnasium. Any remaining glimmers of the prestige of the Egyptian kingship had now long since dimmed – ruined, tarnished and battered by the Ptolemies' violence and incompetence, and left to decay in the shadows of Egypt's most ancient monuments.

Ptolemy XII, a son of Ptolemy IX, then reigned from 80 BC. He gained the nickname 'flute player' because, according to Strabo, he practised the instrument frequently and even held playing contests in the royal palace. Cassius Dio records that he bribed the Romans to support his kingship, taxing the Egyptians to raise the money, and refused to intervene when the Romans took Cyprus, which had effectively been under Egyptian control since Ptolemy I. In 58 BC, the ensuing rebellion chased him out of Egypt and he made his way to Rome, leaving his daughter Berenice IV to rule in his stead. From Rome, Ptolemy planned his return to power, attempting to gather Roman support for his cause. The Egyptians were glad to see him go, and, hearing of his plans, sent a delegation to Rome to argue the case for his continued exile.

Thanks to Ptolemy's scheming, however, few survived the journey to Italy and those that did arrive were too afraid to speak out against him. Though the Romans eventually voted against supporting him anyway, the great general and consul Pompey, along with the general Aulus Gabinius, favoured Ptolemy's restoration to power. With this encouragement, in 55 BC Ptolemy returned to Egypt and had Berenice – his own daughter – put to death. He then ruled with the backing of Roman troops left in Egypt by Gabinius until his death in 51 BC.

In accordance with Ptolemy XII's stipulations in his will, the throne passed to his daughter, Cleopatra VII, and her younger brother, Ptolemy XIII. Continuing a family tradition, in 49 BC they began a war against one another, which ended in Cleopatra being exiled to Syria. A year later, with civil war in Rome now raging, Pompey was defeated by Julius Caesar at the battle of Pharsalus and fled to Egypt, only to be assassinated by order of Ptolemy XIII. Caesar himself then entered Egypt, and, allied with Cleopatra, attempted to bring an end to the dynastic squabbling. War ensued, leaving Ptolemy XIII dead and Cleopatra now ruling alongside the young Ptolemy XIV. Soon after, Cleopatra accompanied Caesar (her lover), their young son Ptolemy Caesarion, and Ptolemy XIV to Rome, remaining there until Caesar's assassination in 44 BC.

Upon their return to Egypt, Ptolemy XIV was himself assassinated and replaced by Caesarion, now crowned as Ptolemy XV.

Cleopatra met and fell in love with the Roman general and politician Mark Antony at Ephesus in 41 BC. They married, and Antony lived in Alexandria when not on campaign. Although previously allied, ongoing political disputes led to war between Antony and Cleopatra's forces on the one hand, and Octavian, the great-nephew and adopted heir of Julius Caesar, as representative of Rome, on the other. With the battle of Actium in 31 BC, ultimately lost by Antony's fleet, the prospect of an Egypt free from Roman rule sank with the burning remains of his ships into the depths of the Ionian Sea. Antony and Cleopatra fled back to Alexandria, where each committed suicide; Cleopatra died on 12 August 30 BC, her story, or myth, forever enshrined in the accounts of classical writers, and inspiring poets and playwrights down through the ages.

Soon afterwards Octavian murdered Ptolemy XV. Now in Alexandria and without opposition, Octavian was proclaimed king of Egypt from the Egyptian new year – 31 August 30 BC. From this moment, Egypt became a Roman province. Before leaving the country, Octavian (Augustus Caesar from 27 BC) visited the tomb of Alexander the Great, and, by touching the corpse of the great empire builder created a physical link between the very beginning of the Ptolemaic Dynasty, their bloody demise and Egypt's future. As a final insult to the Ptolemaic line, he refused to visit their nearby tombs.

## Roman Egypt

Although the arrival of the Romans is often regarded as the end of pharaonic civilization, it is not the end of the pharaonic office. Officially it was now occupied by the Roman emperor, irrespective of whether or not he ever set foot in his newly acquired province. And it truly was *his* province; senators were banned from entering Egypt without the express permission of the emperor and Egyptians were barred from the administration. The country was now overseen by a Roman prefect, an individual appointed directly by the emperor and answerable only to him; this was an unusual situation, as Roman provinces were typically governed by members of the senate. Below the prefect, four regional administrators oversaw the governors of each nome. Egypt's importance, and thus the need for such close control, lay in the fertility of its land. Under this new regime, the country would be little more than a source of grain, feeding the empire and powering its armies.

Nevertheless, traditional temples continued to be built and embellished across the country, with many surviving today – Kom Ombo, Esna, Edfu, Dendera and Philae, for example, were completed or decorated under Roman rule. In each of these temples, the great emperors of Rome are depicted and described as true

The head of a colossal statue of Augustus, from Meroe, Sudan, now in the British Museum, London. Augustus was the first Roman emperor to rule Egypt as pharaoh, marking a new era in Egyptian history.

OPPOSITE **A basalt statue of Queen Cleopatra VII, now in the State Hermitage Museum, St Petersburg, Russia, She reigned as pharaoh during the last years of the Ptolemaic Dynasty, and her life story and relationships with Julius Caesar and Mark Antony continue to excite popular imagination 2000 years after her suicide.**

pharaohs: at Esna, Trajan looms large on the outer wall, gripping hundreds of enemies by the hair and raising his mace high above his head, ready to bring it crashing down upon them; at Dendera, Augustus, Nero, Tiberius, Claudius and Trajan offer to the gods; while the walls of Edfu bear the cartouches of Roman emperors from Augustus to Marcus Aurelius. Although most emperors would never see these carvings, nor perhaps even care about their existence, to the Egyptian priests they represented the continuing presence of the pharaoh – he might now be an absentee-landlord, and sometimes his cartouche might simply read 'Caesar', but at least the divine office remained occupied. So long as Egypt had a king, *maat* had a champion.

Following Augustus' departure, only five Roman emperors visited Egypt. The first of these was Vespasian, who in AD 69 spent an entire winter in Alexandria. Not yet emperor, the main aim of his journey was to collect money for himself and grain for Rome, as well as to gain backing from the Prefect of Alexandria in his bid to become emperor. A public propaganda campaign followed, in which he was proclaimed Serapis incarnate and a son of Amun. Later, having gained the support he needed, and thus control of Rome's grain supply, Vespasian was proclaimed

A relief showing the Roman emperor Trajan making an offering before Hathor and Ihy at the Temple of Hathor, Dendera.

OPPOSITE **A white marble statue of Antinous as Osiris. Antinous, lover of Hadrian, drowned in the Nile during an imperial visit to Egypt, prompting the emperor-pharaoh to commemorate him by founding a city in Middle Egypt near the site of the tragedy. Originally from Hadrian's villa at Tivoli, the statue is now in the Gregorian Egyptian Museum, Vatican City.**

emperor, first in Egypt and soon after in the Roman senate. Curiously, Cassius Dio records that during Vespasian's time in Alexandria, the new emperor displayed supernatural abilities, healing one man's withered hand by stepping on it and another man's blindness by spitting on his eyes. Despite his apparent pretensions as a healer, in public demonstrations the Alexandrians mocked Vespasian and chanted slogans at him for failing to reward them for their role in raising him to the purple. In fact, their only reward was to be taxed relentlessly, and in greater amounts than they had been forced to pay before.

In AD 130–31 Hadrian spent eight to ten months in Egypt, a long visit paid for by the local population. While touring the country he offered sacrifices to the general Pompey, hunted lions to the west of the Nile Delta and visited the Colossi of Memnon at Thebes – the already ancient remains of Amenhotep III's mortuary temple. He also founded the only new Roman settlement in Egypt, Antinoopolis, named after his lover, Antinous, who had drowned in the Nile there. Despite this tragic event, Hadrian was so taken with Egypt that he built up a considerable collection of pharaonic and Egyptianizing art works at his villa in Tivoli, outside Rome, including Nilotic scenes.

Septimius Severus visited Egypt in AD 199–200, leaving a series of administrative reforms and legal judgments in his wake. His main legacy was the granting of city councils to the capitals of Egypt's nomes, thereby allowing them the additional rights already held by Egypt's Greek-style *poleis*, such as Alexandria. Caracalla, Septimius Severus' son, cast a much darker shadow over Egyptian life. Upon hearing of insults directed at him from Alexandria, mainly accusing him of being involved in the murder of his brother and co-ruler, Geta, he set out to exact his revenge on the city in AD 215, under the official pretence that he wished to worship Serapis and visit the tomb of Alexander, whom he regarded as an inspiration. After fulfilling both of these objectives, Caracalla put his true plan into action. In the account of Cassius Dio, he met the city's leading citizens and invited them to dinner, after which he had them put to death. He then sent his soldiers into the city, and they spent days slaughtering its inhabitants and plundering its resources. For much of this time, Caracalla was himself present and had a personal hand in the killing; at other times he sent commands from his quarters in the Temple of Serapis. Foreigners, except merchants, were expelled from the city, and shrines were despoiled. In contrast to Cassius Dio's account, Herodius records that Caracalla's rage was directed exclusively at the city's youth, whom he tricked into assembling on a large plain before ordering his army to massacre them.

The last emperor to visit Egypt was Diocletian, who reigned from AD 284 to 305. He is most notable for reorganizing the Roman provinces, subdividing them throughout the entire empire. Egypt did not escape his reforms: a new taxation system was implemented that ended the special favours shown to the Greek elite, and regional boundaries were restructured, dismantling the age-old nome system. The country's right to a separate coinage from Rome was also revoked. The Egyptians resisted these reforms – revolts erupted across the country, ultimately leading to the complete destruction of Coptos and Busiris. Amid this chaos, Diocletian himself entered Egypt and laid siege to Alexandria; its citizens finally capitulated after eight months, in AD 298. His success was memorialized by the raising of (the so-called) 'Pompey's Pillar' in Alexandria, which once bore a statue of the emperor seated on his horse. Afterwards, Diocletian travelled south to expel Nubian raiders from Upper Egypt, and decided to set Egypt's southern border at its traditional location at Philae, just south of Aswan. The emperor returned to Egypt in AD 302, when he dispensed bread to the people of Alexandria and spoke out against the religion of Manichaeism. In AD 303 he initiated the 'great persecution' against Christians, leading to the deaths of thousands across Egypt.

'Pompey's Pillar' in Alexandria was actually erected under Diocletian to commemorate his successful eight-month siege of Alexandria.

## Diocletian – The Last Pharaoh?

Although Diocletian abdicated in AD 305, retirement from pharaonic office came only with death. In a curious twist of history, however, this was not to be the case for Diocletian. For despite the fact that he died in AD 313, receiving a burial in his palace mausoleum on the Croatian coast at Split, to the Egyptians his reign never ended. With the empire's conversion to Christianity and the banning of pagan temples and cult ceremonies, many of Egypt's temples were converted into Christian churches, but the old ways persisted, especially in the south. And so, to avoid any reference to Christian emperors, the continuing, endless reign of Diocletian was used for dating purposes by Egypt's priests.

The last preserved royal cartouche was carved on a stele from Armant dating to AD 340 – 'year 57 of Diocletian' (27 years after his death); the surrounding text refers to Diocletian as King of Upper and Lower Egypt, Lord of the Two Lands,

Son of Re, Lord of Crowns and Caesar – a true pharaoh with a full titulary. An inscription in Demotic – a late, cursive form of written Egyptian – in the Temple of Isis at Philae includes a mention of 'year 90 of Diocletian', while the last known hieroglyphic inscription, also found at Philae, commemorates the birth festival of Osiris in 'year 110 of Diocletian' – 24 August AD 394. References in Demotic continued: one Demotic graffito at Philae dates to 'year 124 of Diocletian' (AD 407/408), and another to his year 152 (AD 435). The last dated Demotic inscription was written at Philae on 11 December AD 452, corresponding to Diocletian's 169th year as king.

This is still not the end of Diocletian's eternal 'reign', however. Despite his persecution of the Christians, it was his regnal year count – this pagan 'era of Diocletian', as used by the fading and floundering cults of the traditional gods – that the early Coptic Christians adopted for their own dating system (though it is also found in secular texts). Although dates in the 'era of Diocletian' continue to be found in Coptic and Greek texts until the 14th century AD (the 1055th year of his reign), in Nubia from the 8th century AD the same system began to be referred to as the 'era of martyrs' instead – some Copts wanting to connect themselves more with the victims of Diocletian's persecution than with the man himself. Over time it became customary for Copts to date events using this latter system, so that at first it existed concurrently with its identical ancestor before ultimately outliving it. In this form, Diocletian's regnal years continue to be counted, surviving to the present day in the Coptic calendar.

In the light of this, can Diocletian be regarded as the last pharaoh? The Egyptian priests certainly treated him this way. He was the last to be cited in the traditional dating system, the last to hold full pharaonic titles and the last ruler actually to step foot in Egypt, not to mention the last to use his authority to significantly change the country. In one respect, then, with his death in AD 313 the great kingship of Egypt, which had endured for over three thousand years of mortals, back through the age of the spirits of the dead, demi-gods and gods – all the way to the beginning of time – ceased to exist, extinguished with Diocletian's final breath. But from another point of view, the reign of Diocletian never ended, his regnal years forever ticking by to the present day, the eternal holder of an eternal office.

A bust of Diocletian, now in the Chateau de Vaux-le-Vicomte in France. The Egyptians continued to count the years of Diocletian's reign beyond his death and his name was the last to be placed in a royal cartouche.

Khasekhemwy

Djoser

Khufu

# THE PHARAOHS: BRIEF LIVES

The following king list and chronology is based on that proposed by Dodson and Hilton, *The Complete Royal Families of Ancient Egypt* (2004). The name cited for each king is the one by which he is most popularly known; in the majority of cases this is the birth name. Dates are conjectural until 664 BC, when the chronology is secure. Before this time, dates are only provided when reasonably sure, though they are by no means exact.

## PREDYNASTIC PERIOD
**Badarian Culture (5000–4000 BC)**
**Naqada I Culture (4000–3500 BC)**
**Naqada II Culture (3500–3150 BC)**
**Naqada III Culture (3150–3000 BC)**

## EARLY DYNASTIC PERIOD
### The 1st Dynasty (c. 3100 BC–)
**Hor-Aha**
Hor-Aha, meaning 'Horus the fighter', can possibly be equated with Menes of Thinis, referred to by classical authors as the first pharaoh. His 'Dynasty o' predecessor, Narmer, is also a possibility. He is buried at Abydos.
**Djer**
**Djet**
**Den**

**Adjib**
**Semerkhet**
**Qaa**

### The 2nd Dynasty
**Hetepsekhemwy**
**Nebre**
**Ninetjer**
**Weneg**
**Sened**
**Peribsen**
**Khasekhem(wy)**          (2611–2584 BC)
Inscriptions on two royal statues of Khasekhem(wy) from Hierakonpolis refer to the deaths of 47,209 northern enemies, indicative of large scale warfare, while late in his reign, the king changed his name from the Horus Khasekhem, meaning 'Appearance-of-Power', to the Horus and Seth Khasekhemwy, meaning 'Appearance-of-the-Two-Powers'. He is buried at Abydos.

## THE OLD KINGDOM
### The 3rd Dynasty
**Djoser**          (2584–2565 BC)
Djoser (Horus Netjerikhet), along with his architect, Imhotep, was responsible for the first step pyramid and thus also for the first large-scale

use of stone in construction. Despite these achievements, however, little else beyond his Saqqara funerary complex is known of him, except that he commissioned a building at Heliopolis and sent missions to the Sinai to quarry semiprecious stones.
**Sanakht**          (2565–2556 BC)
**Sekhemkhet**          (2556–2550 BC)
**Khaba**          (2550–2544 BC)
**Huni**          (2544–2520 BC)

### The 4th Dynasty
**Sneferu**          (2520–2470 BC)
A son of Huni, Sneferu built three pyramids, including the first smooth-sided 'true' pyramid. He also launched military campaigns into Libya and Nubia and sent quarrying expeditions into the Sinai for turquoise; 40 ship-loads of cedar, probably from the Lebanon, are also reported to have arrived in Egypt during his reign. Sneferu was probably buried in the Red Pyramid at Dahshur, though his nearby Bent Pyramid has also been suggested as a possibility.
**Khufu**          (2470–2447 BC)
The builder of the Great Pyramid at Giza, Khufu also sent expeditions to the diorite quarries northwest of Abu

**Menkaure**

**Userkaf**

**Pepi I**

Simbel and to the quarries of Sinai.
Only one statuette is known of him, a
tiny ivory piece excavated at Abydos.

| Djedefre | (2447–2439 BC) |
| Set?ka | (2439–2437 BC) |
| Khafre | (2437–2414 BC |

Builder of the second Giza pyramid
and also the Great Sphinx.

| Menkaure | (2414–2396 BC) |
| Shepseskaf | (2396–2392 BC) |

## The 5th Dynasty

| Userkaf | (2392–2385 BC) |
| Sahure | (2385–2373 BC) |

Under Sahure, the first recorded
expedition to the land of Punt, located
somewhere on the Red Sea coast,
brought large quantities of myrrh back
to Egypt. The turquoise quarries of the
Sinai were also worked, as well as the
diorite quarries of Nubia. Sahure was
the first king to build his pyramid at
the site of Abu Sir, south of Giza.

| Neferirkare | (2373–2363 BC) |
| Shepseskare | (2363–2362 BC) |
| Neferefre | (2363–2359 BC) |
| Niuserre | (2359–2348 BC) |
| Menkauhor | (2348–2340 BC) |
| Djedkare | (2340–2312 BC) |
| Unas | (2312–2282 BC) |

Unas was the first king to include
the Pyramid Texts on the walls of his
pyramid chambers, at Saqqara.

## The 6th Dynasty

| Teti | (2282–2270 BC) |

Teti initiated administrative reforms
and was, according to Manetho, killed
by his bodyguards. His pyramid is at
Saqqara.

| Userkare | (2270–2265 BC) |

Absent from many king lists, and
regarded by some scholars as a
usurper, Userkare only reigned for a
short time. He was perhaps related to
a king of the 5th Dynasty.

| Pepi I | (2265–2219 BC) |

A son of Teti, Pepi I was responsible
for major building works at various
key sites, including Abydos and
Hierakonpolis, where two copper
statues of the king were found. He
also launched campaigns into Nubia
and southern Palestine, and was the
target of a failed harem conspiracy.
His pyramid is at Saqqara.

| Merenre | (2219–2212 BC) |
| Pepi II | (2212–2118 BC) |

The longest ruling pharaoh, Pepi II
came to the throne at a young age.
As a result of his long reign, many of
his heirs predeceased him, leading to
succession problems that hastened
the collapse of the Old Kingdom. His
pyramid is at Saqqara.

| Merenre? | (2118–2117 BC) |

## THE FIRST INTERMEDIATE PERIOD

### The 7th and 8th Dynasties

**Netjerkare**

**Menkare**

**Neferkare**

**Neferkare Neby**

**Djedkare**

**Neferkare Khendu**

**Merenhor**

**Nikare**

**Neferkare Tereru**

**Neferkauhor**

**Neferkare Pepysonbe**

**Neferkamin**

**Qakare**

**Ibi**

**Neferkaure**

**Neferkauhor**

**Neferirkare**

### The 9th and 10th Dynasties

**Akhtoy I**

**Neferkare**

**Akhtoy II**

**Senen [...]**

**Akhtoy III**

**Akhtoy IV**

**(various)**

**Meryhathor**

**Akhtoy V**

**Merykare**

| ? | (–2040 BC) |

Montuhotep II

Amenemhat III

Wahibre Hor

## The 11th Dynasty

| | |
|---|---|
| Montuhotep I | (2160– BC) |
| Intef I | (–2123 BC) |
| Intef II | (2123–2074 BC) |
| Intef III | (2074–2066 BC) |

## THE MIDDLE KINGDOM
### The 11th Dynasty (continued)

**Montuhotep II**  (2066–2014 BC)
Montuhotep was a Theban king who successfully united the country, thereby ending the First Intermediate Period and instigating the Middle Kingdom. After uniting the country he secured its borders and set about building monuments, including his tomb at Deir el-Bahri in Thebes.

| | |
|---|---|
| **Montuhotep III** | (2014–2001 BC) |
| **Montuhotep IV** | (2001–1994 BC) |

### The 12th Dynasty

**Amenemhat I**  (1994–1964 BC)
Perhaps originally vizier under Montuhotep IV, it is unclear how Amenemhat came to power. He is responsible for founding the city of Amenemhat-Itj-Tawy, just north of the Faiyum, and may have been killed as part of a palace conspiracy. He was buried beneath his pyramid at Lisht, probably close to his newly founded capital.

| | |
|---|---|
| **Senwosret I** | (1974–1929 BC) |

| | |
|---|---|
| **Amenemhat II** | (1932–1896 BC) |
| **Senwosret II** | (1900–1880 BC) |
| **Senwosret III** | (1881–1840 BC) |

Increased centralization led to the weakening of provincial power under Senwosret III. He also expanded Egypt's control of Nubia, setting the country's southern boundary at Semna. After 41 years of rule, he was buried beneath a pyramid at Dahshur, but also had a cenotaph complex built at Abydos.

| | |
|---|---|
| **Amenemhat III** | (1842–1794 BC) |
| **Amenemhat IV** | (1798–1785 BC) |
| **Sobekneferu** | (1785–1781 BC) |

## THE SECOND INTERMEDIATE PERIOD
### The 13th Dynasty

| | |
|---|---|
| **Sobekhotep I** | (1781 BC–) |
| Sekhemkare | |
| Nerikare | |
| **Amenemhat V** | |
| Sehetepibre | |
| **Amenemhat VI** | |
| Smenkare | |
| Iufeni | |
| Hotepibre | |
| Swadjkare | |
| Nedjemibre | |
| **Sobekhotep II** | |
| Reniseneb | |
| **Wahibre Hor** | |
| **Amenemhat VII** | |

| | |
|---|---|
| Wegaf | |
| Khendjer | |
| Smenkhkare | |
| Intef IV | |
| Meryibre | |
| **Sobekhotep III** | |
| Neferhotep I | |
| Sihathor | |
| **Sobekhotep IV** | |
| **Sobekhotep V** | |
| **Sobekhotep VI** | |
| Wahibre Iaib | |
| Merneferre Ay | |
| Ini I | |
| Sankhenre | |
| Mersekhemre | |
| Hori | |
| **Sobekhotep VII** | |
| Ini II | |
| Neferhotep II | |
| [5 unknown kings] | |
| Mer[...]re | |
| Merkheperre | |
| Merkare | |
| ? | |
| **Montuhotep V** | |
| [...]mesre? | |
| Ibi II | |
| [...]webenre | |
| Se[...]kare | |
| Seheqaenre | |
| Sekhaenre | |
| Sewahenre | (–1650 BC) |

Sobekemsaf I

Intef VII

Thutmose III

## The 14th Dynasty
A series of kings of unknown order.

## The 15th Dynasty
**Semken** (1650– BC)
**Aper-Anati**
**Sakirhar**
**Khyan**
**Apophis (Apepi)** (1585–1545 BC)
A Hyksos ruler who faced an attack by the Theban king Kamose, Apophis reigned for about 40 years. An inscription on a scribal palette indicates that he could read hieroglyphs, evidence of an increased Egyptianization among these 'rulers of foreign lands'.
**Khamudy** (1545–1535 BC)

## The 16th Dynasty
**?** (1650 BC–)
**Djehuty**
**Sobekhotep VIII**
**Neferhotep III**
**Montuhotepi**
**Nebiriau I**
**Nebiriau II**
**Semenre**
**Bebiankh**
**Sekhemre-Shedwaset**
**Dedumose I**
**Dedumose II**
**Montuemsaf**

**Montuhotep VI**
**Senwosret IV** (–1590 BC)

## The 17th Dynasty
**Rahotep** (1585 BC–)
**Sobekemsaf I**
**Intef V**
**Intef VI**
**Intef VII**
**Sobekemsaf II**
**Senakhtenre Tao I** (–1558 BC)
**Seqenenre Tao II** (1558–1553 BC)
This king, called 'the brave', fought against the Hyksos occupiers of northern Egypt. He died violently, either by assassination, fighting against enemy combatants or by execution following the loss of a battle. He was buried at Thebes.
**Kamose** (1553–1549 BC)
Little is known of Kamose beyond a campaign that he led against the Hyksos; this took him as far as their capital, Avaris – modern Tell el-Daba. His reign was short, seemingly only four years, and his mummy was found in a wooden coffin in a pit at Dra abu el-Naga at Thebes. Unfortunately, it crumbled to dust before an examination could be undertaken.

## THE NEW KINGDOM
## The 18th Dynasty
**Ahmose I** (1549–1524 BC)
Probably a child when crowned, Ahmose later liberated Egypt from the Hyksos domination and in doing so founded the New Kingdom. He then initiated many construction projects across the country and campaigned in Nubia, retaking territory lost with the collapse of the Middle Kingdom. Although his tomb has not yet been identified, he did build a cenotaph at Abydos – the last royal pyramid constructed in Egypt.
**Amenhotep I** (1524–1503 BC)
**Thutmose I** (1503–1491 BC)
**Thutmose II** (1491–1479 BC)
**Thutmose III** (1479–1424 BC)
Thutmose came to the throne as a child, and initially ruled as co-regent with his aunt Hatshepsut. After her death, he set about consolidating Egypt's control of the Levant, ultimately launching 17 campaigns into the region between his years 23 and 42 as king. His most significant battle occurred in his 23rd year, when he faced a coalition of Asiatics at the city of Megiddo – an event described in detail on the walls of the Temple of Amun at Karnak. In contrast to these Levantine battles,

**Hatshepsut**

**Akhenaten**

**Tutankhamun**

only minor skirmishes occurred in Nubia, which by this time had been annexed. Thutmose built extensively at Karnak, including a temple called the *Akh Menu*, close to the god Amun's sanctuary. He also constructed a mortuary temple at Deir el-Bahri, Thebes, beside that of Hatshepsut, and in his later years built and renovated temples in the provinces and in Nubia. Thutmose III died in the 54th year of his reign and was buried in KV 34 in the Valley of the Kings.

**Hatshepsut** (1472–1457 BC)
After the death of her husband, King Thutmose II, Hatshepsut ruled as queen regent during the infancy of her nephew, Thutmose III, before taking royal titles herself, serving as full co-regent until her death. She is best known for re-initiating contact with the land of Punt, an exotic trading partner of Egypt located somewhere on the Red Sea coast. An illustrated account of the voyage to Punt, including the goods brought back to Egypt, was carved on the walls of Hatshepsut's mortuary temple at Deir el-Bahri, Thebes. In the later reign of Thutmose III and under Amenhotep II her name and monuments were attacked. She was buried in KV 20, in the Valley of the Kings.

**Amenhotep II** (1424–1398 BC)
**Thutmose IV** (1398–1388 BC)
**Amenhotep III** (1388–1348 BC)
**Amenhotep IV /Akhenaten**
(1360–1343 BC)
Akhenaten (initially Amenhotep IV) founded the royal city of Akhetaten as a cult centre for the worship of the sun disc ('Aten'). Complete with government offices and palaces, this was also to be the site of the royal tomb and the burials of his courtiers. Akhenaten commanded the erasure of the god Amun's name wherever it was found, and later extended this ban to all traditional gods. As part of this religious upheaval, he also changed art conventions; people were now depicted with spindly legs, elongated heads and paunches, while the new state god, the Aten, could only be depicted as a disc, floating high in the sky, with rays of light descending from its surface, terminating in small hands. Akhenaten died after 17 years as king and was buried in his royal tomb at Amarna.

**Smenkhkare** (1346 BC)
**Neferneferuaten** (1346–1343 BC)
**Tutankhamun** (1343–1333 BC)
Tutankhamun, the son of Akhenaten and a secondary queen, came to the throne as a young boy. Known as

Tutankhaten while still at Akhetaten, the king was renamed Tutankhamun after moving to Memphis. After the tumult of the Amarna Period, Egypt now returned to its traditional religion. To commemorate this renewal, a large text, today known as the Restoration Stele, was erected in Tutankhamun's name within the Great Hypostyle Hall at Karnak Temple. Construction at the traditional centres of Karnak and Memphis began again, and the abandonment of Akhetaten commenced. Tutankhamun died in his late teens. Recent studies have shown that he suffered from a severe form of malaria and avascular bone necrosis, which meant he had trouble walking. Combined, these conditions may have contributed to his early death. His virtually intact tomb in the Valley of the Kings (KV 62) was discovered by Howard Carter in 1922.

**Ay** (1333–1328 BC)
**Horemheb** (1328–1298 BC)
Probably born in Hnes (Kom el-Ahmar Sawaris), south of the Faiyum Oasis, Horemheb was a military general for most of his career, serving under Tutankhamun, and built a tomb for himself at Saqqara. With the collapse of the 18th Dynasty royal line, Horemheb came to power and

Ramesses II

Merenptah

Ramesses VI

initiated a programme of restoration that continued into the succeeding Ramesside Period. While dismantling Akhetaten, he built extensively at Karnak, including pylon gateways and the first stage of the Great Hypostyle Hall. He also built a royal tomb for himself in the Valley of the Kings (KV 57), but this remained incomplete at the time of his death.

### The 19th Dynasty

**Ramesses I** (1298–1296 BC)

**Seti I** (1296–1279 BC)
Seti led the army during his father's reign and launched a campaign into Syria during his first year as king. He later also quelled a rebellion in Nubia. He constructed a magnificent cenotaph temple at Abydos and was buried in the Valley of the Kings (KV 17).

**Ramesses II** (1279–1212 BC)
Ramesses reigned for 67 years, and in that time presided over great building works and numerous campaigns. His most famous battle, against the Hittites at Kadesh, was depicted and described on temple walls across Egypt and in Nubia. Following the sealing of a treaty with the Hittites, peace also prevailed under Ramesses and lasted beyond his reign. He also developed

the important Ramesside royal city of Pi-Ramesses. Although Ramesses had many wives during his reign, none are more famous than Nefertari, whose tomb in the Valley of the Queens (QV 66) is one of the most beautiful in Egypt. Ramesses himself was buried in KV 7 in the Valley of the Kings.

**Merenptah** (1212–1201 BC)
Merenptah was the 13th son of Ramesses II. He sent campaigns into Nubia and Palestine, and faced a major incursion by the Libyans and Sea Peoples in his fifth year. He also sent grain to the Hittites during a time of famine. He was buried in KV 8 in the Valley of the Kings.

**Seti II** (1201–1195 BC)

**Amenmessu** (1200–1196 BC)

**Siptah** (1195–1189 BC)
Siptah came to the throne as a young boy, during which time effective power rested in the hands of Queen Tawosret, aided by an official named Bay. He reigned for only six years, perhaps contracting polio in that time. He outlived Bay, who was apparently executed in his fifth year, but not Tawosret, who succeeded him as sole ruler. Siptah was buried in KV 47 in the Valley of the Kings.

**Tawosret** (1189–1187 BC)

### The 20th Dynasty

**Sethnakht** (1187–1185 BC)

**Ramesses III** (1185–1153 BC)
Ramesses III faced two invasions by the Libyans and one from the Sea Peoples. He recorded his victories against these enemies on the walls of his great mortuary temple at Medinet Habu. He may have been assassinated as part of a harem conspiracy and was buried in KV 11 in the Valley of the Kings.

**Ramesses IV** (1153–1146 BC)

**Ramesses V** (1146–1141 BC)

**Ramesses VI** (1141–1133 BC)

**Ramesses VII** (1133–1125 BC)

**Ramesses VIII** (1125–1123 BC)

**Ramesses IX** (1123–1104 BC)

**Ramesses X** (1104–1094 BC)

**Ramesses XI** (1094–1064 BC)

**Herihor** (1075–1069 BC)

### THE THIRD INTERMEDIATE PERIOD
### The 21st Dynasty

**Smendes** (1064–1038 BC)

**Amenemnisu** (1038–1034 BC)

**Pinudjem I** (1049–1026 BC)

**Psusennes I** (1034–981 BC)
Psusennes I was responsible for developing the port town of Tanis into a major royal city, building it up using stonework dragged from nearby

Psusennes I

Taharqo

Ahmose II

Pi-Ramesses. His tomb was found at Tanis in 1940 by Pierre Montet and still contained much of his elaborate grave goods.

| | |
|---|---|
| **Amenemopet** | (984–974 BC) |
| **Osorkon the Elder** | (974–968 BC) |
| **Siamun** | (968–948 BC) |
| **Psusennes II** | (945–940 BC) |

## The 22nd Dynasty

**Shoshenq I**     (948–927 BC)

A pharaoh of Libyan descent, Shoshenq I sent a campaign into Palestine – the first since the Ramesside Period – and listed the locations he attacked on the walls of Karnak Temple. Shoshenq also installed one of his sons as high priest of Amun at Karnak, thereby reasserting royal influence over this important office. It is not known where Shoshenq I was buried, though Tanis, Bubastis and Memphis have all been suggested as possible locations.

| | |
|---|---|
| **Osorkon I** | (927–892 BC) |
| **Shoshenq II** | (895–895 BC) |
| **Takelot I** | (892–877 BC) |
| **Osorkon II** | (877–838 BC) |
| **Shoshenq III** | (838–798 BC) |
| **Shoshenq IV** | (798–786 BC) |
| **Pimay** | (786–780 BC) |
| **Shoshenq V** | (780–743 BC) |

| | |
|---|---|
| **Pedubast II** | (743–733 BC) |
| **Osorkon IV** | (733–715 BC) |

## The 23rd Dynasty

| | |
|---|---|
| **Harsiese** | (867–857 BC) |
| **Takelot II** | (841–815 BC) |
| **Pedubast I** | (830–805 BC) |
| **Iuput I** | (815–813 BC) |
| **Shoshenq VI** | (805–796 BC) |
| **Osorkon III** | (796–769 BC) |
| **Takelot III** | (774–759 BC) |
| **Rudamun** | (759–739 BC) |
| **Iny** | (739–734 BC) |
| **Peftjauawybast** | (734–724 BC) |

## The 24th Dynasty

| | |
|---|---|
| **Tefnakht** | (735–727 BC) |
| **Bakenrenef** | (727–721 BC) |

## The 25th Dynasty

| | |
|---|---|
| **Piye** | (752–721 BC) |
| **Shabaqo** | (721–707 BC) |

Following his brother Piye's military incursion into Egypt, Shabaqo set about consolidating Nubian control and afterwards began an extensive building campaign across the country. Shabaqo was buried beneath a pyramid (K.15) at el-Kurru, in modern Sudan.

| | |
|---|---|
| **Shabitqo** | (707–690 BC) |
| **Taharqo** | (690–664 BC) |
| **Tanutamani** | (664–656 BC) |

## THE LATE PERIOD
### The 26th Dynasty

**Psamtik I**     (664–610 BC)

Raised at the Assyrian court, Psamtik returned to Egypt to rule in the name of the Assyrians following their defeat of the 25th Dynasty. Despite his background, he, with the aid of foreign mercenaries, took control of the Delta for himself and by his ninth year also controlled Upper Egypt. He thus began the 26th Dynasty and a new period of unity, called the Late Period. He was buried at Sais.

| | |
|---|---|
| **Necho II** | (610–595 BC) |
| **Psamtik II** | (595–589 BC) |
| **Apries** | (589–570 BC) |
| **Ahmose II** | (570–526 BC) |

Ahmose II came to the throne as part of a military coup to remove the unpopular King Apries from power. He initiated building projects at Sais, Buto, Memphis and Abydos, though little survives. He was buried at Sais.

**Psamtik III**     (526–525 BC)

### The 27th Dynasty

| | |
|---|---|
| **Cambyses II** | (525–522 BC) |
| **Darius I** | (521–486 BC) |
| **Xerxes I** | (486–465 BC) |
| **Artaxerxes I** | (465–424 BC) |
| **Xerxes II** | (424 BC) |
| **Darius II** | (423–405 BC) |

Nepherites I

Ptolemy I

Ptolemy VI or V

### The 28th Dynasty

**Amyrtaeus** (404–399 BC)
Amyrtaeus liberated Egypt from the Persians, but was killed by Nepherites I.

### The 29th Dynasty

**Nepherites I** (399–393 BC)
**Pasherenmut** (393 BC)
**Hakor** (393–380 BC)
**Nepherites II** (380 BC)

### The 30th Dynasty

**Nectanebo I** (380–362 BC)
**Teos (Djedhor)** (365–360 BC)
**Nectanebo II** (360–342 BC)

### The Second Persian Period (The 31st Dynasty)

**Artaxerxes III** (342–338 BC)
**Artaxerxes IV (Arses)** (338–336 BC)
**Darius III** (335–332 BC)

### The Macedonian Dynasty

**Alexander the Great** (332–323 BC)
**Philip III Arrhidaeus** (323–317 BC)
**Alexander IV** (317–310 BC)

### THE PTOLEMAIC PERIOD

**Ptolemy I (Soter I)** (310–282 BC)
**Ptolemy II (Philadelphus)** (285–246 BC)
**Ptolemy III (Euergetes I)** (246–222 BC)
**Ptolemy IV (Philopater)** (222–205 BC)

**Ptolemy V (Epiphanes)** (205–180 BC)
**Ptolemy VI (Philometor)** (180–164 BC)
**Ptolemy VIII (Euergetes II)** (170–163 BC)
**Ptolemy VI (again)** (163–145 BC)
**Ptolemy VIII (again)** (145–116 BC)
**Ptolemy IX (Soter II)** (116–110 BC)
**Ptolemy X (Alexander I)** (110–109 BC)
**Ptolemy IX (again)** (109–107 BC)
**Ptolemy X (again)** (107–88 BC)
**Ptolemy IX (again)** (88–80 BC)
**Ptolemy XI (Alexander II)** (80 BC)
**Berenice III** (80 BC)
**Ptolemy XII (Neos Dionysos)** (80–58 BC)
**Berenice IV** (56 BC)
**Ptolemy XII (again)** (55–51 BC)
**Cleopatra VII Philopater** (51–30 BC)
Cleopatra VII was the last of the Ptolemaic pharaohs. Allied with Mark Antony, she brought Egypt out of decline and even expanded its control. However, with the defeat at the battle of Actium, and Antony and Cleopatra's subsequent suicides, Egypt was absorbed into the Roman Empire.
**Ptolemy XIII** (51–47 BC)
**Ptolemy XIV** (47–44 BC)
**Ptolemy XV** (41–30 BC)

### THE ROMAN PERIOD

**Augustus** (30 BC– AD 14)
**Tiberius** (AD 14–37)

**Gaius (Caligula)** (AD 37–41)
**Claudius** (AD 41–54)
**Nero** (AD 54–68)
**Galba** (AD 68–69)
**Otho** (AD 69)
**Vespasian** (AD 69–79)
**Titus** (AD 79–81)
**Domitian** (AD 81–96)
**Nerva** (AD 96–98)
**Trajan** (AD 98–117)
**Hadrian** (AD 117–138)
**Antoninus Pius** (AD 138–161)
**Marcus Aurelius** (AD 161–180)
**Lucius Verus** (AD 161–169)
**Commodus** (AD 180–192)
**Septimius Severus** (AD 193–211)
**Caracalla** (AD 198–217)
**Geta** (AD 209–212)
**Macrinus** (AD 217–218)
**Didumenianus** (AD 218)
**Severus Alexander** (AD 222–235)
**Gordian III** (AD 238–242)
**Philip** (AD 244–249)
**Decius** (AD 249–251)
**Gallus & Volusianus** (AD 251–253)
**Valerian** (AD 253–260)
**Gallienus** (AD 253–268)
**Macrianus & Quietus** (AD 260–261)
**Aurelian** (AD 270–275)
**Probus** (AD 276–282)
**Diocletian** (AD 284 – abdicated AD 305, died AD 313)

# FURTHER READING

## ANCIENT EGYPT – GENERAL

Brewer, D. J. and E. Teeter, *Egypt and the Egyptians* (2nd ed.; Cambridge: Cambridge University Press, 2007).

Clayton, P. A., *Chronicle of the Pharaohs* (London and New York: Thames & Hudson, 1994).

Dodson, A. and D. Hilton, *The Complete Royal Families of Ancient Egypt* (London and New York: Thames & Hudson, 2004).

Ikram, S., *Ancient Egypt: An Introduction* (Cambridge: Cambridge University Press, 2009).

Kemp, B., *Ancient Egypt: Anatomy of a Civilisation* (2nd ed.; London: Routledge, 2006).

Redford, D. B. (ed.), *The Oxford Encyclopedia of Ancient Egypt* (3 vols; Oxford: Oxford University Press, 2001).

Shaw, I. and P. Nicholson, *The British Museum Dictionary of Ancient Egypt* (London: British Museum, 2008).

Shaw, I. (ed.), *The Oxford History of Ancient Egypt* (Oxford, 2000).

Trigger, B. G. et al. (eds), *Ancient Egypt: A Social History* (Cambridge: Cambridge University Press, 1983).

Wilkinson, T. A. H., *The Rise and Fall of Ancient Egypt* (London and New York: Bloomsbury, 2010).

## KINGSHIP – GENERAL

Bonheme, M.-A. and A. Forgeau, *Pharaon – Les secrets du pouvoir* (Paris: Arman Colin, 1988).

Frankfort, H., *Kingship and the Gods: A Study of Ancient Near Eastern Religion as the Integration of Society and Nature* (Chicago: University of Chicago Press, 1948).

Morris, E. F., 'The Pharaoh and Pharaonic Office' in A. Lloyd, *A Companion to Ancient Egypt*, Vol. 1 (Chichester and Malden, Mass.: Wiley-Blackwell, 2010), 201–17.

O'Connor, D. and D. P. Silverman, (eds) *Ancient Egyptian Kingship* (Leiden: Brill, 1995).

Posener, G., *De la divinité du Pharaon* (Paris: Société Asiatique, 1960).

Shaw, G. J., 'Kingship' in I. Shaw and J. Allen (eds) *The Oxford Handbook of Egyptology* (Oxford, in press).

Shaw, G. J., *Royal Authority in Egypt's Eighteenth Dynasty* (Oxford: BAR International Series, 2008).

Ziegler, C., *The Pharaohs* (London: Thames & Hudson, 2002).

## TRANSLATIONS AND SOURCES

Breasted, J. H., *Ancient Records of Egypt* (5 vols; Chicago: University of Chicago Press, 1906–07).

Caminos, R., *Late-Egyptian Miscellanies* (London: Oxford University Press, 1954).

Cumming, B., *Egyptian Historical Records of the Later Eighteenth Dynasty* (Fascicles I–III; Warminster: Aris & Phillips, 1982–84).

Davies, B. G., *Egyptian Historical Records of the Later Eighteenth Dynasty* (Fascicles IV–VI; Warminster: Aris & Phillips, 1992–95).

Diodorus Siculus, *Library of History* (transl. by C. H. Oldfather; Book I; Cambridge, Mass.: Harvard University Press, 1933).

Frood, E., *Biographical Texts from Ramessid Egypt* (Leiden: Brill, 2007).

Helck, W., *Urkunden der 18. Dynastie* (Fascicles 17–22; Berlin, 1955–58).

Helck, W., *Historisch-biographische Texte der 2. Zwischenzeit und neue Texte der 18. Dynastie* (Wiesbaden: Harrassowitz, 1975).

Herodotus, *The Histories* (transl. by A. de Sélincourt; London: Penguin, 1996).

Kitchen, K. A., *Ramesside Inscriptions, Historical and Biographical* (8 vols; Oxford: Blackwell, 1969–90).

Kitchen, K. A., *Ramesside Inscriptions. Translated and Annotated* (Oxford: Blackwell, 1993– ).

Lichtheim, M., *Ancient Egyptian Literature* (3 vols; Berkeley: University of California Press, 1975–80).

Lichtheim, M., *Ancient Egyptian Autobiographies Chiefly of the Middle Kingdom* (Freiburg, Schweiz: Universitätsverlag, 1988).

Moran, W. L., *The Amarna Letters* (Baltimore and London: Johns Hopkins University Press, 1992).

Parkinson, R., *Voices from Ancient Egypt: An Anthology of Middle Kingdom Writings* (London: British Museum; Norman: University of Oklahoma Press, 1991).

Peden, A. J., *Egyptian Historical Inscriptions of the Twentieth Dynasty* (Jonsered: P. Åström, 1994).

Ritner, R. K., *The Libyan Anarchy: Inscriptions from Egypt's Third Intermediate Period* (Atlanta: Society of Biblical Literature; Leiden: Brill 2009).

Sethe, K., *Urkunden der 18. Dynastie* (Fascicles 1–16; Leipzig, 1906–09).

Sethe, K., *Urkunden des Alten Reichs* (Leipzig, 1933).

Strudwick, N., *Texts from the Pyramid Age* (Leiden: Brill, 2005).

Simpson, W. K. et al., *The Literature of Ancient Egypt* (New Haven and London: Yale University Press, 2003).

Wente, Edward F., *Late Ramesside Letters* (Chicago: University of Chicago Press, 1967).

## CHAPTER 1: PHARAONIC KINGSHIP: EVOLUTION AND IDEOLOGY

Barta, W., *Untersuchungen zur Göttlichkeit des regierenden Königs* (Munich: Deutscher Kunstverlag, 1975).

Goebs, K., *Crowns in Egyptian Funerary Literature: Royalty, Rebirth, and Destruction* (Oxford: Griffith Institute, 2008).

Guilhou, N., 'Myth of the Heavenly Cow' in J. Dieleman and W. Wendrich (eds), *UCLA Encyclopedia of Egyptology* (Los Angeles, 2010), http://digital2.library.ucla.edu/viewItem.do?ark=21198/zz002311pm

Gundlach, R., '"Horus in the Palace": The Centre of State and Culture in Pharaonic Egypt' in R. Gundlach and J. Taylor (eds), *Egyptian Royal Residences, 4. Symposium zur ägyptischen Königsideologie; 4th Symposium on Egyptian Royal Ideology; London, June, 1–5 2004* (Wiesbaden: Harrassowitz, 2009), 45–67.

Hardwick, T., 'The Iconography of the Blue Crown in the New Kingdom', *The Journal of Egyptian Archaeology* 89 (2003), 117–41.

Hornung, E., *The Ancient Egyptian Books of the Afterlife* (transl. by D. Lorton; Ithaca, N.Y.: Cornell University Press, 1999).

Lorton, D., 'Review: Towards a Constitutional Approach to Ancient Egyptian Kingship', *The Journal of the American Oriental Society* 99 (1979), 460–65.

Redford, D., *Pharaonic King-Lists, Annals and Day-Books: a Contribution to the Study of the Egyptian Sense of History* (Mississauga: Benben, 1986).

Shaw, G. J., 'The Meaning of the Phrase m Hm n stp-sA', *The Journal of Egyptian Archaeology* 96 (2010), 175–90.

Wainwright, G. A., 'The Red Crown in Early Prehistoric Times', *The Journal of Egyptian Archaeology* 9 (1923), 26–33.

Wilkinson, T. A. H., *Early Dynastic Egypt* (London and New York: Routledge, 1999).

Wilkinson, T. A. H., 'What a King is This: Narmer and the Concept of the Ruler', *The Journal of Egyptian Archaeology* 86 (2000), 23–32.

Williams, B. et al. 'The Metropolitan Museum Knife Handle and Aspects of Pharaonic Imagery before Narmer', *The Journal of Near Eastern Studies* 46 (1987), 245–85.

## CHAPTER 2: THE STORY OF THE TWO LANDS

Arnold, D., 'Amenemhat I and the Early Twelfth Dynasty at Thebes', *The Metropolitan Museum Journal* 26 (1991), 5–48.

Baines, J., 'Kingship Before Literature: the World of the King in the Old Kingdom' in R. Gundlach and C. Raedler (eds), *Selbstverständnis und Realität: Akten des Symposiums zur ägyptischen Königsideologie in Mainz, 15.-17.6.1995* (Wiesbaden: Harrassowitz, 1997), 125–74.

Barbotin, C., *Ahmosis et le début de la XVIIIe dynastie* (Paris: Pygmalion, 2008).

Baud, M., *Djéser et la IIIe Dynastie* (Paris: Pygmalion, 2002).

Bryan, B., *The Reign of Thutmose IV* (Baltimore: Johns Hopkins University Press, 1991).

Cline, E. H. and O'Connor, D., *Thutmose III: A New Biography* (Ann Arbor: University of Michigan Press, 2006).

Cline, Eric H. and O'Connor, D., *Amenhotep III: Perspectives on his Reign* (Ann Arbor: University of Michigan Press, 1998).

Favry, N., *Sésostris Ier et le début de la XIIe dynastie* (Paris: Pygmalion, 2009).

Gardiner, A. H., *Egypt of the Pharaohs* (Oxford: Clarendon Press, 1961).

Goedicke, H., *Die Stellung des Königs im Alten Reich* (Wiesbaden: Harrassowitz, 1960).

Grajetzki, W., *The Middle Kingdom of Ancient Egypt: History, Archaeology and Society* (London: Duckworth, 2006).

Hari, R., *Horemheb et la reine Moutnedjemet ou la fin d'une dynastie* (Geneva: Editions de Belles-Lettres, 1964).

Johnson, J. H., 'The Demotic Chronicle as a Statement of a Theory of Kingship', *The Journal of the Society for the Study of Egyptian Antiquities* 13 (1983), 61–72.

Kitchen, K. A., *The Third Intermediate Period in Egypt (1100–650 BC)* (2nd ed. with 2nd suppl.; Warminster: Aris & Phillips, 1996).

Leahy, A. B., 'The Libyan Period in Egypt: An Essay in Interpretation', *Libyan Studies* 16 (1985), 51–64.

Lloyd, A. B., 'The Inscription of Udjahorresnet, A Collaborator's Testament', *The Journal of Egyptian Archaeology* 68 (1982), 166–80.

Manetho, *Aegyptiaca* (transl. by W. G. Waddell; London: W. Heinemann; Cambridge, Mass.: Harvard University Press, 1940).

Manuelian, P. Der, *Studies in the Reign of Amenophis II* (Hildesheim: Gerstenberg, 1987).

Peden, A. J., *The Reign of Ramesses IV* (Warminster: Aris & Phillips, 1994).

Ratié, S., *La reine Hatchepsout: sources et problèmes* (Paris: Brill, 1979).

Redford, D. B., *Akhenaten. The Heretic King* (Princeton: Princeton University Press, 1984).

Redford, D. B., *Egypt, Canaan, and Israel in Ancient Times* (Princeton: Princeton University Press, 1992).

Simpson, W. K., 'A Statuette of King Nyneter', *The Journal of Egyptian Archaeology* 42 (1956), 45–49.

Spalinger, A. J., 'The Concept of the Monarchy During the Saite Epoch – An Essay of Synthesis', *Orientalia* 47 (1978), 12–36.

Spalinger, A. J., 'Sovereignty and Theology in New Kingdom Egypt: Some Cases of Tradition', *Saeculum* 47 (1996), 217–38.

Tallet, P., *Sésostris III et la fin de la XIIe Dynastie* (Paris: Pygmalion, 2005).

## CHAPTER 3: BECOMING PHARAOH

Barta, W., 'Thronbesteigung und Krönungsfeier als unterschiedliche Zeugnisse königlicher Herrschaftsübernahme', *Studien zur Altägyptischen Kultur* 8 (1980), 33–53.

Brunner, H., *Die Geburt des Gottkönigs: Studien zur Überlieferung eines altägyptischen Mythos* (Wiesbaden: Harrassowitz, 1986).

Desroches-Noblecourt, C., 'Une coutume égyptienne méconnue', *Bulletin de l'Institut Français d'Archéologie Orientale* 45 (1947), 185–232.

Feucht, E., 'The Xrdw n kAp Reconsidered' in S. Israelit-Groll (ed.), *Pharaonic Egypt, The Bible and Christianity* (Jerusalem: The Magnes Press, 1985), 38–47.

Gardiner, A. H., 'The Coronation of King Haremhab', *The Journal of Egyptian Archaeology* 39 (1953), 13–31.

Griffiths, J. G., 'The Costume and Insignia of the King in the Sed-Festival' in *The Journal of Egyptian Archaeology* 41 (1955), 127–28.

Janssen, R. M. and J. J. Janssen, *Growing Up in Ancient Egypt* (London: Rubicon, 1990).

Leprohon, R. J., 'Patterns of Royal Name-Giving' in E. Frood and W. Wendrich (eds), *UCLA Encyclopedia of Egyptology* (Los Angeles, 2010), http://digital2.library.ucla.edu/viewItem.do?ark=21198/zz001nx697

Leprohon, R. J., 'The Royal Titulary in the 18th Dynasty: Change and Continuity', *The Journal of Egyptian History* 4 (2010), 7–45.

Leprohon, R. J., 'The Programmatic Use of the Royal Titulary in the Twelfth Dynasty', *The Journal of the American Research Center in Egypt* 33 (1996), 165–71.

Murnane, W. J., *Ancient Egyptian Coregencies* (Chicago: Oriental Institute, 1977).

Robins, G., *Women in Ancient Egypt* (London: British Museum Press; Cambridge, Mass.: Harvard University Pres, 1993).

Robins, G., *Reflections of Women in the New Kingdom: Ancient Egyptian Art from the British Museum* (Atlanta: Michael C. Carlos Museum, 1995).

Roehrig, C., *The Eighteenth Dynasty Titles Royal Nurse (mn't nswt), Royal Tutor (mn' nswt), and Foster Brother/Sister of the Lord of the Two Lands (sn/snt mn' n nb t3wy)* (Unpublished PhD Dissertation; University of California at Berkeley, 1990).

Strouhal, E., *Life of the Ancient Egyptians* (Norman: University of Oklahoma Press, 1992).

## CHAPTER 4: BEING PHARAOH

Bell, L., 'Luxor Temple and the Cult of the Royal Ka', *The Journal of Near Eastern Studies* 44 (1985), 251–94.

Blackman, A. M., 'The House of the Morning', *The Journal of Egyptian Archaeology* 5 (1918), 148–65.

Bleiberg, E., 'The King's Privy Purse During the New Kingdom: An Examination of *inw*', *The Journal of the American Research Center in Egypt* 21 (1984), 155–67.

Bleiberg, E., *The Official Gift in Ancient Egypt* (Norman: University of Oklahoma Press, 1996).

van den Boorn, G. P. F., *The Duties of the Vizier, Civil Administration in the Early New Kingdom* (London: Kegan Paul, 1988).

Crowfoot, G. M., and N. de Garis Davies, 'The Tunic of Tut'ankhamun', *The Journal of Egyptian Archaeology* 27 (1941), 113–30.

Davies, N. de Garis, 'The Place of Audience in the Palace', *Zeitschrift für ägyptische Sprache und Altertumskunde* 60 (1925), 50–56.

Decker, W., *Sport and Games of Ancient Egypt* (transl. by A. Guttmann; London and New Haven: Yale University Press, 1992).

Epigraphic Survey, *The Tomb of Kheruef, Theban Tomb 192* (Chicago: Oriental Institute, 1980).

Erman, A. and H. M. Tirard, *Life in Ancient Egypt* (New York: Dover Publications, 1971).

Fairman, H. W., 'The Kingship Rituals of Egypt' in S. H. Hooke (ed.), *Myth, Ritual and Kingship* (Oxford: Clarendon Press, 1958), 74–104.

Gardiner, A. H., 'The Mansion of Life and the Master of the King's Largess', *The Journal of Egyptian Archaeology* 24 (1938), 83–91.

Gnirs, A. M., 'In the King's House: Audiences and Receptions at Court' in R. Gundlach and J. Taylor (eds), *Egyptian Royal Residences, 4. Symposium zur ägyptischen Königsideologie; 4th Symposium on Egyptian Royal Ideology; London, June 1–5 2004* (Wiesbaden: Harrassowitz, 2009), 13–43.

Goedicke, H., 'A Special Toast' in P. Der Manuelian (ed.), *Studies in Honor of Wiliam Kelly Simpson*, Vol. I (Boston: Museum of Fine Arts, 1996), 353–59.

Harris, J. E. and E. F. Wente, *An X-Ray Atlas of the Royal Mummies* (Chicago: University of Chicago Press, 1980).

Hayes, W. C., *Glazed Tiles from a Palace of Ramesses II at Kantir* (New York: Metropolitan Museum of Art, 1937).

Janssen, R. M., and J. J. Janssen, *Egyptian Household Animals* (Aylesbury: Shire, 1989).

Kruchten, J.-M., *Le décret d'Horemheb traduction, commentaire épigraphique, philologique et institutionnel* (Brussels: Éditions de l'Université de Bruxelles, 1981).

Kuhlmann, K. P., 'Throne' in W. Wendrich (ed.), UCLA Encyclopedia of Egyptology (Los Angeles, 2011), http://digital2.library.ucla.edu/viewItem.do?ark=21198/zz0026w9gt

Lorton, D., 'The King and the Law', *Varia Aegyptiaca* 2 (1986), 53–62.

McDowell, A. G., *Jurisdiction in the Workmen's Community of Deir el-Medina* (Leiden: Brill, 1990).

Menshawy, S. El-, 'The Protocol of the Ancient Egyptian Royal Palace' in Z. Hawass and L. Pinch Brock (eds), *Egyptology at the Dawn of the Twenty-First Century: Proceedings of the Eighth International Congress of Egyptologists*, Vol. II (Cairo: American University of Cairo Press, 2003), 400–06.

Peet, T. E., *The Great Tomb Robberies of the Twentieth Dynasty* (Oxford: Clarendon Press, 1930).

Quirke, S., *The Administration of Egypt in the Late Middle Kingdom: The Hieratic Documents* (New Malden: SIA, 1990).

Quirke, S., 'Visible and Invisible: The King in the Administrative Papyri of the Late Middle Kingdom' in R. Gundlach and W. Seipel (eds) *Das frühe ägyptische Königtum. Akten des 2. Symposiums zur ägyptischen Königsideologie in Wien 24.–26.9.1997* (Wiesbaden: Harrassowitz, 1999), 63–71.

Redford, S., *The Harem Conspiracy, the Murder of Ramesses III* (Dekalb: Northern Illinois University Press, 2002).

Simpson, W. K., 'A Protocol of Dress: The Royal and Private Fold of the Kilt', *The Journal of Egyptian Archaeology* 74 (1988), 203–04.

Smith, G. E., *Catalogue Général des Antiquités Égyptiennes du Musée du Caire, Nos 61051–61100, The Royal Mummies* (Cairo, 1912).

Tyldesley, J., *Judgement of the Pharaoh* (London: Weidenfeld & Nicolson, 2000).

Vernus, P., *Affairs and Scandals in Ancient Egypt* (Ithaca, N.Y.: Cornell University Press, 2003).

Vogelsang-Eastwood, G., *Pharaonic Egyptian Clothing* (Leiden: Brill, 1993).

Waseda University, *Studies on the Palace of Malqata* (Waseda University, 1993).

Weatherhead, F., 'Painted Pavements in the Great Palace at Amarna', *The Journal of Egyptian Archaeology* 78 (1992), 179–94.

Wilson, J. A., 'Ceremonial Games of the New Kingdom', *The Journal of Egyptian Archaeology* 17 (1931), 211–20.

## CHAPTER 5: PHARAOHS ON CAMPAIGN

Dar J. C. and C. Manassa, *Tutankhamun's Armies: Battle and Conquest During Egypt's Late 18th Dynasty* (Hoboken, N.J.: John Wiley, 2007).

Edgerton, W. F. and J. A. Wilson, *Historical Records of Ramses III, The Texts in Medinet Habu Volumes I and II, Translated with Explanatory Notes* (Chicago: University of Chicago Press, 1936).

Epigraphic Survey, *Earlier Historical Records of Ramses III* (Chicago: University of Chicago Press, 1930).

Epigraphic Survey, *Later Records of Ramses III* (Chicago: University of Chicago Press, 1932).

Epigraphic Survey, *The Battle Reliefs of King Sety I* (Chicago: University of Chicago Press, 1986).

Gnirs, A. M., *Militär und Gesellschaft. Ein Beitrag zur Sozialgeschichte des Neuen Reiches* (Heidelberg: Heidelberger Orientverlag, 1996).

Gnirs, A. M., 'Ancient Egypt' in K. Raaflaub and N. Rosenstein (eds), *War and Society in the Ancient and Medieval Worlds* (Cambridge Mass.: Harvard University, 1999), 71–104.

Heinz, S. C., *Die Feldzugsdarstellungen des Neuen Reiches: eine Bildanalyse* (Vienna: Österreichischen Akademie der Wissenschaften, 2001).

Iskander, S., *The Reign of Merenptah* (Unpublished PhD Thesis; New York University, 2002).

Partridge, B., *Fighting Pharaohs, Weapons and Warfare in Ancient Egypt* (Manchester: Peartree, 2002).

Redford, D. B., 'Egypt and Western Asia in the Old Kingdom', *The Journal of the American Research Center in Egypt* 23 (1986), 125–43.

Redford, D. B., *The Wars in Syria and Palestine of Thutmose III* (Leiden: Brill, 2003).

Ricke, H., G. R. Hughes and E. F. Wente, *The Beit el-Wali Temple of Ramesses II* (Chicago: University of Chicago Press, 1967).

Schulman, A. R., 'Chariots, Chariotry, and the Hyksos', *The Journal of the Society for the Study of Egyptian Antiquities* 10 (1970–80), 105–53.

Shaw, G. J., 'The Death of King Seqenenre Tao', *The Journal of the American Research Center in Egypt* 45 (2009), 159–76.

Shaw, I., *Egyptian Warfare and Weapons* (Aylesbury: Shire, 1991).

Spalinger, A. J., *Aspects of the Military Documents of the Ancient Egyptians* (New Haven and London: Yale University Press, 1982).

Spalinger, A. J., *War in Ancient Egypt* (Oxford: Blackwell, 2005).

Vandersleyen, C., *Les guerres d'Amosis; fondateur de la XVIIIe dynastie* (Brussels: Fondation Égyptologiqe Reine Élisabeth, 1971).

## CHAPTER 6: ROYAL CITIES

Badawy, A., 'The Civic Sense of Pharaoh and Urban Development in Ancient Egypt', *The Journal of the American Research Center in Egypt* 6 (1967), 103–09.

Baines, J. and J. Malek, *The Cultural Atlas of Ancient Egypt* (rev. ed.; New York: Checkmark Books, 2000).

Bard, K. A., *Encyclopedia of the Archaeology of Ancient Egypt* (London: Routledge, 1999).

Brissaud, P., 'Les principaux résultats des fouilles récentes à Tanis (1987–1997): L'émergence d'une vision nouvelle du site' in P. Brissaud (ed.) *Tanis. Travaux récentes sur le Tell Sân el-Hagar* (Paris: Agnès Vienot Éditions, 1998), 13–68.

Kitchen, K., *Pharaoh Triumphant, The Life and Times of Ramesses II* (Warminster: Aris & Phillips, 1982).

Kitchen, K., 'Towards a Reconstruction of Ramesside Memphis' in E. Bleiberg (ed.), *Fragments of a Shattered Visage; The Proceedings of the International Symposium on Ramesses the Great* (Memphis: University of Memphis, 1993), 87–104.

Lacovara, P., *The New Kingdom Royal City* (London and New York: Kegan Paul International, 1997).

Leclère, F., 'La Ville de Sais à la Basse Époque', *Égypte Afrique et Orient* 28 (2003), 13–38.

Martin, G. T., 'Memphis: The Status of a Residence City in the Eighteenth Dynasty' in M. Bárta and J. Krejci (eds), *Abusir and Saqqara in the Year 2000* (Prague: Archiv Orientalni Suplementa 9, 2000), 99–120.

Naville, É., *Bubastis (1887–1889)* (London: Egypt Exploration Fund, 1891).

O'Connor, D. B., 'Cities and Towns' in *Egypt's Golden Age, The Art of Living in the New Kingdom* (Boston: Museum of Fine Arts, 1982), 17–25.

O'Connor, D. B., 'City and Palace in New Kingdom Egypt', *Cahiers de recherches de l'Institut de Papyrologie et d'Égyptologie de Lille* 11 (1989), 73–87.

O'Connor, D. B., 'Mirror of the Cosmos: The Palace of Merenptah', in Edward Bleiberg (ed.), *Fragments of a Shattered Visage; The Proceedings of the International Symposium on Ramesses the Great* (Memphis: University of Memphis, 1993), 167–98.

O'Connor, D. B., 'The City and the World: Worldview and Built Forms in the Reign of Amenhotep III', in D. O'Connor and E. H. Cline (eds) *Amenhotep III: Perspectives on his Reign* (Ann Arbor: University of Michigan Press, 1998), 125–72.

Shaw, G. J., 'Tanis' in R. Bagnall et al. (eds) *The Encyclopedia of Ancient History* (13 vols; Oxford Wiley, 2012).

Simpson, W. K., 'Studies in the Twelfth Egyptian Dynasty: I–II', *The Journal of the American Research Center in Egypt* 2 (1963), 53–63.

Strudwick, N. and H. Strudwick, *Thebes in Egypt* (London: British Museum Press, 1999).

Thompson, D. J., *Memphis under the Ptolemies* (Princeton: Princeton University Press, 1988).

Wilson, P., *The Survey of Sais (Sa el-Hagar), 1997–2002* (London: Egypt Exploration Society, 2006).

## CHAPTER 7: THE PHARAOH IN DEATH

Arnold, D. and H. E. Winlock, *Tutankhamun's Funeral* (New York: Metropolitan Museum of Art; New Haven: Yale University Press, 2010).

Beinlich, H., 'Zwischen Tod und Grab', *Studien zur altägyptischen Kultur* 34 (2006), 17–31.

Carter, H. and A. H. Gardiner, 'The Tomb of Ramesses IV and the Turin Plan of a Royal Tomb', *The Journal of Egyptian Archaeology* 4 (1917), 130–58.

Dodson, A., 'The Tombs of the Kings of the Thirteenth Dynasty in the Memphite Necropolis', *Zeitschrift für ägyptische Sprache und Altertumskunde* 114 (1987), 36–45.

Dodson, A. and S. Ikram, *The Tomb in Ancient Egypt* (London and New York: Thames & Hudson, 2008).

Eaton-Krauss, M., 'The Burial of Tutankhamen, Part Two', *KMT, A Modern Journal of Ancient Egypt* 21, 1 (2009), 18–36.

Ikram, S., *Death and Burial in Ancient Egypt* (Harlow: Longman, 2002).

Lehner, M., *The Complete Pyramids* (London and New York: Thames & Hudson, 1997).

Lehner, M., 'Niches, Slots, Grooves and Stains: Internal Frameworks in the Khufu Pyramid?' in H. Guksch and D. Polz (eds), *Stationen; Beiträge zur Kulturgeschichte Ägyptens; Rainer Stadelmann gewidmet* (Mainz: Philip von Zabern 1998), 101–13.

O'Connor, D., *Abydos. Egypt's First Pharaohs and the Cult of Osiris* (London and New York: Thames & Hudson, 2009).

Polz, D., 'The Royal and Private Necropolis of the Seventeenth and Early Eighteenth Dynasties at Dra' Abu el-Naga' in K. Daoud, S. Bedier and S. Abd el-Fatah (eds), *Studies in Honor of Ali Radwan*, Vol. II (Cairo: Publications du Conseil Suprème des Antiquités de l'Égypte, 2005), 233–45.

Redford, D. B., *Excavations at Mendes, Vol 1, The Royal Necropolis* (Leiden: Brill, 2004).

Reeves, N., *The Complete Tutankhamun* (London and New York: Thames & Hudson, 1990).

Reeves, N. and R. H. Wilkinson, *The Complete Valley of the Kings* (London and New York: Thames & Hudson, 1996).

Roth, A. M., 'Social Change in the Fourth Dynasty: The Spatial Organization of Pyramids, Tombs, and Cemeteries', *The Journal of the American Research Center in Egypt* 30 (1993), 33–55.

Sagrillo, T., 'The Geographical Origins of the "Bubastite" Dynasty and Possible Locations for the Royal Residence and Burial Place of Shoshenq I' in G. P. F. Broekman, R. J. Demarée and O. E. Kaper (eds), *The Libyan Period in Egypt, Historical and Cultural Studies into the 21st and 22nd Dynasties* (Leiden: Brill, 2009), 341–59.

Spencer, A. J., *Death in Ancient Egypt* (Harmondsworth: Penguin, 1982).

Spencer N. A., 'The Epigraphic Survey of Samanud', *The Journal of Egyptian Archaeology* 85 (1999), 55–83.

Taylor, J. H., *Death and the Afterlife in Ancient Egypt* (London: British Museum; Chicago: University of Chicago Press, 2001).

Wilson, J. A., 'Funeral Services of the Egyptian Old Kingdom', *The Journal of Near Eastern Studies* 3 (1944), 201–18.

## CHAPTER 8: THE LAST PHARAOHS

Anonymous, *The Greek Alexander Romance* (transl. by Richard Stoneman; Harmondsworth: Penguin, 1991).

Arrian, *The Life of Alexander the Great* (transl. by A. de Sélincourt; Harmondsworth: Penguin, 1958).

Ashton, S.-A., *Ptolemaic Royal Sculpture from Egypt: The Interaction between Greek and Egyptian Traditions* (Oxford: Archaeopress, 2001).

Bagnall, R. S. and K. A. Worp, *Chronological Systems of Byzantine Egypt* (2nd ed.; Leiden: Brill, 2004).

Birley, A. R., *The African Emperor: Septimius Severus* (2nd ed.; London: Batsford, 1988).

Bowman, A. K., *Egypt after the Pharaohs* (Oxford: Oxford University Press; Berkeley: University of California Press, 1986).

Cassius Dio, *Roman History* (transl. by E. Cary; 9 vols; Cambridge, Mass.: Harvard University Press, 1914–27).

Herodian, *History of the Empire from the Time of Marcus Aurelius* (transl. by C. R. Whittaker; 2 vols; Cambridge, Mass.: Harvard University Press, 1969–70).

Hölbl, G., *A History of the Ptolemaic Empire* (transl. by T. Saavedra; London and New York: Routledge, 2001).

Lloyd, A. B., 'Nationalist Propaganda in Ptolemaic Egypt', *Historia: Zeitschrift für Alte Geschichte* 31 (1982), 33–55.

Ritner, R. K., 'Egypt Under Roman Rule: The Legacy of Ancient Egypt' in *The Cambridge History of Egypt*, Vol. 1 (Cambridge: Cambridge University Press, 1998), 1–33.

Saunders, N. J., *Alexander's Tomb: The Two Thousand Year Obsession to Find the Lost Conqueror* (New York: Basic Books, 2007).

Williams, S., *Diocletian and the Roman Recovery* (London and New York: Routledge, 1997).

# SOURCES OF QUOTATIONS

Details of the published sources can be found in the Further Reading in the relevant section.

## CHAPTER 1

p. 19 'Re has placed …' (transl. by R. Parkinson, *Voices from Ancient Egypt*, p. 39); p. 22 'breath of life…' Ramesses II, Abydos Temple inscription (transl. by J. H. Breasted, *Ancient Records of Egypt*, III, p. 108, section 265).

## CHAPTER 2

p. 29 'more cruel than…' Manetho, *Aegyptiaca*, Fr 28 (b) (transl. by W. G. Waddell, pp. 61–62); p. 34 'a disciple of …' Stele of Ahmose I, Karnak (transl. by G. J. Shaw from K. Sethe, *Urkunden der 18. Dynastie*, 19, 13–20, 1); p. 34 'more conversant …' Festival Hall inscription of Thutmose III, Karnak (transl. by G. J. Shaw from W. Helck, *Urkunden der 18. Dynastie*, 1271, 19); p. 34 'had seen a …' Papyrus Berlin 3049, vs XVIII–XIX (P. Vernus, 'Un décret de Thoutmosis III relatif à la santé publique (P. Berlin 3049, vs XVIII–XIX)', *Orientalia* 48 (1979), 176–84); p. 40 'As for Pharaoh…' Papyrus Berlin 10487 (transl. following E. F. Wente *Late Ramesside Letters*, p. 53); p. 45 'I have appeared …' The Demotic Chronicle, 5/1-6/8; 5/9–10 (transl. by J. H. Johnson, 'The Demotic Chronicle as a Statement of a Theory of Kingship', p. 63); p. 46 'a few days …' and 'Because the law …' The Demotic Chronicle, 3/21 and 4/12 (transl. by J. H. Johnson, 'The Demotic Chronicle as a Statement of a Theory of Kingship', p. 66).

## CHAPTER 3

p. 50 'God has given …' Tomb of Niankhsekhmet (transl. by G. J. Shaw from Kurt Sethe, *Urkunden des Alten Reichs*, 39, 15); p. 50 'He (the god …' Leather Roll of Senwosret I, Berlin 3029 (transl. by R. Parkinson, *Voices from Ancient Egypt*, p. 41); p. 50 'And his heart …' *The Romance of Setna Khaemwaset and the Mummies* (transl. by R. K. Ritner in W. K. Simpson et al., *The Literature of Ancient Egypt*, p. 455); p. 50 'slid into her…' and 'cleansed herself …' *The Tales of Wonder* (transl. by M. Lichtheim, *Ancient Egyptian Literature*, I, pp. 220, 221); p. 52 'when she was …' Inscription of Ahmose Pennekhbet (transl. by G. J. Shaw from K. Sethe, *Urkunden der 18. Dynastie*, 34, 16–17); p. 52 'because of the …' Inscription from the mortuary temple of Prince Wadjmose, Thebes (transl. by C. Roehrig, *The Eighteenth Dynasty Titles Royal Nurse (mn't nswt), Royal Tutor (mn' nswt), and Foster Brother/Sister of the Lord of the Two Lands (sn/snt mn' n nb t3wy)*, p. 24 n. 58); p. 52 'because of my …' Senenmut statue Chicago 173800 (transl. by P. F. Dorman, *The Monuments of Senenmut* (London and New York, 1988, p. 124); p. 53 'one who hears …' Statue text of Amenhotep Son of Hapu, from *Karnak* (transl. by E. Feucht, 'The Xrdw n kAp Reconsidered', p. 39); p. 54 'I have sent …'

Amarna letter EA 180 (transl. by D. Redford, *Egypt, Canaan and Israel*, p. 198); p. 55 'with his own fingers' Tomb of Senedjemib Inti (transl. by G. J. Shaw from K. Sethe, *Urkunden des Alten Reichs*, 60, 8); p. 55 'with his own two …' Stele of Usersatet (transl. by G. J. Shaw from W. Helck, *Urkunden der 18. Dynastie*, 1343, 11); p. 55 'proficient in …' *The Teachings for King Merikare* (transl. by V. Tobin in W. K. Simpson et al., *The Literature of Ancient Egypt*, pp. 154–55); p. 55 'a boy's ear …' Papyrus Anastasi III, 3/10-4/4 (adapted from transl. by R. Caminos, *Late-Egyptian Miscellanies*, p. 83); p. 57 'enjoying …' Block from Sphinx Temple, Giza (transl. by G. J. Shaw from K. Sethe, *Urkunden der 18. Dynastie*, 91, 14); p. 60 'When there was …' Inscription of Weni (transl. by N. Strudwick, *Texts from the Pyramid Age*, p. 353); p. 60 'Maintain your …' *The Teachings of Amenemhat* (transl. by V. Tobin in W. K. Simpson et al., *The Literature of Ancient Egypt*, p. 168); p. 61 'one who placed …' (K. A. Kitchen, *Ramesside Inscriptions. Translated and Annotated*, IV, 364, 5 and 371, 8–9); p. 61 'the great enemy' Ostracon IFAO 1864 (see P. Grandet, 'L'execution du chancelier Bay O.IFAO 1864', *Bulletin de l'Institut Français d'Archéologie Orientale* 100 (2000), pp. 339–45); p. 62 'The Egyptians objected …' Herodotus, *The Histories*, Book II, 167 (transl. by A. de Sélincourt, p. 196); p. 63 'the guards, …' *The Instruction of Ankhsheshonqy* (transl. by R. K. Ritner in W. K. Simpson et al., *The Literature of Ancient Egypt*, p. 501); p. 63 'Menkheperre …' Inscription of Amenemhab (transl. by G. J. Shaw from K. Sethe, *Urkunden der 18. Dynastie*, 895, 17-896, 8); p. 66 'He assumed …' The Great Sphinx Stele of Amenhotep II (transl. adapted from B. Cumming, *Egyptian Historical Records of the Later Eighteenth Dynasty*, I, p. 20); p. 69 'Priest of the …' Stele of Semty the Younger (transl. by M. Lichtheim *Ancient Egyptian Autobiographies*, pp. 96–97); p. 69 'the Chamberlain …' Inscription of Amenhotep (transl. by A. H. Gardiner, 'The Coronation of King Haremhab', p. 26); p. 69 'Oh happy day …' Composition of Amennakht, Ostracon CGT 57001, recto, reign of Ramesses IV (transl. by A. McDowell, *Village Life in Ancient Egypt: Laundry Lists and Love Songs* (Oxford, 1999), p. 159).

## CHAPTER 4

p. 73 '(it was) his …' *The Instruction of Ankhsheshonqy* (transl. by R. K. Ritner in W. K. Simpson et al., *The Literature of Ancient Egypt*, p. 501); p. 74 'The equipment of …' (transl. by N. Reeves, *The Complete Tutankhamun*, p. 159); p. 75 'great lord of …' Inscription of Montuhotep (transl. by J. H. Breasted, *Ancient Records of Egypt*, I, p. 257, section 533); p. 78 'the priest of …' False Door of Geref from Saqqara (transl. by N. Strudwick, *Texts from the Pyramid Age*, p. 273); p. 78 'In the morning …' and 'For there was …' Diodorus Siculus, *Library of History*, Book I, 70 (transl. by C. H. Oldfather, Vol. 1, pp. 243, 245); p. 79 'When I was

…' Inscription of Kaihap Tjeti (transl. by N. Strudwick, *Texts from the Pyramid Age*, p. 287); p. 84 'Remember the day …' and 'As to the …' Papyrus Koller and Papyrus Turin C and D, and Papyrus Turin A vso. 3, 9–10 (transl by. A. M. Gnirs, 'In the King's House: Audiences and Receptions at Court', pp. 28–29, 40); p. 84 'It happened …' *The Instruction of Ankhsheshonqy* (transl. by R. K. Ritner in W. K. Simpson et al., *The Literature of Ancient Egypt*, p. 500); p. 84 'Because of my …' Tomb of Hesi (transl. by Nigel Strudwick, *Texts from the Pyramid Age*, pp. 276–77); p. 84–85 'When His Majesty …' Tomb of Ptahshepses, (transl. by N. Strudwick, *Texts from the Pyramid Age*, pp. 304–05); p. 85 'Now the *sem*…' Tomb of Rawer (transl. by N. Strudwick, *Texts from the Pyramid Age*, pp. 305–06); p. 85 'law which is …' *The Duties of the Vizier*, (transl. by G. P. F. van den Boorn, *The Duties of the Vizier*, p. 147); p. 85 'who laid down …' Festival Hall inscription of Thutmose III, Karnak (transl. by G. J. Shaw from W. Helck, *Urkunden der 18. Dynastie*, 1269–1272); p. 85 'who establishes laws …' Amenhotep III at Luxor Temple, forecourt architrave (transl. by B. G. Davies, *Egyptian Historical Records of the Later Eighteenth Dynasty*, IV, p. 16); p. 85 'who is knowledgeable …' Tutankhamun Restoration Stele (transl. by B. G. Davies, *Egyptian Historical Records of the Later Eighteenth Dynasty*, VI, p. 33); p. 86 'The kings were …' Diodorus Siculus, *Library of History*, Book I, 71 (transl. by C. H. Oldfather, Vol. 1, pp. 246–47); p. 87 'until Pharaoh …' The Tomb Robbery Papyri (transl. by A. McDowell, *Jurisdiction in the Workmen's Community of Deir el-Medina*, p. 242); p. 87 'Pharaoh caused …' *The Instruction of Ankhsheshonqy* (transl. by R. K. Ritner in W. K. Simpson et al., *The Literature of Ancient Egypt*, p. 503); p. 87 'He was put …' Papyrus Mayer A12, 26 (transl. by A. McDowell, *Jurisdiction in the Workmen's Community of Deir el-Medina*, p. 243); p. 88 'Do not distinguish …' *The Teachings for King Merikare* (transl. by G. J. Shaw from W. Helck, *Die Lehre für König Merikare* (Wiesbaden, 1977), p. 36); p. 89 'It is he who …' *The Duties of the Vizier* (transl. by G. P. F. van den Boorn, *The Duties of the Vizier*, p. 276); p. 90 'If you are …' *The Maxims of Ptahhotep* (transl. by V. Tobin in W. K. Simpson et al., *The Literature of Ancient Egypt*, p. 136, 140); p. 90 'Now with regard …' Unknown person, Giza (transl. by N. Strudwick, *Texts from the Pyramid Age*, pp. 322–23); p. 91 'The one whom …' *The Loyalist Instruction* from the Sehetepibre Stele (transl. by W. K Simpson et al., *The Literature of Ancient Egypt*, p. 174.); p. 92 'send your daughter …' Amarna letter EA 99, 10–15 (transl. by A. R. Schulman, 'Diplomatic Marriage in the Egyptian New Kingdom', *The Journal of Near Eastern Studies* 38 (1979), p. 183); p. 92 'From time …' Amarna Letter EA 4 (transl. by W. L. Moran, *The Amarna Letters*, pp. 8–9); p. 92 'For His Majesty …' Inscription of Khamaat (transl. by N. Strudwick, *Texts from Pyramid Age*, p. 304); p. 95 'every god who …' and 'festival of Washing …' The Konosso Stele of Thutmose IV (transl. by B. Cumming, *Egyptian Historical Records of the Later Eighteenth Dynasty*, III, p. 252); p. 99 'I did not plan …' Obelisk inscription of Hatshepsut, Karnak Temple (transl. by M. Lichtheim, *Ancient Egyptian Literature*, II, p. 27); p. 103 'As I am in …' Tomb of Ineni (adapted from transl. by H. Goedicke, 'A Special Toast', p. 357); p. 103 'one brought me …' Tomb of Senemiah (adapted from transl. by H. Goedicke, 'A Special Toast', p. 357); p. 104 'Give thanks for …' *The Teachings for King Merikare* (transl. by W. K. Simpson et al., *The Literature of Ancient Egypt*, p. 156); p. 107 'the delight of …' Inscription of Ankhkhufu (transl. by N. Strudwick *Texts from the Pyramid Age*, p. 263); p. 107 'bring me 18 …' Tomb of Paheri (transl. by E. Strouhal, *Life of the Ancient Egyptians*, p. 133); p. 108 'He used

to …' Herodotus, *The Histories*, Book II, 172–74 (transl. by A. de Sélincourt, p. 198); p. 110 'The Osisris …' Sarcophagus of Ta-Miu (transl. by. R. M. Janssen and J. J. Janssen, *Egyptian Household Animals*, p. 17); p. 110 'His Majesty then …' The Victory Stele of Piye (transl. by R. K. Ritner in Simpson et al., *Literature of Ancient Egypt*, p. 376); p. 111 'with his buttocks …' *The Adventures of Setna and Si-Osire* (transl. by R. K. Ritner in William K. Simpson et al., *The Literature of Ancient Egypt*, p. 481); p. 112 'He (the king) …' Inscription of the nomarch Kheti (transl. by W. Decker, *Sport and Play*, p. 91); p. 113 'slew seven lions …' Armant Stele of Thutmose III (transl. by B. Cumming, *Egyptian Historical Records of the Later Eighteenth Dynasty*, I, p. 8); p. 114 'Take care! …' Inscription from Medinet Habu (transl. by J. A. Wilson, 'Ceremonial Games of the New Kingdom', p. 213).

## CHAPTER 5

p. 118 'Stout-hearted …' *The Story of Sinuhe* (transl. by M. Lichtheim, *Ancient Egyptian Literature*, I, pp. 225–26); p. 118 'I have made …' The Semna Stele of Senwosret III (transl. by R. Parkinson, *Voices from Ancient Egypt*, pp. 43–45); p. 118 'Look, I am …' The Kamose Stelae (W. Helck, *Historisch-biographische Texte*, 93, 2, 4–5); pp. 120–21 'Enter combat …' Victory Stele of Piye (transl. by M. Lichtheim, *Ancient Egyptian Literature*, III, p. 69); p. 121 'one waded …' Victory Stele of Psamtik II (transl. by M. Lichtheim, *Ancient Egyptian Literature*, III, p. 85); pp. 121–22 'was happy …' Seti I, Karnak Temple (transl. by The Epigraphic Survey, *The Battle Reliefs of King Sety I*, p. 21); p. 122 'Bring forth …' Ramesses III, Medinet Habu (transl. by W. F. Edgerton and J. A. Wilson, *Historical Records of Ramses III*, p. 35); p. 126 'When he …' The soldier Amenemhab (transl. by G. J. Shaw from K. Sethe, *Urkunden der 18. Dynastie*, 890, 12–13); p. 128 'May our …' The Annals of Thutmose III, Karnak Temple (transl. by G. J. Shaw from Kurt Sethe, *Urkunden der 18. Dynastie*, 649–51); p. 130 'Prepare yourselves …', 'His Majesty set …' and 'Then His Majesty …' The Annals of Thutmose III, Karnak Temple (transl. by G. J. Shaw from Kurt Sethe, *Urkunden der 18. Dynastie*, 655–56; 657, 215; 657, 16); p. 130 'caused the Nile …' Ramesses III, Medinet Habu (transl. by W. F. Edgerton and J. A. Wilson, *Historical Records of Ramses III*, pp. 54–56); p. 130 'Forward against …' Victory Stele of Piye (transl. by M. Lichtheim, *Ancient Egyptian Literature*, III, p. 76); p. 132 'the spoil which …' Inscription of Seti I at Karnak Temple (The Epigraphic Survey, *The Battle Reliefs of King Sety I*, p. 38); p. 135 'How faint …', 'Stand firm …' and 'Have I not …' The Kadesh Poem (transl. by M. Lichtheim, *Ancient Egyptian Literature*, II, p. 67, p. 68, pp. 69–70); p. 136 'We have begged …' Ramesses III, Medinet Habu (transl. by W. F. Edgerton and J. A. Wilson, *Historical Records of Ramses III*, p. 84); p. 136 'they were made …' Amada inscription of Merenptah (transl. by K. A. Kitchen, *Ramesside Inscriptions. Translated and Annotated*, IV, p. 2); p. 136 'driving donkeys …' Karnak inscription of Merenptah (transl. by K. A. Kitchen, *Ramesside Inscriptions. Translated and Annotated*, IV, p. 6); p. 136 'with the joy …' Amada and Elephantine Stele of Amenhotep II (transl. by G. J. Shaw from W. Helck, *Urkunden der 18. Dynastie*, 1297–98, 2); p. 137 'I brought spoil …' Autobiography of Ahmose Son of Ibana (transl. by M. Lichtheim, *Ancient Egyptian Literature*, II, p. 13).

## CHAPTER 6

p. 144 'I have raised …' *The Teachings of King Amenemhat* (transl. by V. Tobin in W. K. Simpson et al., *The Literature of Ancient Egypt*, p. 170); p. 144 'Then his Majesty …' Victory Stele of Piye (transl. adapted from R. K. Ritner in W. K. Simpson et al., *The Literature of Ancient Egypt*, p. 378); p. 145 'a chalice of …' Papyrus Harris 500 (transl. by K. Kitchen, *Pharaoh Triumphant*, p. 116); p. 145 'His Majesty saw …' Victory Stele of Piye (transl. by M. Lichtheim, *Ancient Egyptian Literature*, III, p. 75); p. 145 'The like of …' Papyrus Sallier IV (transl. by K. Kitchen, *Pharaoh Triumphant*, p. 115); p. 149 'Stronger is Thebes …' Papyrus Leiden I, 350, I:13ff (transl. by K. Kitchen, *Pharaoh Triumphant*, p. 119); p. 153 'His Majesty has …' P. Anastasi II (transl. by K. Kitchen, *Pharaoh Triumphant*, p. 119); p. 154 'Everyone has …' P. Anastasi II (transl. by R. Caminos, *Late Egyptian Miscellanies*, pp. 37–38); p. 155 'embellished more …' Stele of Intef (transl. by G. J. Shaw from K. Sethe, *Urkunden der 18. Dynastie*, 975, 7–8); p. 155 Golden cubit from the tomb of Kha (transl. by B. Cumming, *Egyptian Historical Records of the Later Eighteenth Dynasty*, III, p. 191); p. 155 'Get on with …' Papyrus Anastasi III (transl. by K. Kitchen, *Pharaoh Triumphant*, p. 122); p. 158 'With regard to …' Inscription of Debehen (transl. by N. Strudwick, *Texts from the Pyramid Age*, p. 271); p. 159 'he found the …' Abydos inscription of Ramesses II (transl. by K. Kitchen, *Pharaoh Triumphant*, p. 45); p. 160 'A king

who …' Leather Roll of Senwosret I, Berlin 3029 (transl. by M. Lichtheim, *Ancient Egyptian Literature*, I, p. 117).

### CHAPTER 7

p. 172 'We took our …' (transl. by A. J. Peden, *Egyptian Historical Inscriptions of the Twentieth Dynasty*, pp. 245–57); p. 173 'I saw to …' Tomb of Ineni (transl. by G. J. Shaw from K. Sethe, *Urkunden der 18. Dynastie*, 57, 3–5); p. 178 'In the family …' Herodotus, *The Histories*, Book II, 169 (transl. by A. de Sélincourt, p. 196–97).

### CHAPTER 8

p. 188 'He put his …' Arrian, Book 3, *Arrian's Life of Alexander the Great* (transl. by A. de Sélincourt, p. 94); p. 192 'the crossroads of …; Dio Chrysostom of Prusa, *Oration*, 32.36 (transl. by A. K. Bowman, *Egypt after the Pharaohs*, p. 218); p. 192 'the first city …' Diodorus Siculus, *Library of History*, Book 17, 52 (transl. by C. H. Oldfather, Vol. 8, p. 269); p. 192 'The city has …' Strabo, *Geography* 17, 1.8; (transl. by A. K. Bowman, *Egypt after the Pharaohs*, p. 206).

# ACKNOWLEDGMENTS

I would like to thank Robert Twigger for his inspiring words and the key role he played in making this book a reality, and also the editorial, design and production team at Thames & Hudson for giving me the chance to realize my dream. I would also like to thank Dr Edgar Pusch for commenting on the section on Qantir and for supplying information on his work. Many thanks go to Dr Campbell Price and Henning Franzmeier for their valuable comments and advice during the writing of the manuscript, and I gratefully acknowledge the German Archaeological Institute (DAI), Cairo, and the Egypt Exploration Society, London, for the use of their libraries during my research. My family have always provided support for my Egyptological endeavours over the years, but my most heartfelt and deepest thanks must go to my wife, Julie Patenaude, to whom this book is dedicated, for putting up with my obsessive dedication to making this book as complete as possible, and for reading and commenting on the various drafts of the text throughout the writing process.

# SOURCES OF ILLUSTRATIONS

a = above, b = below, c = centre, l = left, r = right

1 Egyptian Museum, Cairo; 2–3 Collection Dagli Orti/Egyptian Museum, Cairo/The Art Archive; 4 Brooklyn Museum, Charles Edwin Wilbour Fund; 7 Photo Sandro Vannini; 8 Collection of George Ortiz, Vandoeuvres/Werner Forman Archive; 9 Photo Albert Shoucair; 10 Philip Winton/ML Design © Thames & Hudson Ltd, London; 11 Werner Forman Archive; 13 Collection Dagli Orti/ Egyptian Museum, Cairo/The Art Archive; 14 Hirmer Fotoarchiv; 15 British Museum, London; 16a, b DAI, Cairo; 17a Ashmolean Museum, Oxford/Werner Forman Archive; 17b Ashmolean Museum, Oxford; 18a Photo Jürgen Liepe; 18b Egyptian Museum, Cairo; 19 Musée du Louvre, Paris; 20al Ägyptisches Museum, Staatliche Museen zu Berlin; 20ar Metropolitan Museum of Art, New York. Rogers Fund and Edward S. Harkness Gift, 1914. Acc. no. 14.3.17. Metropolitan Museum of Art/Art Resource/Scala, Florence; 20b Photo Jürgen Liepe; 21a, b Photo Rob Koopman; 22 Egyptian Museum, Cairo; 23 Andrea Jemolo/akg-images; 25 Musée du Louvre, Paris; 26ar British Museum, London; 26cr British Museum, London; 26bl Ashmolean Museum, Oxford/The Art Archive;

28, 30 Photo Jürgen Liepe; 31 © Roger Wood/Corbis; 32 Egyptian Museum, Cairo; 35 Heidi Grassley © Thames & Hudson Ltd, London; 36 Egyptian Museum, Cairo; 37 Trustees of the British Museum, London; 38 Erich Lessing/akg-images; 39 Courtesy Oriental Institute Museum, University of Chicago; 42 Musée du Louvre, Paris; 43 Egyptian Museum, Cairo; 44 Ägyptisches Museum, Staatliche Museen zu Berlin; 45 British Museum, London; 47 Aidan Dodson; 49 Egyptian Museum, Cairo; 50 From Naville, É., *The Temple of Deir el Bahari*, Vol. 2, pl. XLVII, 1896. Heidelberg University Library; 51 Erich Lessing/akg-images; 52 British Museum, London; 54 Photo Sandro Vannini; 56a De Agostini Picture Library/akg-images; 56b Werner Forman Archive; 57 Richard Mortel; 58 British Museum, London; 59 Photo Kenneth Garrett; 61 Francis Dzikowski © Theban Mapping Project; 62 Egyptian Museum, Cairo; 64a Walters Art Museum, Baltimore; 64b Courtesy Oriental Institute Museum, University of Chicago; 65 Photo Sandro Vannini; 66 Werner Forman Archive; 67a Courtesy Oriental Institute Museum, University of Chicago; 67b From Lepsius, K. R., *Denkmäler aus Ägypten and Äthopien*, Part III, vol. V, p. 37, pl. 36. 1849–59. Universitäts- und Landesbibliothek Sachsen-

Anhalt, Halle (Saale); **68a** Gianni Dagli Orti/The Art Archive; **68b** Trustees of the British Museum, London; **69** Werner Forman Archive; **71** Photo Kenneth Garrett; **72a, c** Courtesy Institute of Egyptology, Waseda University; **72b** Robert Harding; **73** Egyptian Museum, Cairo/Werner Forman Archive; **74a** Metropolitan Museum of Art, New York. Rogers Fund, 1911 Acc. no. 11.215.451. Metropolitan Museum of Art/Art Resource/Scala, Florence; **74b** Egyptian Museum, Cairo; **75** Photo Sandro Vannini; **76a** Museum of Textile History, Borås; **76bl** World Museum, National Museums Liverpool; **76br** Museum of Textile History, Borås; **77a** Robert Harding Productions; **77b** © Andrew McConnell/Alamy; **78** Photo Sandro Vannini; **80** ML Design, after P. Lacovara, *The New Kingdom Royal City*, p. 116, fig. 23. KPI, 1997; **81** Photo Scala, Florence; **82a** Courtesy Oriental Institute Museum, University of Chicago; **82b** From Ziegler, C., *The Pharaohs*, p. 288, fig. 25. Thames & Hudson Ltd, London, 2002; **84** *The Metropolitan Museum of Art Bulletin*, vol. 21, no. 12, fig. 5, December, 1926; **87** World Museum, National Museums Liverpool; **88a** From Kitchen, K. A., *Pharaoh Triumphant*, p. 47, fig. 16. Aris & Phillips Ltd, 1982; **88b** Egyptian Museum, Cairo; **89** Gianni Dagli Orti/Musée du Louvre, Paris/The Art Archive; **91** Ägyptisches Museum, Staatliche Museen zu Berlin; **92** Metropolitan Museum of Art, New York. Rogers Fund 1941. Acc. no. 41.2.10. Metropolitan Museum of Art/Art Resource/Scala, Florence; **93a** Photo John Ross; **93b** British Museum, London; **94, 95** Courtesy Oriental Institute Museum, University of Chicago; **96** Heidi Grassley © Thames & Hudson Ltd, London; **97a** Photo Albert Shoucair; **97b** British Museum, London; **99** Gianni Dagli Orti/Luxor Museum, Egypt/The Art Archive; **100** © Roger Wood/Corbis; **101** Egyptian Museum, Cairo/Werner Forman Archive; **103** Photo Sandro Vannini; **105** From Smith, G. E., *Catalogue of the Royal Mummies in the Museum of Cairo*, 1912; **106** Egyptian Museum, Turin; **107** British Museum, London/Werner Forman Archive; **108a** From Dodson, A. and Ikram, S., *The Tomb in Ancient Egypt*, p. 118, fig. 108. Thames & Hudson Ltd, London, 2008; **108b** Werner Forman Archive; **111** Philippe Maillard/akg-images; **113** Nick Jakins; **114** Courtesy Oriental Institute Museum, University of Chicago; **115a** Robert Harding; **115b** Gianni Dagli Orti/Egyptian Museum, Cairo/The Art Archive; **117** Egyptian Museum, Cairo; **119** Patrick Landmann/Getty Images; **120, 121, 122** Courtesy Oriental Institute Museum, University of Chicago; **123a** New York Public Library, USA/Bridgeman Art Library; **123bl** From Pusch, E. B., 'Pi-Ramesse-geliebt-von-Amun, Hauptquartier Deiner Streitwagentruppen', in: Eggebrecht, A. (ed.), *Pelizaeus-Museum Hildesheim, Die Ägyptische Sammlung*. Verlag Philip von Zabern, Mainz, 1993. Courtesy Dr. Edgar B. Pusch; **123br** Egyptian Museum, Cairo; **124a** New York Public Library, USA/Bridgeman Art Library; **124b** Courtesy Oriental Institute Museum, University of Chicago; **125al** Egyptian Museum, Cairo; **125ar** Photo A. J. Veldmeijer. Courtesy SCA/Egyptian Museum Authorities; **125b** Bibliothèque Royale, Brussels; **127a** Courtesy Oriental Institute Museum, University of Chicago; **127b, 129A** Ägyptisches Museum, Staatliche Museen zu Berlin; **129b** Peter Bull Art Studio © Thames & Hudson Ltd, London; **131** British Museum, London; **132l** Gianni Dagli Orti/The Art Archive; **132r** Courtesy Oriental Institute Museum, University of Chicago; **134–35** Red Lion Prints © Thames & Hudson Ltd, London; **136a** Egyptian Museum, Cairo; **136b** Photo Reno Raaijmakers/© Amsterdam City Walks; **137** Gianni Dagli Orti/The Art Archive; **139** Heidi Grassley © Thames & Hudson Ltd, London; **140a** Ägyptisches Museum, Staatliche Museen zu Berlin; **140b** DAI, Cairo; **141** Photo Kenneth Garrett; **142** Ivan Vdovin/age fotostock/Robert Harding; **143** Philip Winton © Thames & Hudson Ltd, London; **146** ML Design after Kitchen, K. 'Towards a Reconstruction of Ramesside Memphis' in Bleiberg, E. (ed.), *Fragments of a Shattered Visage; The Proceedings of the International Symposium on Ramesses the Great*, p. 100, fig. 2. Memphis, Tenn., 1993; **147** Trustees of the British Museum, London; **148a** From Manniche, L., *Lost Tombs*, pl. 8. Kegan Paul International Ltd, London, 1988; **148b** Werner Forman Archive; **149** Watercolour by Jean-Claude Golvin. Musée départemental Arles antique. © éditions errance; **150a** Egyptian Museum, Cairo; **150b** Courtesy The Amarna Trust; **151a** ML Design © Thames & Hudson Ltd, London; **151b** Eastwood Cook, Modelmakers, based on a design by Michael Mallinson; **152** British Museum, London; **154l, 154r** From Pusch, E. B., 'Pi-Ramesse-geliebt-von-Amun, Hauptquartier Deiner Streitwagentruppen', in: Eggebrecht, A. (ed.), *Pelizaeus-Museum Hildesheim, Die Ägyptische Sammlung*. Verlag Philip von Zabern, Mainz, 1993. Courtesy Dr. Edgar B. Pusch; **155** Courtesy Oriental Institute Museum, University of Chicago; **156l** Courtesy Sarah Parcak, University of Alabama, Birmingham; **156r** British Museum, London; **157** Penelope Wilson; **158** Salinas Regional Archaeological Museum, Palermo; **160** Jochen Schlenker/Robert Harding; **161** Werner Forman Archive; **163** James Morris/akg-images; **164a, b** British Museum, London; **165** Günter Dreyer/DAI, Cairo; **166** Bildarchiv Steffens/akg-images; **167** Photo Kenneth Garrett; **168** Petrie Museum of Egyptian Archaeology, University College London; **169** Photo Jon Bodsworth. Courtesy Vincent Brown, www.pyramidtextsonline.com; **170** Hervé Champollion/akg-images; **171a** Photo Jürgen Liepe; **171b** Egyptian Museum, Cairo; **172** British Museum, London; **173** Amanda Lewis/iStockphoto.com; **174** Alberto Siliotti/Geodia, Archivio Image Service; **175b** Philip Winton © Thames & Hudson Ltd, London; **176** Egyptian Museum, Turin; **177** Egyptian Museum, Cairo; **178** Giovanni Mereghetti/Marka/Robert Harding; **179** © Robert Harding/Robert Harding World Imagery/Corbis; **180a** From Lehner, M., *The Complete Pyramids*, pp. 26–27. Thames & Hudson Ltd, London, 1997; **180b** From Smith, G. E., *Catalogue of the Royal Mummies in the Museum of Cairo*, 1912; **181, 182a** Egyptian Museum, Cairo; **182b** Philippe Maillard/akg-images; **183a** Photo Sandro Vannini; **183b** Egyptian Museum, Cairo; **184** Photo Sandro Vannini; **185a** Francis Dzikowski © Theban Mapping Project; **185bl, bc** Photo Albert Shoucair; **185br** Egyptian Museum, Cairo; **186** Gianni Dagli Orti/The Art Archive; **187** Photo John Ross; **189** Collection Dagli Orti/The Art Archive; **190a** Numismatic Museum, Athens; **191** fotoVoyager/iStockphoto.com; **192** Watercolour by Jean-Claude Golvin. Musée départemental Arles antique. © éditions errance; **193** Jane Taylor/The Art Archive; **194a** British Museum, London; **194b** Gianni Dagli Orti/Collection Antonovich/The Art Archive; **195** Metropolitan Museum of Art, New York. Rogers Fund, 1920. Acc. no. 20.2.21. Metropolitan Museum of Art/Art Resource/Scala, Florence; **196** Ägyptisches Museum, Staatliche Museen zu Berlin; **197** Werner Forman Archive; **198** Hermitage Museum, St Petersburg; **199** British Museum, London/Werner Forman Archive; **200** Garry J. Shaw; **201** Photo Scala, Florence; **202** Gianni Dagli Orti/The Art Archive; **203** Château de Vaux-le-Vicomte, France; **204l** Ashmolean Museum, Oxford/The Art Archive; **204c, r** Egyptian Museum, Cairo; **205l** Museum of Fine Arts, Boston; **205c** Photo John Ross; **205r** Brooklyn Museum, Charles Edwin Wilbour Fund; **206l** Photo Jürgen Liepe; **206c** Egyptian Museum, Cairo; **206r** Photo Jürgen Liepe; **207l** British Museum, London; **207c** Trustees of the British Museum, London; **207r** Egyptian Museum, Cairo; **208l** Metropolitan Museum of Art, New York. Rogers Fund 1929. Inv. no. 29.3.2. Metropolitan Museum of Art/Art Resource/Scala, Florence; **208c, r** Egyptian Museum, Cairo; **209l** Egyptian Museum, Turin; **209c** Egyptian Museum, Cairo; **209r** British Museum, London; **210l, c** Egyptian Museum, Cairo; **210r** Ägyptisches Museum, Staatliche Museen zu Berlin; **211l** Musée du Louvre, Paris; **211c** British Museum, London; **211r** Yale University, Peabody Museum, Barringer Collection

# INDEX